Management Strategies for Today's Project Shop Economy

MANAGEMENT STRATEGIES FOR TODAY'S PROJECT SHOP ECONOMY

Glenn Bassett

Q

QUORUM BOOKS

New York • Westport, Connecticut • London

658.5
B31m

Library of Congress Cataloging-in-Publication Data

Bassett, Glenn.
   Management strategies for today's project shop economy / Glenn
Bassett.
    p. cm.
   Includes bibliographical references and index.
   ISBN 0–89930–574–1 (alk. paper)
   1. Organizational change. 2. Job enrichment. 3. Production
management. I. Title.
HD58.8.B373   1991
658.5—dc20   90–20712

British Library Cataloguing in Publication Data is available.

Library of Congress Catalog Card Number: 90–20712
ISBN: 0–89930–574–1

First published in 1991

Quorum Books, 88 Post Road West, Westport, CT 06881
An imprint of Greenwood Publishing Group, Inc.

Printed in the United States of America

The paper used in this book complies with the
Permanent Paper Standard issued by the National
Information Standards Organization (Z39.48–1984).

10 9 8 7 6 5 4 3 2 1

CONTENTS

Preface   vii

Introduction   xi

1. Fundamentals of Capacity   1

2. Tools and Work: The Tyranny of the Machine   23

3. Theory of Value   39

4. Capacity Strategy and Management of Bottlenecks   55

5. Scheduling Rules   75

6. Scheduling and Motivating Workers   113

7. Putting Quality First   135

8. Principles of Work Flow   153

9. Human Skill and Adaptation   171

10. Compensation and Reward Systems for the Project Shop   189

11. Where Can Efficiency Be Found?   211

12. Conclusion: Operations Policy and Practice in the
    New Era   231

Bibliography   239

Index   241

PREFACE

This book is about the merger of knowledge from formerly independent management domains. The subject matter taught in every college or university is fragmented and segregated into detached, isolated islands of theory or practice. It is a useful way to deal with the incredible variety of human knowledge. Elizabethan theatre is taught as if it were without relation to statistics, American history, psychology or the physics of optics. Occasionally, circumstances conspire to put one teacher or scholar in touch with two or more formerly independent domains. The opportunity to interrelate what are usually separate disciplines opens a window on fresh dimensions of knowledge and understanding.

The management of human resources is typically taught in the American business schools as if it were independent of the laws of economics, the rules of accounting, the principles of marketing or the methodology of production operations. The individual student is left to integrate these separate domains as best he or she is able. Few teachers are called on to cross the boundaries of these precincts of knowledge. The purity—perhaps even the sterility—of each isolated island of knowledge is thereby ensured.

I was offered the unusual opportunity to break through the boundaries of academe and teach in two usually separate areas: human resources and production operations. The opportunity flowed from the confluence of two chance combinations of these ordinarily disparate subjects: a Ph.D. in management taken at a university where the business faculty was composed half-and-half of operations researchers and social psychologists and a teaching assignment in a university where the behavioral and operations disciplines resided in the same department of the business school. Preaching from both pulpits flowered naturally from these roots.

My approach to these separate academic domains might well have remained simply and ingenuously schizophrenic, though, had not other factors contributed to an emerging awareness of the opportunity for connecting them. One of those factors was the opportunity to teach the capstone course in business strategy—an assignment that requires integration of disparate business subjects through use of the case method. The second factor arises out of the industrial dynamics of the current age; it is manifest in the flight to the Third World of labor intensive commodity manufacture and the naive discovery by Japanese manufacturers of synergy in worker motivation combined with operations methodology through quality circles. Like an image emerging from blankness on an instant photograph, the picture of an economy shifting from domination by mass production toward a supremacy of custom and short-run output came increasing sharper. The natural fit of motivational and human resources considerations to operations methods and principles within the frame of that image slowly became discernible.

When, for instance, one begins to examine problems of job stress within the context of waiting line and capacity theory, fresh insights come into view. Quality problems on the moving assembly line are freshly illuminated by principles of feedback and goal setting out of the behavioral literature. The ability of participation to forge commitment to a decision course or the motivational power of job enrichment to increase productivity is irrelevant until high worker skill and self-direction required by the project shop replaces the narrow specialization of work required by mass output systems. The presumed motivating power of pay linked to output dispels like dew on the morning grass when innovative approaches to scheduling work and leisure time around customer demand are examined. The assumed efficiency of continuous, high capacity production flow disappears when the cost of poor quality and the loss of labor output from conservative flow-pace standards is calculated. The power of each body of literature to illuminate and enrich the other is awesome.

The present text represents the beginning description of opportunities for integration of these rich and formerly separate disciplines of work analysis. It suggests some of the many possibilities that exist for richer understanding of work and worker effectiveness. It even hints at the potential for combining large parts of these two bodies of knowledge into a department of academic discipline in its own right. Though exploratory and occasionally tentative, some elements are almost revolutionary in quality. It is highly technical in spots and richly rhetorical in others. Overall, it is "a whole 'nother way" of looking at work and organization in an age of rapid technological change.

A major premise of the perspectives offered here is that mass commodity output systems are a brief detour off the main highway of human (and humane) work methods. The mechanical mindlessness of the moving assembly line is not the final or best or even the most efficient design for encouragement of productive output. Better designs have prevailed before and will prevail again in the broader scope of history. Western civilization has, though, gone at least a century and a half lacking experience with these other ways of work. It must rediscover them. An examination of the flow of recent history will help supply a perspective on this opportunity. The meat of this argument, though, is in the demonstration of positive impact from applying the correct operating methods to project shop management. From an examination of these methods it will soon become apparent that efficiency no longer counts.

INTRODUCTION

In the stream of natural history 150 years is the smallest speck of dust on the surface. To a single living human being, it is an eternity of time in which all that can be has been. Western society is presently at or near the end of a brief century and a half of machine worship. Work and life-style have above all been shaped by and fitted to the needs or limitations of machinery during this brief span of history. An unparalleled affluence of commodity products and an unquenchable appetite for more of everything is one result. The distortion of human life by the twin slave masters of overspecialization in work and passive overconsumption of goods is another. Together they undermine human health and despoil the human ecosystem with pollution.

The end of that age is at hand. Humankind is on the threshold of a transition that returns it to life that is paced by natural seasons and the whims of human need. It represents a major departure from familiar patterns of work life that could initially frighten and confuse. It will, though, be an easy adjustment because it is better suited to the natural makeup of humans. The age of machine paced, mass commodity output offered economic security in return for mind-numbing work. Security is now taken as a given. Mass production by automated factories is already displacing large numbers of unskilled and semiskilled workers. The past 150 years are an aberration that will soon pass. The skilled worker who is master of the machine will replace the assembly line drudge. His workplace will be the project shop.

The greatest part of human history is characterized by custom, short-run production. Before the nineteenth century, ships, chariots and weapons were produced in quantity only in time of war. But none was mass produced to standard. Each was handcrafted. Every nail was forged from head to point by a skilled blacksmith. An apprentice may have fired the furnace or hefted the bellows, but forging the end item was the craftsman's skill and pride. Each thrust of the needle through the hide of the shoe was purposefully independent. Every piece of pottery or china was individually handformed and fired. Each was produced to satisfy a specific customer demand. Abundant harvests were occasion for consumption against the seasons of scarcity. Storehouses held only those foods that would withstand spoilage. A late winter fast marked their depletion. Weapons might be saved from the last war, but rust and rot were their natural enemy. Only those kept active for the hunt were fully reliable. Human life was driven by the cycles of nature and the whims of the human spirit.

In the history of industry and technology, assembly line production of commodity goods is a very brief and recent chapter. Standardized products and services produced in very large quantities appeared in Western society only around the middle of the nineteenth century. The transformation of warfare from a contest of wit and skill into a contest of industrial logistics arrived with the American Civil War. The newly created commodity production capability of the northern states was pitted against the agricultural and cottage industry of the South. What meager supply of European arms production the South could run past the Union blockade kept the competition from being excessively uneven. Finally, in the hail of death rained on their respective armies, the North simply overwhelmed its adversary with superior depth of supply. The superiority of mass commodity supply was amply proven.

It is easily overlooked that the skill and courage of a less mechanized agricultural economy made the outcome of the Civil War a precious near thing. The brutal single-mindedness of a Ulysses S. Grant was well served by the industrial powerhouse that stood behind him. The strategic brilliance of Lee and his lieutenants was most of what prevented Grant's onslaught from quick success. Had Lee enjoyed full access to offshore arms production, it is doubtful that skill and spirit would have yielded to brute force. Commodity production obtains its edge from advantage and urgency. Competition and ambition are its natural foundations.

During an interim century and a half, the power of commodity production to drive competition and serve ambition has been demonstrated to excess. The two most destructive wars in human history were fought upon an exploding base of technological advance. The material wants of humankind (in Western society, at least) are now supplied in opulent abundance *because* of commodity production. One may question whether the quality of human life has advanced or retreated as a result of technological progress, but there is no argument that social change of unparalleled magnitude has occurred in the span of less than two lifetimes.

Remarkably, as access to technological progress and mass supply extends to ever further corners of the earth, it is human skill that limits its further advance. The function of competition and ambition ultimately was to motivate mastery of new technological complexity. The advantage of a great production plant was in amplification of superior knowledge and skill on the part of a technological elite through the hands and feet of raw, unskilled laborers driven by ambition to better their lives. A society without a technological elite or lacking ambition among its laboring class cannot withstand the harsh discipline required by mass commodity production.

In parallel fashion, competition and ambition must run their course. When the fire to master nature is snuffed by abundant affluence and leisure, when ambition to improve one's lot fades to complacent consumption of plentiful goods, the thrust driving mass production weakens. The machinery of mass commodity production migrates naturally to new concentrations of competition and ambition. They leave behind a culture accustomed to cheap abundance, seeking self-expression in the special, the uncommon, the custom product and service. They revert to the dominance of a project shop economy.

An economy characterized by mass production of commodity goods and services is inherently unstable. It is an interim, transitional stage that takes humankind from subsistence to abundance. In subsistence, one must live by one's wit. In abundance, one may choose to live either by one's wit or on society's surplusses. During the intermediary transition, one lives on one's ambitions. Those who join the journey from subsistence to abundance must accept the discipline of ambition. As with any great social transition, dropping out on the way is economic suicide. Once the journey is finished and abundance obtained in the fabled land of milk and honey, dropping out is little more than independent self-expression.

The transmutation of culture through abundance and standardized technology ends in full scale reversion to nonstandardization. Ambition is now played out in the search for individual uniqueness. Competition is against one's own personal standards of excellence. But technology has introduced powerful new tools: materials, ideas, power sources, operating methods. Ambition and competition demand their mastery as the ticket of entry to the arena. Lack of ambition or competitiveness consigns one to subsistence on the waste thrown off by an affluent society. Those unprepared for the new age are the orphans of mass production, whereas the ambitious share in opulence that puts the ancient kings of Egypt or Mesopotamia to shame. The unskilled labor that once manned mass production lines no longer has employment.

Reversion to nonstandardized product or service is culture shock. Little has changed in the past 150 years of mass commodity production systems. Suddenly, it passes. It is as if a very advanced culture opened at its core to reveal a lost culture of primitives. Surely, the reemphasis of craftsmanship and quality discovered in the reversion reveals a value lost or diminished by standardized mass production. But the sharp retreat from efficiency and cost control is disorienting. Custom production is still so labor intensive, so wedded to trial and error, so inefficient in achieving the ultimate result. Mass production has accustomed us to a smooth precision, an exactness in minimum cost execution, which custom product and service can never possess. The tools of mass production conferred great clarity and power on the producer. Commodity production provides a baseline of comfort and affluence never before known, available to all who will serve its machinery. But it also produces faceless uniformity. When, finally, demand shifts inevitably to the unique, the custom, the individualized, the costly, the inefficient product and service, it is a cataclysm. The new challenge is to provide custom, short-run output of highest quality at the lowest, most competitive cost.

But neither workers nor managers are prepared for the extent of the transition demanded of them. Their first impulse is to dismiss this challenge as inherently inconsistent and unreachable. Cost is a function of efficiency, which in turn is a function of sales volume. It is the classic cost/volume strategy that has driven the economy all our lifetime and most of our grandparents'. But wait—there are competitors, Japanese notably, who seem to have abandoned a cost/volume philosophy successfully in favor of production to exact demand and who comfortably tolerate marginally, even underutilized, resources. Is there, in fact, a path that leads to high precision, high quality, custom, short-run output at low cost? If there is, we had better locate it quickly if the United States is to retain its vaunted and much valued position of dominance in the world economy.

Is it possible, for instance, that a century and a half of mass production emphasis has produced methods and values that are fundamentally antithetical to low-cost custom, short-run production? It is clear that mass production methodology is difficult to transfer to the project shop. Materials flow technology, for instance, is simplified by mass production to a lock-step flow that can be exactly timed and controlled. Just-in-time flow technology is the natural state of mass production. Work-in-process (WIP) inventory accumulates principally at weak points and bottlenecks in the flow. If it is easier to let inventory build than to fix the weakness or bottleneck, WIP becomes a solution. It is generally a bad solution because of the ease with which marginal or unacceptable quality can be hidden in the WIP queue, but it is a quick and appealing solution to competitive, ambitious managers who focus on the near-term payoff.

Materials flow in a project shop changes daily with each new project that comes through the door. Work-in-process is a way of life. The job of management is to prevent work from becoming stalled in the WIP queues. Otherwise, the same problems of marginal or unacceptable quality found in mass production are inflicted on the job shop with none of the opportunities for efficiency in system flow enjoyed in the commodity production setting.

The explosive advance of technology and operations methodology that has accompanied the age of commodity production has primarily served mass production methods. The giants of the age of scientific management,

Frederick Winslow Taylor, Henry L. Gantt, Frank Galbraith and Lillian Galbraith, all focused on maximized use of the production machine at minimum labor cost. Economic Order Quantity (EOQ), an early, powerful model of cost optimization, focuses on cost trade-offs of setup versus inventory holding. In the framework of mass commodity production, inventory serves to reduce high changeover cost and simultaneously buffers uncertainty of demand. It goes unnoticed that the best possible cost situation exists when there is neither setup nor inventory cost.

Linear programming (LP), perhaps the most sophisticated quantitative decision support tool ever devised for application to production, deals in optimization of the trade-off between limited pools of resources that are in heavy, constant demand. Application of LP to custom, short-run production may require a job-by-job analysis of cost and profitability in an often dynamic and unpredictable market. The job that is profitable in today's mix of work is marginal in tomorrow's. The priority in a project shop is to keep work flowing into the shop. Costing must be accomplished one job at a time. The LP may be useful in allocating scarce machinery or labor in a commodity shop but cannot survive in the absence of constraints on output. Service that attracts customers requires extensive excess capacity of machinery, equipment and skill to do the job. Cost/volume is replaced as a strategy by cost/work-mix. That mix is not likely to be sufficiently stable to permit mathematical optimization.

Flexible reallocation of resources at a moment's notice is the strength of the project shop. Some repeat, short-run orders may be useful to stabilize work flow through the shop, especially when setup and turnaround times are short, but short runs don't contribute to stabilizing of production flow. Quick response to the unanticipated is a project shop's forte. If quantitative decision tools are to be applied in a job shop, they must be computerized, user friendly, as well as applicable job-by-job and to the current aggregate of work in-house.

The genius of production methods and operations research that supported the growth of commodity production must be rediscovered for application to custom, short-run, project shop production and service requirements. For this to occur, the shift in foundation assumptions on which project shop performance rests must be discovered and articulated. The movement toward custom product and service is already well advanced. U.S. agriculture, mechanized, chemically enriched and genetically enhanced, is capable of feeding not only this nation but much of the rest of the world with less than 5% of our working population applied to its requirements. Profit in the sale of food has shifted toward specialized crops or processing of food. Potential is greatest in the production of healthier, more varied and more exotic specialty crops.

Manufacturing, at midcentury the dominant economic force, shrinks yearly as a proportion of the labor force. The competition is more often won today by the company that is first to the market with technological advance. Research and development (R&D) is indispensable to competitive success. The wave of the future must certainly be products manufactured individually to the exact specifications of the buyer. In the process of reaching for that technological utopia, the delivery of mass produced commodity products and services will require ever fewer human hands. The automated factories of tomorrow's world will echo agriculture in employing fewer than 5% of the labor force. Designed for flexibility and programmed variation on the base product, built for ease of changeover to other product lines, the flexible, automated factory will become a variety of the project shop.

With the service economy rapidly replacing manufacturing as the dominant user of labor, just as manufacturing formerly replaced agriculture, mass production methods are rediscovered for application to efficiency of service delivery. Hospitals, banks, fast-food chains, law firms, mass transit service and service provisioners of many other sorts effectively use existing production methodology to reduce cost and increase efficiency. Ultimately, the labor used by this sector also will shrink. Finally, all paths lead back to custom production and service as the broad base of economic activity, raised economically high on a foundation of low-cost commodity products and services.

Advanced economies have already turned the corner with agricultural and manufacturing efficiency. The philosophy and methodology of mass production is firmly established to support any further refinement needed. It is the custom, short-run job shop product and service that now leads the tide of economic change and advance. A fresh foundation of philosophy, theory and methodology is needed to support that leadership.

This book provides a preliminary and elemental foray into the emerging age of project shop operations management. It explicates the basic philosophical shifts that are necessary to move from a mass output to a project shop economy. It describes some of the basic operating methods that apply to the management of project operations. It explores the impact of this change on workers by tracing the transition of work roles from mass output to project shop jobs. It provides a partial answer to why the Japanese can find no basis for a distinction between operations management and human resources management. Effective management of quality is found to require worker control over the pace and pattern of production. Participation—at an appropriate level—and autonomy—within reasonable limits—are unavoidable elements of a well-managed project shop. Individual growth and adaptivity are indispensable adjuncts to project shop flexibility and success.

On a technical front, the project shop requires of management a full appreciation of the relationship between capacity utilization and level of service. A fresh, even revolutionary relation of worker to his or her tools is needed. Effective scheduling and work flow are discovered to be dependent on identification of bottlenecks. Limitation in either machine capacity or human skill may create a bottleneck. Cost efficiency turns principally on effective scheduling of labor within the framework of equipment and tool availability. Complexity of the operation makes systematic data gathering and analysis a fundamental task of the project shop manager. These are just the beginnings of the new operations methods and perspectives required for managing project shop operations.

Fortunately, many familiar operations concepts can be productively applied to project shop operations management. In many ways, it is the philosophical foundation that changes most. Once the new vision is captured, most of the traditional tools of operations management, waiting line theory, scheduling, Monte Carlo stimulation, materials flow, inventory control, statistics and probability, all find a useful application. The point of view of the operations manager is more critical to progress than his or her specific kit of tools. In these pages, we shall sketch in broad strokes that point of view and suggest new applications for familiar tools. In so doing, the foundation for the age of the project shop will be described.

1

FUNDAMENTALS OF CAPACITY

"Running at max capacity is efficient but ineffective."

Eskimos, it is reported, use twenty different words to denote snow. Two separate roots distinguish falling from fallen snow, and some eight to ten unique variations on these roots allow still further differentiation. Some, perhaps, serve purely esthetic ends. Most permit useful differentiation of the qualities of snow as they shape the daily existence of these hardy arctic dwellers. Snow is a basic element in their lives. The varied ways in which it is used or can limit activity are of greatest importance to an Eskimo.

Managers, however, have only one word for capacity. If you attend closely to its use, you may discriminate subtle varieties of meaning from situation to situation. But the word itself does not change to reflect shadings of meaning. Operations managers, especially, seem to employ a limited vocabulary to describe their experience, letting the terms be defined by the immediate circumstances of work. There is parsimony in this practice, but there is imprecision too. Advancement of the art of management requires increased differentiation of concepts. Capacity is as good a place as any to start.

Capacity most often is used to describe the throughput or output capability of machines and related production systems. But there are at least four distinct meanings that are connoted in the term *capacity* from time to time or place to place. Understanding operations management requires that these different shadings of meaning be identified and made explicit.

VARIETIES OF CAPACITY

First is system output capacity. This is systemic or temporal capacity. Maximum output is described as a quantity "x" in "y" amount of time.

Time is fundamental to this meaning of this capacity because time is the basic constraint on it. When you need more output, you merely keep the system churning until demand is satisfied. When time is limited, capacity is limited. For the moment, we will ignore shortages of input to the system, viewing them merely as the output of other systems constrained by their own temporal capacity. Later in chapter 4 we will find that a mismatch in the temporal capacity of sequenced systems—a bottleneck—is a fundamental problem for any kind of operations flow.

The second quality of capacity that impacts operations is that of structural capacity. This refers to load carrying limitations on a system or machine that, if exceeded, result in breakdown and damage to the system and perhaps also to people or equipment around it. This may also describe the useful life of a system that is subject to wear with use. Most systems do ultimately wear out with use, but those that are ruggedly designed and well maintained may be used as if they might go on operating forever. The point at which it breaks down or self-destructs when driven beyond its structural limits describes a system's structural capacity.

The third quality of capacity that must be recognized as a factor in operations is recovery capacity. Every operating system needs preventive maintenance and care. Without attention, it may lose output efficiency, wear more quickly or break down more often. Some systems, human particularly, are subject to fatigue that disperses with rest or diversion. Overheating of machinery may be harmless as long as operations are brought to a halt and a period of cooling is permitted. Breakdown in even a critical system element is a minor matter as long as replacement parts and skilled maintenance labor are available to effect rapid repair. The tires on an Indianapolis race car are replaced in seconds so that the racer may recover his position on the track. Recovery capacity in the pit is critical to winning the race.

A fourth quality of capacity is found in the capacity for flexibility or adaptation. An athlete's ability to run the one-hundred-yard dash is entirely separate from his ability to throw the discus. The ability of a patent law office to handle criminal cases is likely to be minimal. The ability of a production line to turn out refrigerators is entirely different from a machine shop's ability to turn out a custom die mold. A rare athlete might compete in both the dash and the discus throw, an unusual attorney might handle patent and criminal cases, but a refrigerator production line is totally unsuited to production of precision steel parts. Specialized design and organization of any performance system limits its flexibility and adaptability. The more specialized the system, the less its flexibility, and the more costly is adaptation to new tasks.

Clearly, these are all significant, relevant meanings of capacity. They have a practical implication for the management of work systems. Most experienced managers will recognize the differences connoted by the varying contexts in which the term *capacity* is used. Why the fuss? It has to do with the way we understand production and service capacity when planning and managing our businesses. Output (temporal) capacity dominates every argument that pertains to capacity planning. Structural, recovery and adaptive capacity have little or no place in the creation of basic capacity strategy for the typical business operation.

THE DOMINANCE OF TEMPORAL CAPACITY

Capacity plans for virtually all kinds of production or service systems are founded on measures and estimates of maximum output (temporal) capacity. Less than full capacity use is presumed to be wasteful and inefficient. The objective of a prudent, efficient operations manager is to obtain every last ounce of output from every system and worker every working day. Inefficiency is the enemy of profit.

Western economy is driven by an expectation of near-term payoff, usually in the form of profits that produce dividends on equity or interest on loaned resources. Competition and ambition demand the maximum temporal output to meet the demands of investors, lenders, workers and customers. The productive system is a golden goose. Our expectation is that it will deliver the maximum output of golden eggs so that these diverse constituencies may enjoy maximum, near-term payoff. It will never do to let output proceed on less than maximum pace; we must have full gratification *now*.

Indeed, the demand for immediate gratification may require that we risk surpassing structural limits or sacrifice recovery and flexibility needs for a higher short-term payoff. Competitive impatience and ambition for the maximum payoff demand full scale temporal output. Capacity planning of business operations recognizes and addresses the maximum near-term temporal capacity potential of the system solely and exclusively.

Once the imperative of maximum short-term temporal output is accepted, everything else about the production system must follow. Maximum output requires steady, predictable market demand subject only to gentle up or down shifts that can be buffered by price change, inventory accumulation, planned capital investment in new plant or calculated liquidation of excess capacity. A labor supply that is dependable and easy to replace is needed to ensure independence from scarcity of skill or fickle human commitment. Unskilled or semiskilled workers who can be trained quickly and replaced are ideal. Worker attendance on the job is crucial to obtaining maximum output. Absence causes valuable equipment to be idled, which cuts output. Workers (as well as managers) are impressed into servitude by the high capacity output system.

The flow of material and supply through the system must be precisely organized and regulated. When the system is weak or undependable, buffer inventories of work-in-process must be tolerated to decouple operations. The offending system element is thereby isolated to prevent its disease of inefficiency from spreading. The moving assembly line, a balanced production flow system with highly specialized, low skilled labor at every workstation, is the direct product of maximum capacity planning. The imperative of temporal capacity maximization is the mother of mass commodity production.

By way of contrast, there are many elements in our way of life that are managed otherwise. Maximum use is of little importance with personal tools and equipment such as automobiles, vacuum cleaners, washing machines, private homes, public highways, or TVs. For low-cost efficiency of machinery used in washing clothing, a public laundromat is hard to improve on. But unless the laundromat is exceptionally convenient to home and shopping, the added personal time demanded, not to mention the additional cost and risk in transport of laundry to and from a laundromat, makes the home washer more efficient.

Few personal automobiles get anything near maximum usage. Buses and taxis that have long hours of use each day are only slightly more rugged in design from a private automobile and may receive more frequent maintenance to support more intense usage. They are more efficiently used. The value of the personal car, though, rests on its flexible accessibility. The fifteen-minute auto trip into town replaces a forty-five minute bus trip or a two-hour walk. The walk might be healthier, but the savings in time for added work or leisure generates unmistakable value for the average person. To offset less than maximum use, the resale value of a car is partly based on mileage usage. Depreciation is allocated between age and use. If one chooses to use one's auto only rarely, full value of use can still be obtained by owning it longer. The expectation of heavy use to obtain maximum payoff from auto ownership plays a major role in the valuation of a used car.

Competition and ambition drive the resale value of minimally used private autos down more than is necessary only because ours is a society oriented to maximum use and payoff. In society's infatuation with industrial progress, the new, the advanced, the different, has come to be associated with increased value. Much of what is scrapped is simply out of date—passe. Most still has utility and value. A minimum of maintenance would restore it. We overlook structural, recovery and adaptive capacity in these resources. Our lives are shaped by the imperative of maximum output, earliest payoff, temporal capacity. We are enslaved by our competition and ambition.

Many of our gravest social and economic ills flow from our overconcern with temporal capacity. Waste and poverty, boom and bust, war and environmental destruction, all flow directly from it. Until recent times, technological progress was sufficient payoff in itself to offset those penalties. The tide is turning. We have discovered that, though full capacity output provides a high rate of return on investment, it does not yield the highest quality of life. Efficiency has a cost; it fails to recognize the uniqueness of each human being. Efficiency makes workers, customers, even managers, mere cogs in the system of output.

Efficiency is purchased at the cost of individual choice. Efficiency requires that people be servants of machines. Maximum temporal capacity utilization yields efficiency. What does it take to turn the tables? How is the machine returned to the status of being our servant? If that, indeed, is our purpose, we must begin with abandonment of the imperative of maximum temporal capacity output as our exclusive foundation for planning, financing and managing production and service operations.

TEMPORAL CAPACITY AND MASS COMMODITY OUTPUT

Mass commodity output, whether of product or service, assumes the desirability, even the necessity, of getting as close to 100% temporal capacity utilization as possible or practical. Operating at exactly 100% capacity against demand is theoretically unsound because any small increase in demand then throws the system into a hopelessly backlogged state. America's crisis of gasoline availability in 1974 and 1978 resulted from a very slight shortfall in supply against demand—several percentage points at most. The closer a system works to maximum capacity, the larger must be the buffer inventory of finished goods to absorb brief surges in demand comfortably. These are fundamental points that are clarified with the help of quantified models and simulations of capacity later in this chapter.

The point that must be made about mass commodity output systems is that very special conditions must be satisfied for them to work at all. Raw material must be in abundant supply. Any shortage or potential shortage must be offset through stockpiles or substitutes. This is equally a requirement of an automobile factory, a fast food chain or a hospital's blood bank. The Federal Reserve exists to ensure that banks need never run out of money—a condition that would be ruinous to the bank and potentially calamitous to the economy as a whole if widespread. Full capacity system operation and inventory are inseparable. When inventory is impossible, as with many kinds of service, operating at full capacity means a great sacrifice in level of service.

Mass output requires that manpower be abundantly available with little limitation on replacement availability. Unemployment is essential to a full capacity output economy because *any* shortage of labor to support the system instantly impairs the system's efficiency. Unskilled or semiskilled labor requiring minimum training and experience is the broadest base of manpower. Skilled manpower is more costly (though not necessarily so in terms of output effectiveness) and is in shorter supply. Shortages of skilled labor require a period of training during which the system must be suboptimized. Shortages of unskilled or semiskilled labor can usually be overcome with small adjustments in the wage scale.

Bottlenecks result in a waiting line of work-in-process (or customers) that must accumulate in front of the bottleneck. The queue grows endlessly until the elements of the system preceding the bottleneck are shut down and the excess is worked off at the bottleneck. The technical aspects of bottlenecks are discussed fully in chapter 4. For purposes of this discussion, it is sufficient to state that, in a full capacity utilization output system, *any* bottleneck has the potential to create intolerable inventory holding problems, which forces reduced capacity utilization in all elements of the system preceding it. Running at full capacity is an all or nothing matter that permits neither bottlenecks nor adaptation to excess demand.

Mass commodity output systems demand a precise balance of work flow from entry to exit of the system. They are designed so that each workstation is the waiting line of work for the next. The Japanese did not invent just-in-time (JIT). What they did was recognize that anything less than a continuous, queueless just-in-time flow of work is a corruption of the continuous flow system. Decoupling a continuous work flow system at points of weakness reduces the need to solve bottlenecks, problems of poor maintenance, substandard skill, absenteeism and all other deficiencies of the system. In addition, the pileup of WIP at the decouple point becomes a convenient place to bury poor quality work. JIT is merely the proper discipline to keep continuous flow output systems healthy (Ohno, 1988; Shingo, 1988).

Finally, continuous flow output systems assume that every machine is well maintained and working correctly, that every worker is trained and on the job with the correct tools and that nothing will go wrong while the system is in operation. When any of these assumptions is violated, the potential for a bottleneck is created that instantly invalidates the entire purpose of a full capacity output system.

Things do, however, go wrong. The moving assembly line must be stopped for the series of cars that are missing two wheels, thereby idling scores of workers until the problem is cleared. Japanese automakers, at least, have the wisdom to expect workers to contribute to the solution of the problem when the line must be stopped and even give workers authority to stop it. The line at the ten-minute car lube shop stalls when the improperly trained worker strips the threads while forcing an oil filter onto the block. Morning coffee runs out when the petcock is left open on the cafeteria line, leaving customers to pile up in the service aisle. Full capacity is a nice theory. It suggests large, early payoff for effort, but it requires the utmost planning, discipline and good luck to work.

THE ILLUSION OF FULL CAPACITY OUTPUT

True full capacity production with continuous flow systems is an improbable ideal. It has been more than forty years since we have seen round the clock operation that obtained true "full capacity" of production systems during World War II. The increase in output made possible by twenty-four hours' scheduling of output at that time was astonishing. But full capacity output systems are poorly fitted to human and social needs. Highly automated, integrated systems like petroleum cracking plants, public utilities or steel foundries function twenty-four hours a day, but even these operations are paced so that only minimum labor routines and simple monitoring are required on the night shift. Activities requiring decisions are made only on the day shift on week days when management and staff are scheduled to work. Only a real emergency will bring the experts out nights or weekends. The "real" business is conducted only on weekday shifts. It is only as integrated, automated manufacturing emerges on the crest of advancing technology that true full capacity utilization of mass commodity output systems will again become possible. Even then it may be impractical to monitor breakdowns during night hours. The best systems will monitor for problems and shut down automatically until the maintenance engineer arrives the next morning.

Full capacity output is ultimately an illusion, if not a deception. The structural capacity of a full capacity output system may be impossible to measure because there is no way to press the system to its limits without creating horrendous bottlenecks. Recovery capacity may be imponderable because of the complexity of the system. Adaptation capacity has long since been sacrificed to the narrow worker specialization and exact work flow balance necessary to achieve full capacity system design. A refrigerator compressor plant is useless for making air-conditioner compressors, even though the principal difference is only in design and performance specifications. A cafeteria does not lend to servicing a formal banquet, a gas station is not a suitable arrangement from which to sell sporting equipment. Full capacity, efficient output makes it difficult if not impossible to satisfy alternative capacity needs and requirements.

Automated, integrated, *flexible* production systems are now on the drawing boards of U.S. industry to reintroduce adaptivity. For true commodity output needs, they are probably the ultimate production system. Even so, there will be constraints on variety or scope of output introduced by capacity for variety in raw materials and in capacity for variety in machine applications. Robust engineering design of such systems may satisfy recovery capacity needs. Truly robust systems, though, will probably take several generations of system evolution to arrive, and early versions will be subject to severe unreliability. Automation in its earliest stages typically requires prodigious inputs of maintenance. Capacity for recovery is low in any new technology. Ultimately, the ideal of continuous flow, full capacity output production and service systems may be approximated for most major commodity items. We can perhaps look forward to the fully automated cereal packaging line or the highly automated hospital somewhere in the future.

At that point, commodity manufacture will probably absorb the same small proportion of labor—less than 5% of the labor force—that agriculture came to require early in this century as food production became increasingly mechanized and technologized. How then will the remainder of the labor force be occupied?

THE COMING AGE OF THE PROJECT SHOP

The new demand for labor will undoubtedly come from custom, individualized products and services, either as modifications of commodities or unique offerings. Custom, short-run output is destined to become the norm of the economy. Already, it has substantially displaced large scale commodity output as the primary source of new manufacturing jobs. The ubiquitous job shop is fast becoming the backbone of the economy.

The term *job shop* is closely associated with machine tools and engineering design because they have been common job shop activities for several decades. On close inspection, a wide variety of other common job shop types can be found in present day commerce. The custom kitchen cabinet shop, the movie studio, a hospital emergency room, the auto repair garage, a dental or orthopedic prosthetic lab, the typical printing shop, all are examples of job shop operations that deliver custom or short-run product and service. The job shop operates on a project basis. To identify better the wide range of products and services that are subject to delivery in this mode, we shall henceforth refer to this kind of operation as a *project* shop.

A project shop presents a wholly new set of problems with respect to efficiency, cost and customer service. Many if not most of the special requirements for efficiency in a continuous output system cannot be satisfied by the project shop. It is impossible to eliminate and very difficult to avoid bottlenecks in a project shop. The flow of work from stage to stage is not easily subject to being organized or balanced. Work arrives unscheduled or semischeduled if not randomly at any workstation. The mix of work changes from day to day, week to week, month to month. Bottlenecks migrate from place to place depending on mix of work. To the orderly eye of an experienced continuous process operations manager, it is chaos.

If not entirely chaotic, it certainly represents complexity. The experience and custom of operations management suggests the need for balanced flow, elimination of bottlenecks, improved use of machine capacity. The result from applying these solutions is likely to be an increase in complexity or greater chaos. The operating methodologies developed to support continuous flow, full output systems are ill suited, if not utterly inappropriate, to the project shop setting.

The principal empirical operations research carried out on project shop operations was accomplished by R. W. Conway, W. L. Maxwell and L. W. Miller (1967) in their classic and extensive study of job sequencing methods.

The conclusion of these authors was that the shortest processing time job prioritizing rule reduces mean job completion time more than any other rule. In chapter 5, the uses and deceptions of this rule will be examined carefully. Sequencing according to shortest processing time (SPT) has its uses, but it is a weak foundation on which to manage project operations if used alone. The most significant element in managing the project shop, level of equipment capacity utilization, was ignored in this simulation research for the sake of simplicity in modeling. For the twenty intervening years those principles on which project shop work flow is managed have, as a result, begun and ended with SPT prioritizing.

By implication, the remainder of project shop operations problems are left to be solved with existing operations methodology taken from continuous flow output systems. Most such methodology just does not fit. Full capacity output planning does not work for the project shop. A fresh point of departure is needed. Capacity is the most appropriate place to begin.

SERVICE AND CAPACITY: WAITING LINE THEORY

Clarity of the argument requires a technical argument. The starting point for examination of project shop capacity issues will be queueing, or waiting line theory. Waiting line theory, developed in 1905 by A. K. Erlang as a tool for analysis of telephone customer service requirements, permits estimation of waiting line (queue) length and customer waiting time required for service. Figure 1–1 illustrates the simplest form of this model, the single channel, single phrase, negative exponential queueing model.

The mathematical model on which waiting line theory is based demonstrates the inevitable countervailing relationship between capacity utilization and customer service as measured by waiting time for service. Figure 1–2 illustrates the relation predicted by the waiting line model for number of jobs (customers) in the waiting line as a function of level of capacity utilization under conditions of unscheduled, random arrivals at the threshold of service. The model illustrates in dramatic fashion the peculiar character of unscheduled work flow.

At relatively low levels of use, under 50%, for instance, the average waiting line is less than a single job. The peculiarities of randomness, however, retain the potential for an occasional short waiting line simply because two or three jobs can, by chance, arrive simultaneously. Still, the workstation is idle more than half of its available time.

At capacity utilization levels around 60% to 70%, a short waiting line is typical, though it is still likely that a job will arrive when the station is empty. At utilization levels of 80% or above, an empty workstation is occasionally encountered, but the event is increasingly rare. The typical waiting line is lengthy, and waiting times are extended. At utilization levels above 90% the curve rockets off the graph. In theory, the waiting line

Figure 1–1
Single Channel Service Model

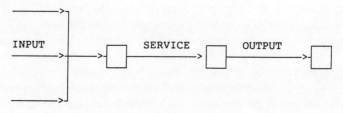

$$\text{Length of Waiting Line} = \frac{\lambda^2}{\mu(\mu - \lambda)}$$

$$\text{Time in Waiting Line} = \frac{\lambda}{\mu(\mu - \lambda)}$$

λ = average arrival rate of customers or jobs

μ = average rate at which customers or jobs are serviced

becomes infinitely long at 100% capacity utilization. Whether this is fully realistic or not may be subject to debate. But anyone who braved the waiting lines for gasoline during the shortages of the 1970s discovered how quickly lines grew toward infinity at only a percentage point or two over full capacity demand. Figure 1–2 illustrates these points graphically.

The waiting line model demonstrates why continuous output systems *must* be balanced so that work (projects, customers, gallons, autos, toasters, etc.) flows from stage to stage in exact, lock-step sequence. If each stage were independent of the previous and flow was random rather than scheduled, full capacity utilization would create the potential for an infinite waiting line in front of every workstation That, indeed, is approximately the dilemma of the project shop.

In the absence of organized, scheduled work flow through stages of the system, long queues of work form in front of high capacity utilization work stations. Scheduling work in a project shop is something of a contradiction in terms. Random work arrival means that the system is at the mercy of the customer's whim. Unique work flow patterns for different kinds of jobs defeat any attempt at balanced work flow. Workstations function as independent systems, each with its own work queue. Expediting does nothing other than to change the sequence of jobs in the queues. Putting the smallest SPT jobs through a station first may sometimes help. The more fundamental solution is to build slack into capacity that will permit reduction of or adjustment around the bottlenecks.

Waiting line theory permits simulation of how waiting time is exacerbated

Figure 1–2
Length of Waiting Line as a Function of Capacity Utilization at Independent Workstations

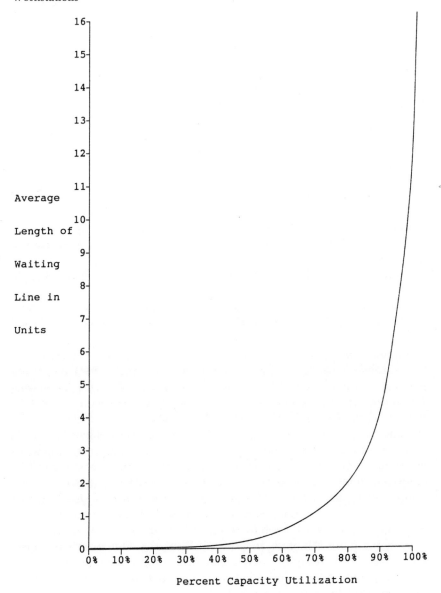

by high capacity utilization. Because it is a robust model, a single phase, single channel, negative exponential queue model, the simplest available, can serve effectively to demonstrate the point (Table 1–1). Any arrival flow sequence characterized by normally distributed but random variability will produce a waiting line. From Table 1–1 it can be determined that, at 99% capacity, the average queue is thirty times as long as at 80% (98.1/3.2), one hundred times as long as at 60% (98.1/0.9). At 95% capacity, the average queue is more than five times longer than at 80% (18.05/3.2) and ten times as long as at 60% (18.05/0.9). A geometric increase in job flow delay due to queueing is encountered as capacity utilization approaches 100%, and theoretically, the queue stretches to infinity when use hits 100%.

Project shops receive work at the customer's convenience. The aggregate business level may be relatively predictable over time, but points in time of arrival distribute more like customers walking into a bank or driving up to a gas pump. Task elements and task sequences vary unpredictably, approximating a random rate and path of flow from station to station. A classic work queueing problem results at entry to the system and at many or all of the steps a job must pass through. As long as full capacity utilization is the major policy for achieving efficiency, delay is an unavoidable concomitant of cost control. Timely service is available at the high cost associated with low capacity utilization or at another customer's expense in added delay.

Delays at very high levels of capacity utilization can be enormous. To illustrate, we can once again use the single phase, single channel negative exponential queueing model as the basis for an estimate. Table 1–2 demonstrates how a three-stage job that requires one week (5.0 days) of total labor/machine time for actual performance, when subject to queueing delays at multiple workstations, could take more than three weeks (16.0 days) to flow through an 80% capacity house or eighteen weeks (91.1 days) in a 95% capacity operation. Table 1–3 illustrates how a four-stage job requiring 1.0 day of actual process time would require more than 3.0 days at 80% capacity utilization and more than 17.0 days at 95% utilization.

Aside from frustrations at delay, significant quality problems are likely to be introduced because delay increases the opportunity for damage or deterioration of WIP staged in the queues. More frequent miscommunication of specifications occurs as the job requires refamiliarization with specifications after each delay in the queue. Queueless job flow *does* have an impact on quality in various ways. The likelihood of delay itself is increased because it is easier for the job to become lost in the system. The longer the queues, the more elaborate and costly will be the administrative control systems needed to locate jobs. As a consequence, high utilization of machines and manpower in a project shop can increase the cost of schedule administration. Expediters are indispensable!

Tables 1–2 and 1–3 are, in essence, rudimentary simulations of produc-

Table 1-1
Queue Length as a Function of Capacity Utilization

Percent Capacity Usage	Ratio of Arrival Rate to Service Rate*	Average Queue Length	% of Time 2 or More Jobs are in the Queue	% of Time 3 or More Jobs are in the Queue
99%	19.8/20	98.1	98.01%	97.03%
95%	19/20	18.05	90.25	86.74
90%	18/20	8.1	81.0	72.90
80%	16/20	3.2	64.0	51.2
70%	14/20	1.63	49.0	34.3
60%	12/20	0.9	36.0	21.6
50%	10/20	0.5	25.0	12.5
40%	8/20	0.27	16.0	6.4
30%	6/20	0.13	9.0	2.7
20%	4/20	0.05	4.0	0.8
10%	2/20	0.03	1.0	0.1

* Queue length is dependent solely on the ratio of arrival to service. Absolute numbers vary as a function of unit of time employed but do not influence queue length. Numbers used are arbitrarily chosen to fit the selected capacity utilization level.

Table 1-2
Queue Delay as a Function of Capacity Utilization with a Three Element Task Requiring One Week Actual Working Time

Job Elmt	Working Time	Daily Arrival Rate	95% Ave. Capacity Service	Queue* Length (days)	80% Ave. Capacity Service	Queue* Length (days)	60% Ave. Capacity Service	Queue* Length (days)
A	2 days	.5	.526	36.6	.625	6.4	.833	1.80
B	1 day	1.0	1.053	17.9	1.25	3.2	1.667	.90
C	2 days	.5	.526	36.6	.625	6.4	.833	1.80
TOTAL 5 days				91.1		16.0		4.50

			50% Ave. Capacity Service	Queue* Length (days)	30% Ave. Capacity Service	Queue* Length (days)
A	2 days	.5	1.0	1.0	1.67	.26
B	1 day	1.0	1.0	1.0	1.67	.26
C	2 days	.5	2.0	1.0	3.33	.13
			1.0	1.0	1.67	.26
				3.0		0.65

$$* \quad \frac{\lambda}{\mu(\mu - \lambda)}$$

14

Table 1-3
Queue Delay as a Function of Capacity Utilization with a Four Element Task Requiring One Day of
Actual Working Time

Job Elmt.	Working Time	Daily Arrival Rate	95% Ave. Capacity Service	Queue* Length (days)	80% Ave. Capacity Service	Queue* Length (days)	60% Ave. Capacity Service	Queue* Length (days)
1	1 hour	1.0	1.053	17.9	1.25	3.2	1.667	.90
2	2 hours	.5	.526	36.6	.625	6.4	.833	1.80
3	3 hours	.33	.35	47.1	.412	9.8	.555	2.64
4	2 hours	.5	.526	36.5	.625	6.4	.833	1.80
TOTAL 8 HOURS				138.1		25.8		7.14

Job Elmt.	Working Time	Daily Arrival Rate	50% Ave. Capacity Service	Queue* Length (days)	30% Ave. Capacity Service	Queue* Length (days)
1	1 hour	1.0	2.0	1.0	3.33	.13
2	2 hours	.5	1.0	1.0	1.67	.26
3	3 hours	.33	.67	1.5	1.11	.38
4	2 hours	.5	1.0	1.0	1.67	.26
				4.5		1.03

$$* \quad \frac{\lambda}{\mu(\mu - \lambda)}$$

tion flow that assume each workstation is operating at the specified average percent capacity utilization. That is, there are no bottlenecks in the flow process. Realistically, each workstation might be assigned its own average level of capacity utilization. Inescapable bottlenecks in the system—machines or skills that deserve higher capacity utilization in the cost calculus and that thereby influence queue length and flow time through the system—could be specifically evaluated for trade-off between capacity utilization gained and impact on the queue. Indeed, modeling existing capacity availability and labor loading with simulation has potentially great power to assess equipment mix, to fix capacity utilization in light of service and quality standards and to identify bottlenecks or allocate labor skill mix to cover the required job mix. Rudimentary and preliminary simulations of the effects of bottlenecks on work flow are presented in chapter 4. The skill and equipment capability required to accomplish more complex and sophisticated simulations are available and adequate to the task (Solomon, 1983). They merely await reform of the criteria against which project shop effectiveness is to be measured.

NOW OR NEXT SCHEDULING IN THE PROJECT SHOP

The fundamental reform required for managing a project shop effectively is abandonment of traditional modes and standards of maximum capacity utilization. One standard that deserves to be transferred intact, however, is the requirement for just-in-time work flow. Engineering design of continuous flow full capacity systems assumes now or next queueing. The WIP queues in such systems are a corruption. To approximate continuous flow service and flow control in a project shop, that level of overcapacity which permits substantial elimination of queues *must* be sought and tolerated. The right level of suboptimization is the proper objective. Efficiency of work flow is now defined by the lack of a queue at each workstation. The correct criterion for project shop work flow effectiveness is the same as for continuous flow; it is queueless, now or next work flow from station to station, made possible by built-in excess equipment capacity. One of the by-products of JIT work flow in the project shop, as in continuous flow, is increased quality.

In project shops that propose to give JIT quality and service, the new rule of thumb must be that every job is either in process now or next in line. "Now or next" is the guiding principle of JIT. The single phase, single channel negative exponential queueing model can again be referenced to determine that capacity utilization at or below 60% (see Table 1–1) is necessary to reduce average queue length to this level. Tables 1–2 and 1–3 demonstrate that, with a multistage, short-run operation, exceptionally fast service requires *very low* levels of machine capacity utilization. A job that must be finished in actual process time plus no more than 20% flow delay might require average capacity utilization of 30% or less.

RETURN ON INVESTMENT AND UNDERUTILIZATION OF CAPACITY

The major impediment to implementing a general policy of excess equipment capacity will be the need for high cash flow from maximum use of expensive new equipment to pay off the debt on interest, or dividend on equity, expected by lenders and investors. High effective yield on interest and investment rates that have recently characterized financial markets are potentially a major barrier to a widespread policy of underutilized capacity. In the longer run, effective yield on money will most likely subside to more modest, traditional levels. The United States in the second half of the twentieth century, though, is on the go-go track of wealth accumulation. Competitiveness and ambition drive most economic decisions. The transition from full capacity utilization policy to one of slack, suboptimized capacity may require an interim strategy of cost and price adjustment. The answer is to use pricing that is adjusted to yield the return on investment (ROI) equivalent of full capacity utilization in calculating the cost effectiveness of new project shop equipment.

Commodity products can be forecast closely enough to provide immediate service of customer demand out of inventory (another kind of queue). Inventory control is fundamental to cost control. Quality is designed, inspected or reworked into the product. But short-run and especially one-of-a-kind project shop production cannot be inventoried. Customer demand can be satisfied only by quicker flow through the production system. Reduced capacity utilization satisfies this criterion, even though it requires suboptimized, underutilized capacity. Underutilization is no problem if price can be increased enough to raise return on investment to the same level as might be obtained at full capacity utilization. When price can be raised based on improved service and quality, the problem is solved. To obtain sufficient return from jobs on newly financed project shop machinery at the expected level of slack in use required for improved service and quality, price must be increased to yield the desired return on investment. Reduced capacity utilization thus becomes a straightforward question of ROI.

Table 1–4 displays the effect of progressive reductions in percent of capacity on pretax ROI goals of 24.0% and 18.0%. At 60% capacity utilization (average queue length of 0.9), the ROI must be priced at 40.0% of cost to equal 24.0% at full use. This means only a 12.9% increase in overall price. At capacity utilization as low as 30.0%, the ROI is set at 80.0% of job cost to yield the equivalent of 24.0% on 100.0% use but demands a price premium of only 45.0%. At the same 30.0 percent utilization rate a more modest goal of 18.0% pretax ROI can be approximated by setting a 60.0% ROI margin over cost to establish the price. This requires only a 36.0% price increase.

This is an extremely conservative analysis, which assumes that 100%

Table 1–4
Return on Investment as a Function of Capacity Utilization

Percent Capacity Utilized	% Margin Required for 24% ROI	Price Increase Required to Maintain ROI at 24%	% Margin Required for 18% ROI	Price Increase Required to Maintain ROI at 18%
100%	24.0%	0.0%	18.0%	0%
95	25.0	0.8	18.9	0.8
90	26.7	2.2	20.0	1.7
85	28.2	3.4	21.2	2.7
80	30.0	4.8	22.5	3.8
70	34.3	8.3	25.7	6.5
60	40.4	13.2	30.0	10.2
50	48.0	19.4	36.0	15.3
40	60.0	29.0	45.0	22.9
30	80.0	45.2	60.0	35.6
20	96.0	58.1	72.0	45.8

capacity utilization is practical in a full capacity, continuous flow shop. In fact, something like 85% is probably more realistic as a normal base even for most continuous flow operations. If 24% ROI is normally achieved on prices at 85% capacity utilization, suboptimization at 60% utilization requires a price increase of less than 10% to maintain the pretax ROI equivalent of 24% at the higher level of capacity utilization. Even a modest increase in service or quality could make that a genuine bargain. From this perspective, improved service and quality are merely a matter of how much premium the customer is willing to pay for service.

In the longer term, project shop capacity underutilization as a management policy has high potential to change the basic rules of investment return. Project shop equipment must be more flexible and adaptable than continuous flow equipment. The investment decision that justifies an automated home appliance production line must take into account the size of the mass market available, the effect on market share of increased capacity and the potential for obsolescence of both product and production line. The investment choice that justifies an automated bagle baking machine looks at exactly the same factors. Investors expect both of these mass production, continuous flow machines to run flat out at maximum capacity generating ample cash to cover operating expense, pay back principle and generate an attractive ROI. If the market lasts longer than conservative estimates for its survival, the surplus is all gravy and can be applied to the next high risk investment. These are not available options in the project shop.

DESPECIALIZATION OF PRODUCTION EQUIPMENT

Continuous flow process equipment is highly customized, expensive to engineer and install and useless for almost any other purpose than that which it is specifically designed for. If the product or service fails, the equipment is little better than junk. The expense of clearing it out to return the plant to bare walls and open floor for other use may be nearly as costly as building a new plant. Given the specificity of plant layout required for continuous run efficiency, the building itself may be useless for most other applications. The adaptive capacity of full output capacity, continuous flow design is often extremely low. Payoffs from such plant investment may be high, but risk is also high. Continuous flow is typically a maximax decision strategy.

A project shop depends on equipment that is general purpose. There is no easy calculation of maximum flow or layout efficiency. Equipment does not (or should not) quickly go out of date. It may be superceded by more efficient equipment that does the same work, but it will not necessarily be obsoleted. High cost, efficient equipment will likely require large demand to justify investing in it. Less specialized equipment will often be more cost effective on custom short-run jobs simply because its investment payback is so small an element of the job price.

Equipment that serves custom, short-run production and service needs must be inherently more flexible. It must have greater adaptive capacity. Its output capacity can be scheduled over an extended term of use. Like the private automobile, it will give the same amount of service with either high capacity use or low capacity use as long as it is appropriately maintained by its owner. Liquidated, used equipment from project shop industry is an attractive cost investment for startup or expansion of other operations. The printer who is skilled in the use of old, even obsolete, general purpose printers that are easily set up may be at a competitive advantage on small jobs even against a large, automated print shop. The larger shop is likely to have about an equivalent setup cost for the small job but may be forced to obtain an investment return on automated equipment that exceeds the small printer's labor. Even under conditions in which efficiency of automated equipment beats out the labor cost of the small shop, falloff in orders due to competition or economic distress may place severe financial stress on the automated shop. Under the same conditions, the small printer merely turns off the power, locks his doors and goes on an extended vacation.

Full capacity utilization, continuous flow production systems are cost efficient only with large scale commodity production. Their inflexibility is a major risk. Unexpected falloff in demand spells financial disaster. If the continuous flow system is weak structurally or has poor recovery capacity, costs mount. Correction of system defects is expensive because it is likely to take the system out of operation for an extended time, defeating full capacity objectives.

Surplus-capacity, variable flow systems are more cost effective with custom, small jobs in an unpredictable market that requires flexible response. They are less risky and more adaptable to economic ups and downs and better long-term financial investments.

LABOR UTILIZATION: FLEXIBILITY = EFFICIENCY

Habits of labor utilization also tend to be carried over from continuous flow operations into project shops. The use of queues to keep pressure for production high and the unrelenting stress of continually arriving work are likely to be used to "motivate" production. High capacity utilization with lengthy queues at workstations is seductive for project shop operations managers because long queues of work make scheduling personnel easy. Each worker is simply assigned to a workstation until work is complete or priorities dictate reassignment to another station that may already have a waiting queue of work. Control of work assignments is made simple. That makes it easier for managers to apply the required large amounts of time on the telephone explaining why the job is late.

The downside of this arrangement—aside from poor turnaround and service—is the loss of control over jobs buried in queues and a decrease in quality brought on by the press for maximum quantity output combined with the ease with which poor quality is hidden in long queues of waiting work.

Long queues of work are indicative of bottlenecks in capacity, and there is sound purpose in shifting resources onto bottlenecks. But when high capacity utilization is the policy of the project shop, the name of the game becomes "chase the bottleneck." In eliminating the current bottleneck, the next bottleneck is created. A general crisis orientation prevails. Organization of any kind is rendered difficult if not impossible.

Nonetheless, the one capacity usage that can and must be maximized in a project shop for cost efficiency's sake is labor cost. Equipment will wait patiently without noticeable complaint or cost until it is called to use; people must be applied as fully as possible if their hourly pay is to generate a billable product and service. Conversion to now or next JIT project shop work flow based on surplus machinery capacity requires a revolution in the application of labor capacity.

First, workers must often flow with jobs, sometimes in a pattern that permits shifting from one project to another and back again as the need requires. Rigid specialization of skill and work function is a liability in the project shop. Capacity for adaptation and flexibility of labor is a necessity. Jobs may sometimes be carried through from start to finish by the same worker, with waiting time in successive station queues applied either to quality inspection or in assisting to eliminate an emergent bottleneck. These will be highly enriched jobs with heavy loadings of task variety, responsibility and autonomy. They may also require extensive variety of skill. Quitting at 4:30 P.M. when the bottleneck remains unresolved or there is only one more process to finish the job will typically become unthinkable. Tasks and overtime are likely to be self-assigned. Self-designated flexible schedules that assign accountability for queue delay and bottlenecks will be a necessity.

Indeed, the really significant revolution in work brought about by the age of the project shop will be a revolution in managing labor capacity. Achievement of near-full capacity output with workers will call for nothing less than maximum self-direction against specified work priorities, flexibility in work schedules and mastery of multiple work skills. Ultimately, the narrow task specialization associated with labor intensive, continuous flow operations must be replaced by highly skilled, self-managed workers in automated, integrated factories as well as in custom, short-run project shops.

The adaptive flexibility of labor will become a pillar of project shop effectiveness. Capacity for labor adaptivity is potentially expandable to almost any extent needed through use of external, subcontract project shops and cottage industry. Graphics or copy work that can be accomplished with a personal computer with desktop publishing or similar software extends the range of skilled resources for creative writing and design to any experienced individual who has his or her own computer system. The future of public relations and advertising will probably be with the project shop. The individual worker who owns and maintains his or her own special equipment is a potential building block for a network of custom workers who are infinitely flexible and responsive. Perhaps the extended vision of project shop operations includes widespread independent contractors self-contained in ability and machinery to accomplish complex, custom and short-run tasks, united by a network of mutual referral and assistance, coordinated by a master tracking and scheduling system somewhere at the core. In the nearer term, perhaps, that is a lot how the typical project shop may also look, the major difference being the payrolling of workers and central ownership of production equipment.

Capacity is the critical variable to managing custom, short-run operations of any kind. The greatest part of operations management methods is suited principally if not solely to continuous flow, mass output operations. The limitations and weaknesses of these methods, even as applied to continuous flow, are unmistakable. Uncritical transfer of existing operations methodology to project shops is ineffective, costly, foolish. Effective, efficient management of project shop operations requires a new perspective on equipment capacity usage and leads potentially to a revolution in the application of labor resources. The general principles on which the new era of project shop management must be founded are clear enough. Only the specifics remain to be developed in the chapters that follow.

2

TOOLS AND WORK: THE TYRANNY OF THE MACHINE

"Specialized tools diminish human skill."

This chapter discovers the axioms of custom, short-run operations tool usage. We shall describe how the human toolmaker is retrofitted to his or her tools, how repetitive use of tools without an offsetting balance in physical activity can distort and injure the human body, how tools controlled at a distance by faceless technicians make automatons of workers and how anything that can be done efficiently by a human can be done more efficiently by a machine. It will be argued that when workers are not in control of their tools, they cannot be made responsible for their use, but that workers must never be permitted to corrupt tools by using them to generate paid leisure or avoid vigorous work activity. It will also be proposed that the availability of slack paid labor time merits the substitution of low-tech, high worker activity tools for high-tech, minimal activity tools whenever that is feasible.

As with the proscription of planned excess capacity offered in the previous chapter, these axioms will initially appear at odds with sound operations practice. We will find, however, that it is those outmoded operations practices designed to maximize efficiency of continuous flow operations that are unsound for application to custom, short-run operations. New methods and revised tools are needed for the new age.

A recurring theme in science fiction literature is that of the self-programmed and self-maintained robot that faithfully carries out all of its master's orders. In the ages before dominance of technology, it was the genie in a bottle that realized everyone's fantasy of wealth and power. What stands out about these phantasms of productive power is their remarkably humanoid qualities. They comprehend the needs of the situation with uncanny precision, respond effectively to satisfy it fully but then retire silently into the background to await the next call to duty. They are uncomplaining servants who require neither our thought nor care to continue working flawlessly.

It is impossible to miss the human qualities of such machines—their versatility, capacity to self-correct errors of communication, their goal orientation in the face of ambiguity. Some humans who are strictly disciplined to their duty, responsive to constituted authority and uncomplaining in their performance are hard to differentiate from machines. The phantasm of robot or genie echoes the reality of disciplined human skill and capability. The human being is the best and most powerful general purpose production tool imaginable. In our ability to create new tools that extend our work capability still further, we are truly a magic making genie.

But we have appetites and impulses. If our service to our master does not fulfill our own needs, we may not continue to perform. In a highly organized economy fulfillment is commonly offered in the form of wages, which allow satisfaction of nonwork related needs. In return for wages, we are expected to play the role of robot or genie, dutifully satisfying the demands of our masters who may be either bosses or customers. The wage bargain classically entails acceptance of duty, which requires full submission to higher authority. Only those who accumulate or inherit wealth are exempted, and even they are subject to dominance by government authority.

In its democratic form, the wage bargain makes us all both servants and masters as we seek favorable terms of economic exchange with our neighbor. Those who cannot accept the responsibility of duty as well as those who fall victim to the arrogance of domination must lose out in the exchange. The former will not be sought out for their services, the latter will find no one willing to serve. There is reciprocity of duty and command under democracy, which penalizes both irresponsibility and haughty self-importance between neighbors and fellow citizens.

MACHINES: OUR SERVANTS AND MASTERS

As the tools of humankind have increased in complexity, reciprocity of duty and command has been modified. Machines intervene in human relationships. They take on the qualities of servant or master. They disappoint with inadequate service when capacity to adapt in pursuit of the goal is lacking. They impose harsh demands for performance without appreciation of human limits. Machines are insensitive to human feeling or purpose. But the productive power of machines is too great to permit their abandonment. In our lust for wealth and power we have loosed the genie of machinery only to become its bondsman. The machine is humankind's universal, modern tyrant.

Some machines whimsically mame or kill. Autos and aircraft are the most common offenders in this category, but industrial equipment also contributes its share of mayhem. Improperly used or maintained, knowingly or unknowingly damaged, constructed with hidden flaws, the machine turns on humankind destructively. For the sake of wealth and power, we entrust our lives to machines and are recurrently betrayed.

Machines insult, affront and abuse human beings, sometimes destroying their self-confidence or self-esteem. Complexity that challenges mastery intimidates those uninitiated in the use of a computer. The auto that stalls stubbornly in the middle of an expressway or on a deserted road or at the height of a severe storm is a cruel joke. The precision power tool that demands muscular strength and coordination discourages its use by the weak or the lazy. Inanimate objects though they be, machines can make us feel stupid and inept. If we are so easily defeated by a dumb tool, how can we hold up our head in pride?

Machines also diagnose injury or disease. They permit use of highly specialized skill at distant places with minimum loss of travel time between. They eliminate the grinding, physically debilitating labor that once crippled workers. They produce abundance of food and goods and deliver them quickly to buyers. Machines have liberated us from want and drudgery.

Machines echo the master–servant roles of humans. They are both tyrant and emancipator. But they fail to offer the comfortable reciprocity of balance in relationships available between humans. Somehow, we must find alternative terms on which to relate to our machines.

PEOPLE SHAPE MACHINES; MACHINES SHAPE PEOPLE

We may begin by pulling back the curtain in the temple of Oz to discover the concealed truth; the machine is never more than an extension of a human being. Even though we cannot easily find the person, one is behind the scene, operating his or her machinery, plying his or her tools. The machine is the mask behind which shy or even faint-hearted wizards of technology manipulate society.

Restoration of reciprocity through alteration of the servant-master relationship in a way that successfully penetrates this modern screen of technology requires first that the fashion in which machines tyranize or liberate be understood. Understanding begins with the axiom that although people shape tools, tools also shape people. When a powerful tool is invented to offset an inventor's infirmity, the shape of the invention invites healthy users to adopt the equivalent weakness that permits the tool to be applied with greatest efficiency. In many instances the tool could easily be redesigned so that it would not foster atrophy or distortion of the human mind or body. Such redesign is rarely considered, however. The norm is unconcern with weakness engendered by it as long as the tool is sufficiently efficient and powerful.

Basically, all general-purpose tools are the most benign. The wedge, lever, mallet, knife and wheel enable us to accomplish more with available strength. Their worst harm results from misuse or breakage, which injures the user. Fortunately, such potential for harm is more than offset by the potential for injury that arises out of attempting to accomplish the same end with the unaided human body. Skill in application of basic tools rewards the user with both increased work output and reduced risk of injury once the skill is mastered.

Our principal tool of the mind, language, has a powerful impact on the shape of the human body. Talking disciplines the lungs. It exercises face and neck muscles that go unused by the simple grinding action of chewing food. Early use of speech develops strength in muscles that are critical to sensory alertness. Spoken language creates the potential for coordinated group action. It is the foundation of teamwork. Direction by authority, instant focus of attention on critical events, teaching or role forming through story telling, all depend on spoken language. Mastery of spoken language is the foundation of leadership through the use of simple, dramatic words. The king who was not also an effective battlefield orator was less likely to prevail over his enemy.

The invention of written language arose out of the need for reliable records for commercial transactions. The fallibility of memory over extended time or distance creates the need for authentic written records. Reading and writing call into play only the small muscles of the hand and the eyes. Stone or clay tablets were worked from a kneeling position on the floor. The parchment writing surface was only a little better. Sitting on the floor or at a table, hunched over the writing surface for long hours to make or read records, led to atrophy of the major musculature of the body. It was no handicap for a cleric or scholar to be crippled or weak. If he did not begin in a state of infirmity, he might end in it after years of physical inactivity. He was quickly disabled at his occupation, however, by common diseases of the hands and eyes such as arthritis or astigmatism. But arthritis did not prevent reading the existing records, and arthritic scholars could dictate to their disciples. Astigmatism disabled reading until the lens was invented to correct the distorted visual image. Blindness was overcome through the invention of the braille alphabet. The disabling infirmities of the first tool were either offset by the invention of others or overcome with specialization of labor. Tool invention begets tool invention.

THE RISKS OF TOOL USAGE

Variety in the use of physical tools that draws many muscles and senses into play promotes strength and health. Overspecialization with tools that stress limited muscle systems can bring about atrophy in the underused muscles. Good health requires that narrow, limited muscle use be offset by activity that tones the unused muscles as it strengthens the overused ones.

When possible, tools must be redesigned to use a broader range of musculature while avoiding misuse or damage to working muscle systems. The impact on human strength or health of tool use, casual or intensive, must be considered in designing and applying them in use. Only by anticipating and offsetting the undesired effects of tool usage on human beings can the physical tyranny of tools be overcome. Ergonomic design of tools is desirable. The physical debilities of tool design can and should be avoided. The pervasiveness of tool use as a substitute for human energy, though, requires that muscle atrophy from tool use be offset with restorative exercises.

Professional athletes, for instance, do not maintain their muscular strength and resilience solely from playing at their sport. Baseball players must respond explosively to the ball but, for more than 95% of the time on the field or at bat, are merely "at the ready." Baseball does not provide sufficient cardiovascular stress to qualify as a health building activity. Maintaining physical tone and stamina must take place off the field.

Golf exposes players to fresh air and a brisk walk. The muscular strength and coordination needed to play the game successfully, though, must be developed independent of the game. To obtain sufficient aerobics value from golf to qualify as a healthy activity, it would be necessary to play twenty or thirty full eighteen hole rounds every week.

Football, the most physical of popular U.S. sports, demands a balanced program of weight lifting or nautilus exercises as a foundation for play. Without a regimen of activity designed to foster maximum strength and stamina, it is dangerous for a player even to go on the field.

An airline pilot must be physically and mentally alert continually while at the controls of his craft. His reflexes must be tuned and quick. Yet flying is a thoroughly sedentary activity. The pilot spends most of the time seated watching the controls of his plane. The work pattern of bus and truck drivers is little different. All of these tools of transport require maximum alertness and quickness of response to crisis. Yet none provides even basic muscular or aerobic exercise. Remaining strong and balanced in health requires a regimen of physical activity off the job.

The job of air traffic controller, one of the most stressful known, permits virtually no major physical response in the performance of work. Stress, indeed, is partly correlated with the presence of high crisis demand without counterbalanced physical activity. When the momentary effects of stress are chemically washed away with alcohol or a tranquilizer, physical adaptability to stress can be weakened yet further. The human body is designed to go into muscular action under stress. Many critical tools of our age make little or no provision for bodily physical involvement of the user.

Some tools have the potential for direct physical injury to their users. Excessive noise from machinery can destroy hearing in related frequency ranges. Stamping or forming presses can crush fingers and hands. Scaffolding can collapse and hurl workers to the ground. Dust and noxious chemicals from processing operations will impair lungs or eyes. High speed cutting equipment may shatter, hurling fragments with the force of a hand grenade. The worker who gains confidence in his tool becomes overconfident, fails to take precautions and exposes himself to harm.

Workers on assembly line or continuous flow jobs often repeat small physical movements over and over, overstressing small, critical muscle systems to the point of injury or disease. Repeated use of small hand tools that require a firm grasp can result in carpal tunnel syndrome, which will totally disable a hand if not treated surgically. The human body adapts to the circumstances of its use. Sometimes that adaptation is healthy, sometimes harmful.

The great danger in specific tool use or general work activity is overroutinization of the work. Narrow speciality, excessive repetitiveness and grinding routine cut deep groves into human muscular and nervous systems. Every human habit or routine should be subject to evaluation for the damage it may do. Blisters or calluses form at points of physical wear on hands or feet. If excessive, they may become chronic open sores. With care, the skin toughens and strengthens to absorb greater wear at the heaviest points of use. Success in strengthening and adapting to habitual patterns of physical stress appears mostly to require patience and discipline as nerves and tissues are stressed almost to but never beyond the breaking point. Even the use of vocal cords in speech or song is subject to gradual strengthening with disciplined practice but will generate blisters (nodules) if rushed.

PHYSICAL CONDITIONING AND VARIETY OF ACTIVITY

Tool use at work must be balanced by compensating activity that strengthens the body as a whole. Those nerves and muscles that support tool use directly must be carefully trained and developed. The entire regimen of life must be built around a balance of physical and mental activity that offsets the excesses of work routine. When work requires very little physical activity or cardiovascular exertion, breaks from the workplace should encourage vigorous exercise. The use of calisthenics to start the Japanese auto assembly line worker's day is not merely a team building activity; it contributes directly to improved health and more effective use of tools.

The appeal of farming to those who appreciate that way of life arises out of the great variety of work activity that is demanded. There is limited routine, usually involving feeding of stock or maintenance of machinery. Otherwise, the seasons of the year drive the schedule. A series of sixteen-hour days may be required to plant or harvest the crops. There will be long, lazy days in the summer as the crops drink up sunlight or long cozy nights in the winter after the work is done. The demand for time is real, urgent and immediate when it occurs. Everything depends on timing. The physical and psychological satisfactions of farming as a way of work and life are sufficiently attractive, indeed, that it attracts more adherents than the shrinking employment base can support. Too many farmers today are ready to accept a marginal wage from their effort for the sake of the quality of life it offers. There are important lessons for the way that work is organized in these observations from farming.

The natural variety of activity necessary to survive created the strong, healthy human body through a thousand millennia of evolutionary times. Injury, disease and natural predators took their toll through prehistoric eons, but the demands of successful living were sufficient to maintain health. The rush for wealth and the good life obscure the basic requirements of human health. Flaccid, sedentary, overspecialized activity supported by excesses of food and alcohol, punctuated by bursts of energy and excitement, is popularly touted as the best available approximation of paradise. In fact, it is the sure road to a purgatory of poor health.

TOOLS AND FACTORY WORK

The transition from a largely agricultural, subsistence economy of the seventeenth century to the custom, job shop economy of the twenty-first century passes through a long period of overspecialized, overroutinized, continuous flow tool and machine use. As the great age of industrialization began almost two hundred years ago, the risk of disease and injury from working the soil was no worse than the risk of disease and injury working the machine. The major difference was the regularity of year-round income. Technology promised salvation from the uncertainties of subsistence agriculture. Life was cheap, but technology was valuable. Men were joined with tools that were patently injurious. Labor was physically hard, agricultural and factory alike. Life on all terms was harsh. But the dirty, brutal factory or cold, poorly lighted office offered some small increment of added security over the whimsey of nature on a farm.

With accumulation of wealth and broadening of the investment base of machinery, expectations for comfort and safety escalated. Comfort and safety, in that order, evolved as the imperatives of tool design in the present age. Adaptation to the abrasive effect of tools on the body is somewhat tolerable as long as comfort cushions the injury. The promise of future comfort and convenience is worth the risk today. Retirement is our reward. Technology is the road to retirement. We cheerfully serve it in hope and confidence for a future of leisure. The loss of fifteen lives in the construction of the Brooklyn Bridge was no more undue risk than the loss of eight lives one hundred years later (1990) to explore outer space. Per passenger mile, airplanes are much safer than trains, vastly safer than private autos. In our competitive impatience, these are small costs in risk of human life to pay for progress.

Indeed, war, murder and drugs snuff out lives on a faster and larger scale than ever imagined for mere industrial tool use risks. Yet because so many hours of a life are committed to the use of production machines and tools, they must inevitably shape experience, attitude, value and preference in far greater depth. The tools a worker uses to gain a livelihood form his physical and mental character. The tools of work shape us daily more intensively than do any others. Tools of work have become crutches and prosthetics. Without them we are powerless. They are the foundation of our wealth and power. We are dependent on them for our living. It is a habit of nearly two hundred years standing.

As the industrial revolution entered on its transitory stage of continuous flow production nearly two centuries ago, specialized labor working repetitively with crude and sometimes dangerous tools offered efficiency that increased productivity tenfold to a thousandfold. Adam Smith's (1982) description of the efficiencies of the skill specialized pin "manufactory" offers insight into the increases in productivity possible from basic improvements in production methods built around specialization of labor.

The important business of making a pin is . . . divided into about eighteen distinct operations. . . . I have seen a small manufactory . . . where ten men only were employed and where some of them consequently performed two or three distinct operations . . . but though they were . . . indifferently accommodated with the necessary machinery, they could, when they exerted themselves, make among them about twelve pounds of pins in a day. There are in a pound upwards of four thousand pins of a middling size. Those ten persons, therefore, could make among them upwards of forty-eight thousand pins in a day. Each person, therefore, making a tenth part of forty-eight thousand pins, might be considered as making four thousand eight hundred pins in a day. But if they had all wrought separately and independently, and without any of them having been educated to this peculiar business, they would certainly not each of them have made twenty, perhaps not one pin in a day. (p. 110)

The discovery of great efficiencies in small matters of work specialization and organization *was* the industrial revolution. Simple tools employed by specialized workers in the context of organized work flow was the definition of a factory. Frederick Winslow Taylor (1911) and other proponents of "scientific management" carried the revolution forward by redesigning simple tools and calculating optimum physical work loads. Frank Gilbreth and Lillian Gilbreth (1924) showed how organizing workstations for maximum efficiency could increase output dramatically. Ergonomics, the scientific study of interface between people and machinery, continues to carry the grand tradition of efficiency seeking in the workplace still further.

Methods of motion economy and fatigue reduction are by now well established and widely communicated even though still commonly ignored. The observation that "hand and body motions must be the simplest possible to perform the work" or that "ballistic movements are faster and more accurate than slow, steady movements" offer specification for more effective use of the human body. The requirement that "hands should be relieved of any job that can be done by a jig or fixture" and that "levers and controls should be operable with the least change in body position and greatest mechanical advantage" specify critical aspects of tool design efficiency. Specifying that "gravity feed should be used wherever possible" and that "tools should be in a known, fixed position" provides direction for organizing the workplace (Barnes, 1968).

The difficulty with many of these wonderful objectives and principles lies in the assumption that the work to be done can be performed within a context of a stable, unchanging repetitive work flow. Carried to their furthest limits, principles of production efficiency require minimum muscular movement of the head, hands and feet in the service of the simplest possible repetitive motions. The more powerful solution to efficiency is to automate all of these motions and to use a robot to perform them. The first axiom of labor efficiency is that *anything that can be done efficiently by a human can be done more efficiently by a machine.*

The only reason that everything repetitive is not done by machinery is that machines are frequently more costly and less reliable than humans. Widespread introduction of robotics into industry in recent years has served as a dramatic reminder of the first axiom of tool innovation: *"every new tool breaks down more often, takes longer to perfect and is harder to master in use than expected by at least a factor of ten."* I have seen a business organized around a very costly and complex piece of automated machinery that replaced simpler and more flexible but less efficient equipment requiring higher skill. This machine, however, was so hopelessly unreliable, so continually subject to breakdown and malperformance, that it ultimately brought the business down. At liquidation, the reputation of the equipment was so universally bad that a reasonable return to the owner in salvage value was not available. Untested, untried tools are dangerous. Innovative systems of automation are costly investments at best. Automation in the workplace is no easy answer. Typically, it requires an investment in design and test shakedown that only a major mass commodity market will support.

The three axioms of machine usage are summarized in Figure 2–1.

MASTERY AND OWNERSHIP OF TOOLS

The tool is no better than its inventor, no more powerful or effective than its skilled user. It is dependent on human skill and knowledge for maintenance and repair. A great factory or, for that matter, any well designed continuous flow output system is an efficient tool designed by creative technicians. Often it can be operated and maintained only by those same highly skilled and experienced technicians. The tightly organized, continuous flow system of production or service output is, in its dependency upon exceptional skill and knowledge and, sometimes even courage, most deficient in those

Figure 2–1
First Axioms of Machine Usage

A Practical Compendium of Rules

for Managing Machinery and Tool Usage

The First Axiom of Ergonomics:

The tools shaped by man reciprocally shape him.
He creates machines and is then recreated
by them.

The First Axiom of Efficiency:

Anything that can be done efficiently by a
human being can be done more efficiently
by a machine.

The First Axiom of Tool Innovation:

Newly innovated machinery breaks down
more often,
takes longer to perfect, and is harder to
master in use than expected
by a factor of ten.

moments of crisis or breakdown. Workers in such a system are themselves little more than general purpose tools. They monitor its operation for continuity of flow, perform simple functions that are too expensive to automate and follow instructions written in an operations manual. The real controller of this tool is hidden behind a screen in the temple of Oz. The sense that many workers have of being "cogs in a machine" is justifiable.

The economic advantage of unskilled labor rapidly erodes when workers have no control, no choice in how the machine is used. Lacking satisfaction in his work, the "cog in a machine" worker is indifferent to the work itself and will test the value of his labor to the maximum. He will insist on increased compensation until, ultimately, it becomes cost effective to replace his labor with a machine. Labor strikes are often little more than a bet by workers that it is more costly for management to mechanize its labor than to pay the workers more. But satisfaction with the work itself offsets the need for more pay by reducing indifference to the job. Indifference undermines interest or concern with quality of work, thereby further accelerating the movement to automation. Work or tools that supply enjoyment do not require premium pay. They become the stuff of avocations.

The answer to worker commitment and effectiveness—*motivation* is a common catchword for this concern—is to put workers back in charge of their tools. On a moving assembly line, this may be as simple as permitting workers to stop or set the pace of the line. Instruction in the technical design of the system may be necessary to permit adequate understanding of its workings. Participation in the solution of its operating problems with training and technical assistance can become highly satisfying for workers on a continuous flow production system. A worker will sabotage the system if that is the only control option available. Sabotage can be active destruction or it can be passive. A worker, for instance, can ignore or obscure incipient breakdown in the form of wear or other problems. But with knowledge of the system's purpose, he may help redesign and maintain it for greater efficiency or reliability of operation.

The major difference between Japan and the United States in industrial organization is the spirit of teamwork between engineers, technicians and workers that prevails in Japan versus the adversarial spirit that characterizes those same relationships in the United States. A long United States tradition of efficiency measures imposed on workers from above by engineers, especially industrial engineers, has created a climate of distrust and competition between workers and technicians. Suggestion plans in industry frequently fail because engineers feel that workers are trying to do their jobs. Workers, on the other hand, fear that technicians won't give them credit for their good ideas. The status barriers between workers and technicians grow rather than diminish with frequency of contact. Suggestion plans highlight the weakness of relations at this crucial interface. Technicians and engineers more easily acquire a sense of personal ownership of the system. Workers who adopt such an attitude are seen by technicians as competitors for control of the system. Engineers design and apply tools. Workers do as they're told. But in the absence of cooperation and shared ownership of tools, inefficiency in use of tools is inevitable. Workers will see to it.

The fundamental and fatal error of the Soviet economy is the placement of control over machine use solely in the hands of technicians—economic planners—most of whom are far distant from the production machinery. Managers and workers alike are excluded from choice in the application of machinery to economic purpose. The result is ongoing gross misuse of resources that has no remedy. Some misuse is the result of bad planning. Some flows from worker sabotage and mischief. Most is directly caused by the absence of ownership and responsibility over the tools of production among those whose lives are directly and daily shaped by them.

The social system that emerges around the control and use of a complex production system determines the effectiveness of its use. U.S. engineers and technicians hold fast to the utopian dream of the robot factory that dispenses with recalcitrant, uncooperative laborers altogether. They solve the social problem by dispensing with the society. In time, they will probably approximate that laborless ideal in those pervasively automated, continuous flow commodity production systems that emerge. Soviet planners pursue the ideal of optimum application of state owned resources whereby every worker is assured secure employment and no one wields private economic power. Americans are nearer to realization of production efficiency than are the Russians, but neither adequately addresses the need for worker control over the use of tools to achieve genuinely effective use of those tools.

The vast new realm of custom, short-run production picks up where commodity production leaves off. It permits a radically revised ethic of tool ownership and use. If the tool use conventions of the old continuous flow systems are transferred intact to the new ones, there will be great losses in effectiveness.

PRACTICAL MAXIMS OF TOOL USAGE

Sound tool usage must be approached on two grounds; first, tools must not be allowed to become either crutches or prosthetics; they must be prohibited from accommodating weakness or laziness. Second, workers must have a choice of tools and be able to exercise effective control over their use in service of the purposes of the organization. The first ground is addressed by sound human engineering of tools and by addressing the real economics of labor versus energy use in marginal situations. The second is partially resolved by encouraging worker ownership of tools. This can be directly brought about through offering low effective rate loans (3% or 4% plus the prevailing inflation rate, for instance) guaranteed by the government so that workers may purchase their own tools. Outright ownership is not essential, though, to creating a sense of choice and control over tool use. Tools that are too expensive or technically sophisticated to permit individual ownership can be privately owned and managed or cooperatively held. The key is the social structure employed to coordinate their use.

REVOLUTIONIZING WORK SYSTEMS

Custom, short-run operations will require powerful, flexible tools. A few will be specialized, most will be multipurpose, some will be general purpose. Relatively high worker skill will be called for. Responsibility for effective use and maintenance will rest with the prime user or user group. Many skilled artisans will own their machinery and contract its use out on a job-by-job basis. Privately or cooperatively held equipment will require an exact record of use for capacity management and maintenance purposes but will be available for use on a low capacity or exactly scheduled basis to workers assigned responsibility for completion of jobs. Instead of workers staying busy with work that has no priority, which ensures that labor and equipment at least will not go idle, equipment capacity will be loosened to the level required by market demand for service, 60% and less, and labor will be scheduled to avoid wasted time waiting in line for equipment or machinery. Workers will follow the work through, often from start to finish. The social system that supports custom, short-run production will be crucial to the success of such schedules.

The center of custom, short-run operations will be a job scheduler that assigns jobs and allocates machine time to workers based on negotiated or accepted time standards. The scheduler may be a computer or a human dispatcher. Independent or cottage industry will be expected to own sufficient equipment capacity and work on a flexible schedule to allow work to be assigned on a strict turnaround contract controlled by a lateness penalty. The difference will be that whereas machinery and equipment are not worker owned, reliable access to it based on job need will be guaranteed by the scheduling system. Tools not owned by workers must be applied at a low enough level of capacity so that all workers are assured availability of adequate capacity through adjustment of work or machine use schedules.

The social system that coordinates custom, short-run operations will be a loose network of skilled operatives, with guaranteed equipment access schedules or with personally owned machine time, carrying out the assigned project work. Workers will be responsible for staying busy on the assigned projects and will directly see to the correction of problems like materials shortages or machine failure. They will also be held directly responsible for the quality of the final product.

Workers who must coordinate with one another either to accomplish work as a team or to pass work back and forth successfully will constitute ad hoc project teams for which coordination time is scheduled as part of the job. The social system on which custom, short-run operations is founded will necessarily be flexible and fluid. It will account for capacity utilization in temporal, recovery and adaptive terms. Communications will be driven by need and planned into time allocations.

Tool availability will be strictly controlled in terms of marginal utility of labor and machine operation cost. This is a simple but revolutionary principle that departs dramatically from the habits and policies of efficiency that drive continuous process operations. The principle can be stated as follows: when workers have adequate time in their work schedule to use a low-tech, even rudimentary, tool to accomplish a job, they *must* use the low-tech tool in place of a high-tech tool when the high-tech tool consumes fuel, adds to maintenance costs, depreciates in value with use or raises capacity utilization above standard through use. Alternatively, if a rudimentary tool costs about the same in use as the high-tech tool but requires vigorous physical activity of aerobic or variable quality and also refreshes skill in its use, the low-tech tool *must* be used when workers have slack time in their personal schedules.

Efficiency is never served when a backhoe is used to plant a rose bush. That the worker knows how to use the backhoe skillfully and can dig a planting hole in ten seconds versus the two minutes required with a shovel is not an acceptable argument. The real cost of using the backhoe is clearly greater, the difference in time is inconsequential, the vigorous exercise of digging is healthy and practice using the shovel is desirable. The backhoe is a prosthetic that contributes to indigence and, eventually, to atrophy of the major muscles. The spare time gained will never be used productively. Such use of high-tech tools is lazy and irresponsible.

When time is no issue in the production or delivery schedule, it is irresponsible to use a forklift truck when a hand truck will do the job. A power press is not appropriate when slack time is available and a hammer and hand held die will do the job. A computer should not be powered up when the message can easily be written by hand or printed on a standard typewriter. The automobile in the driveway should not be started up and driven to the corner market when there is plenty of time to walk in the fresh air.

Sound argument can be made on several levels for implementing and enforcing a policy of low-tech equipment usage when labor use is slack. It is a useful way to sensitize workers to cost reduction opportunities that preserve wage earning opportunity. In some cases it may even result in substantial cost savings. Of greatest importance, it directly establishes the principle that it is improper to use high-tech equipment to create paid, personal leisure time that will not be put to productive use. It offers the option of increased unpaid personal leisure to those willing to invest in ownership of the machines, equipment and tools of output. It promotes the proposition that all work should be healthy, stimulating activity that contributes to economic purpose. It is a fundamental policy statement for the age of custom, short-run operations output.

Affluence and wide availability of high-tech tools breeds laziness and waste, which directly defeats the gains in efficiency of mass, continuous flow production. The likelihood is that it may even result in a net loss of health due to indigence. This should be cause to pause and rethink the economics of tool use efficiencies. Regrettably, Americans have come to the point where the right to misuse high-tech equipment as personal crutches or prosthetics is taken for granted. Teaching workers to save fuel and tool capacity by opting for healthy exercise will not be easy. The opportunity to practice low-tech tool usage will seldom be seen as an advantage by most workers. But the end of the mass production age, the rising price of fuel and the deteriorating health of sedentary, minimally active American workers will finally demand it.

The priorities of the new operations age will be revised. The manner in which tools shape bodies and lives of workers must be closely scrutinized.

People shape tools. Tools, in turn, shape people. Work that requires adaptivity to the special and custom requirements of the market requires healthy, active, adaptive workers. Excess equipment capacity must be available if custom, short-run operations are to compete effectively in a service and quality oriented market. Self-indulgent misuse of capacity as a prosthetic or crutch must be recognized as an intolerable economic and human waste.

Workers must, nevertheless, have freedom and sway over the use of their tools that permits experiment and discovery. They must be permitted, even actively encouraged, to play with their tools as an alternative to idleness. Skill in the use of tools arises out of a combination of experiment driven by necessity and mastery through play. The recreational value of a tool must be recognized. It is inappropriate that an auto be driven to the corner store for milk when a walk will do the job. But a drive into the mountains to fish or climb can be productive and beneficial. The difference may at first seem contradictory. It serves, nonetheless, the objective of reorienting work values toward more effective tool use based on flexibility, service response and quality of output. It simultaneously observes the calculus of marginal utility of labor versus machinery and promotes human health.

The new age of custom, short-run production will be built on older, preindustrial values in many ways. These values will, no doubt, seem strange at first. Excess capacity to ensure customer service; use of low-tech tools to reduce cost, preserve excess capacity and discourage unproductive, paid leisure; emphasis on personal control over the tools for one's job, opportunity for choice in their productive and recreational use, all are, at the outset, directly contrary to nearly all existing policies and practices of the mass commodity economy. It is mass production, though, that is the digression from sound social and economic principle. The project shop only returns to the best lessons of the past in its application of tools. Tool users will be all that much better off for it.

3

THEORY OF VALUE

"Commodities are a way station on the highway to affluence."

Henry Ford once announced that his customers could have any color car they wanted as long as it was black. Ford put the nation on wheels by focusing narrowly on efficiency and mechanical function. In less than two decades the Model T got Americans into the habit of using the motor car. Once the market for motoring was formed and paved roads became common, the low-cost efficiency of elementary function lost its appeal. The car buying public began to expect comfort, styling and individuality in their autos. Ford's Model T was a commodity product, mass produced on one of the earliest continuous flow assembly lines. Once the commodity offering served its purpose of habituating the market to the affordability of the basic product, the Model T, for all its inherent engineering genius, was just a cheap car.

Ultimately, that is the fate of all commodity products. With success, the efficiency, initially indispensable in creating mass demand, no longer counts. A small excess of a commodity is a glut on the market that depresses prices and profits, thereby defeating the benefits of efficiency. An excess of supply drives price—and value—down. Rarity bids it up. The only way to prevent excess supply from poisoning the market when demand is saturated is to keep it off the market or dump it remotely with discriminatory pricing. Scrapping or demolishing is generally the safer option. When abundance of a crop drives the price too low for the harvest to be profitably brought in, a farmer is usually better off plowing part or all of it under. American managers are so distressed by the waste of a product that most attempt to recover part of their cost regardless of the risk to market value. For the most part this is the result of a lifetime orientation toward efficient cost/

volume output employing the continuous flow commodity output model of production.

As the basic commodity needs of customers are satisfied by continuous flow, high efficiency mass production, the value and profitability of commodities decline. Existing plant, equipment and labor skill are exploited in a war of capacity utilization that can only be won by the lowest price at an acceptable level of quality. A stronger competitive strategy emerges from the smoke of this battle in the form of segmentation of the market to meet specialized, variegated need. The more a product is specifically customized to customer requirements, the higher its value to the customer. High profitability dictates limitation of commodity output capacity and a shift toward custom, short-run output. Once the bloom is off the commodity, the greatest profit is obtained from individualized, one of a kind and limited run output.

SUPPLY AND DEMAND FOR UNIQUE PRODUCTS OR SERVICES

These assertions are virtually economic truisms: Price rises when demand exceeds supply; it falls when supply exceeds demand. Excess capacity can create a glut on the market. Cheap equals plentiful; plentiful equals cheap. As long as we talk large numbers, there is little doubt about the correctness of these principles. When we come down to one, two or three of a kind items, though, it's hard to be certain these rules still apply. They were written to describe a real, existing supply, not output capacity potential. Some kinds of styling, clothing for instance, are difficult to put a price on until they have been created and worn. If one of a kind is created and not acceptable, there is no demand. It is automatically without value. Much the same fate befalls many clothing styles, which means that style pricing must always account for the risk of style rejection. Perhaps one of a kind pricing must also account in some way for the risk of nonacceptance of the final product.

One of a kind items such as works of art and jewelry or architecturally unique homes are typically priced to cover their market singularity. They are then held in inventory until the right buyer comes along. If a buyer does not appear in a reasonable time, they may be sacrificed, modified or scrapped. For examples such as these, the standard rules of pricing still seem to apply. For the moment, then, let's assume that the law of supply and demand applies equally to commodity and to custom output, to inventoried stock as well as to output potential.

UTILITY IN THE PRESENCE OF SCARCITY AND PLENTY

In theory, the basis of economic value is utility. Utility has to do with satisfaction of physical, material human need. A product's or service's value diminishes as soon as demand has been satisfied. But value increases as a result of insufficient supply. The law of supply and demand depends on utility. People need food, shelter and clothing. They need basic tools and materials. They need security and self-esteem. Products or services that supply these needs have value up to the point where need is satisfied. If food is in severe short supply, need is greater, partly because of nutrition deficits that occur in famine, partly because of fear of starvation. Both a physical and a psychological basis for need can be identified. The widespread prevalence of obesity in affluent America demonstrates the persistence of psychological need well beyond the point of satisfaction of physical need for food. The same persistence of psychological need beyond the minimum physical basics can be identified in those who require palatial shelter, regal clothing, vast monetary wealth, absolute security, constant affection, or those who demand excitement at a level of high personal risk of harm. Human need is not fixed. It expands in the presence of plenty and contracts in the event of scarcity. Something more than mere utility must be invoked to account fully for demand.

Abundance does curious and special things to demand. It changes the value of goods and services qualitatively. Plenty can create outright contempt for the basics of life. The Garden of Eden was a place of such abundance that all the physical needs of mortal man and woman were immediately provided for by nature. Physical need was fully met. The utility of these provisions was taken for granted by its tenants. In the absence of want, physical need was superceded by curiosity—the psychological need for stimulation that always emerges from the background when satisfaction is attained. The Eden of unlimited satiation is intolerable and, hence, an unstable state. The desert of risk and challenge always wins out. If it didn't, there could be no law of supply and demand.

Utility is the first element of the value equation. Utility is made clearest when, in the absence of goods and services that satisfy utility, value is driven up sharply by deprivation due to shortages. Food prices vary annually as a function of seasonal plenty or scarcity. When an overall shortage of food arises, the prices of all foods rise. When an overall glut of food exists, the prices of all foods fall. Air and water are used without concern for their utility when plentiful. High altitude flying, though, demands that a scarcity of oxygen in that rare atmosphere be anticipated with a supplementary supply from the oxygen tank, even though the enclosed cabin is pressurized to increase the density of the air. A substantial price must be paid for breathable air and the risk of depressurization in a jet aircraft.

Clean, potable water is rarer than air. Population density and heavy industrial use can put severe pressure on water supplies. Conflict between mining and agricultural interests for access to water off the Rocky Mountain watershed has existed for more than a century. Sewage and industrial effluent in the great midcontinent rivers severely limits industrial and population growth along their banks, where, once, plentiful fresh water and cheap water transport made them magnets of economic growth. Utility, like the plenitude of Eden, goes unnoticed until it is absent.

The fresh energy of youth has no value until it wanes in sickness or old age. The security of home goes unnoticed until breached by break-in and robbery. Freely tendered love and devotion are cheap until lost. The things we can least do without, the most fundamental dependencies of need, we may scorn when in abundance. Experience makes a difference, of course, but the greater the abundance, the greater the insulation from harsh experience.

THE SHIFTING REFERENCE POINTS OF VALUE

In the early years of the industrial revolution when the difference between want and plenty was still fresh in the memory of the work force, the product of mass commodity production was highly valued. Indeed, the discovery of a way of life free of daily concern for satisfaction of basic utilities was downright emancipating. A seventy hour work week in a dingy factory was a noble and invigorating crusade for the betterment of humankind. Henry Ford's $5.00 workday on a moving assembly line made a secure middle-class wage earner out of the penniless, unskilled laborer.

Approximately sevenscore years later—about the passage of a lifetime— a secure middle-class job and paycheck are assumed as one's birthright. Food is abundant, often in excess supply. Clothing has become a throwaway item. Passing children's pants, shirts and dresses on to the succeeding generation is almost unheard of. Housing, temporarily abundant in the building boom that followed World War II, is either in great excess in those parts of the country where economic dislocation is severe or excessively tight where affluence sets the standard for living space five times greater than the square footage per occupant fifty years earlier. Tax incentives for home ownership make a first and even second home one of the best investments available to the wage earning middle class. Every child has his or her own room, TV, and, when old enough, automobile. Americans, even those in relative poverty, are characterized by a contempt for the basic utilities of life.

In less than four decades, new classes of utilities have been created in the form of computers and calculators. Computing technology exploded into prominence, created unparalleled excitement for its productive power and has already become a ho-hum utility for the newest generation. The pace of computing advance has been a dazzling, dizzy one. In the forties, crude monstrosities as large as a small house were set to work on the highest priority engineering and financial control problems of industry. A small army of programmers and maintenance technicians was required to keep them running. In the fifties, commercial time-sharing on telephone lines put computing within reach of high level technicians in the largest companies.

In the seventies, the first personal, hand held calculators, some more powerful than the earliest full scale computers, came on the market at prices of $500 or more. Within fifteen years, the same tool could be purchased for $5.00. As the eighties approached, the personal computer was invented. The first had computing power equivalent to many existing mainframe computers of only a decade earlier. Within a decade of its introduction, the standard PC has achieved computing power more than one hundred times greater than at its inception *at no increase in price*. Yet the personal computer and its little brother, the hand held calculator, have already become commonplace utilities. Only the fastest, most technologically advanced equipment excites interest from today's computer accustomed worker technocracy.

Yet the change in personal effectiveness, productivity and satisfaction experienced by those who have experienced the transition is exciting and real almost beyond belief. It has been a spectacular era. As one who has followed it from start to present, who wrote more than six books on a typewriter and carried out one major piece of statistical research on a mechanical calculator, I can offer my personal experience of this change. The word processor has doubled my productivity; I can draft the same amount of copy in half the time once required, exclusive of typing the finished copy. Long hours are no longer needed to retype illegible notes. There is no struggle to find a cheap, willing typist to do my drudge work. Editing and spell checking are virtually automatic on the computer.

As a high speed number cruncher, the computer has been even more helpful. In 1958, to satisfy the requirement for a master's thesis, I calculated fifty-three correlation coefficients on sixteen variables across a sample base of thirty-six people. A total of eighty hours of time went into the project. For its time it was an impressive piece of individual effort by any standard. Twenty years later under a consulting contract that required calculation of more than 1,000 correlation coefficients on 150 people across forty-eight variables, four hours of setup time for programming and data entry were required. The entirety of output was generated on the printer in another four hours. My output, in very conservative terms, was increased by a factor of twenty, while the time shrank by a factor of ten—or twenty if you consider direct labor only. My personal productivity increased by a factor of at least two hundred, perhaps four hundred times or more. The memory of hard labor for significantly less output remains fresh. The computer is still a genie in my book. For some of the new generation, it is already their dreariest drudgery.

In the absence of comparative experience, the value of utility is determined strictly by supply and demand. Abundance of a good or service can lead to indifference or contempt among those who have never known want of it or to comfort in knowledge of that abundance among those who have known scarcity. Experience shapes response to scarcity.

HUMAN RESPONSE TO SCARCITY AND PLENTY

Scarcity and plenty are qualitatively distinct events and experiences. Scarcity rewards foresight and exertion. It punishes passivity and indifference. In scarcity, scrappers and risk takers survive. There are clear winners and losers. For those who have known the dread of scarcity, losing is intolerable. In abundance, anyone who is not a complete fool can find a winning niche. Only the confused or grossly incompetent perish. There is all the difference in the world between the experience of abundance and scarcity.

It is impossible for anyone who has never known real scarcity of food, clothing and shelter to understand the readiness, even the rush, to accept risk that characterizes the actions of competitors in scarcity. Risk of life for a major payoff is unthinkable for the protected child of abundance. It is more likely to be judged the best shot at survival by heirs of grinding poverty. Scarcity puts one's life at risk regardless. In an economy of scarcity, the hungry are natural predators. The well fed are natural victims. The experience of scarcity generates either aggressive response of self-defense or passive acceptance of extinction.

The shift from abundance to scarcity reactivates the preexisting response tendency in those who understand the implications of scarcity. The inexperienced are instantly put at a disadvantage. They are ready neither to undertake risk aggressively nor to conserve resources against decline. This introduces opportunity for the aggressive and experienced to seize advantage over the inexperienced and unprepared. Significant shifts in positions of wealth and status can occur in a sudden transition from plenty to scarcity. Opportunism pays!

The value of scarce goods and services increases naturally with scarcity and is then amplified by hoarding. Those experienced with scarcity buy up the existing stock to ensure their own need and as a speculative investment. Those experienced but passive reduce their dependence on it to a minimum. The inexperienced foolishly bid up the price in a desperate move to preserve their accustomed standard of living. Sudden scarcity is an occasion of great threat and opportunity, depending on experience and readiness to respond.

Value of goods and services is, without doubt, determined in part by their utility. The relative abundance or scarcity of those goods and services—supply and demand in the classic economic sense—increases or decreases their price. Human experience further shapes response to abundance or scarcity. Inexperience with scarcity amplifies a tendency to be scornful of cheap abundance. Experience with scarcity confers tactical advantage in response to its reappearance. Experience and inexperience amplify the natural shifts in utilitarian value brought about by plenty and scarcity.

FROM WAGE SLAVERY TO THE LABORING REVOLUTION

The dawn of the industrial revolution was a time of widespread experience of scarcity. But the industrial revolution, with its sharp emphasis on full utilization of production capacity, its continuous flow output and its narrow specialization of worker skill, was also an enormous departure from the preceding millennia of craftsmanship dedicated to a lifetime of meaningful production. The nearest analog to factory employment is the institution of slavery. Slavery was not exclusively applied to acts of menial labor; it was, however, always labor forced under threat of death, which supported the luxury life-style of the rich and powerful. The industrial revolution was built on the surplus population that arose out of an expanding food supply made possible by improved agricultural methods. It was further sustained by cheap foodstuffs from fertile foreign lands imported by a global mercantile fleet. Those without inherited land on which to farm were forced into the urban mercantile centers to find work or starve. Laborers literally went to work in factories of the eighteenth and nineteenth centuries under threat of death as slaves had before them. Plant owners enjoyed the same luxury as slave owners. Laborers complied willingly because the surplus of goods and services realized through mass production promised to become the touchstone of wealth and plenty even for the laboring masses.

Slavery has seldom been as harsh as the storybooks make it out to be. The slave was an important asset to his owner. He had to be kept healthy enough to be an effective worker. A degree of mutual dependency between owner and slave was inevitable. History books record the discomfort of masters who lost the services of an effective, devoted slave. Thomas Jefferson is said to have made a beloved mistress of one slave. But there were costs to owning slaves. They had to be fed and housed. Slaves would escape or go beserk. Some had to be punished as an example to all. Employment of freemen at a living wage transferred the responsiblity for health, self-development and self-maintenance to the laborer. Punishment for the effect of example need be no more severe than loss of wage employment. Compared to the slaves in an economy based on slavery, free wage laborers are vastly easier to manage and replace. It is necessary only to pay enough to sustain life with a little left over for self-indulgence on holidays. One must not overpay drudgery labor, lest the laborer accumulate excess and escape from the drudgery of wage bondage.

Dependence of factory owners on labor, nonetheless, was nearly complete. Without labor the factory would close. Wages that held laborers close to the edge of destitution and desperation made idleness the lesser of evils. Reliable, consistent attendance on the job (still a major concern of mass production management) required payment of a minimal living wage. The best factory employee is one characterized by a complacency born of rising above the despair of poverty, who expects nothing better. Satisfaction of basic need made possible by mass commodity production raises the aspiration of laborers. Karl Marx evoked the cry of exploitation and called for class warfare. Samuel Gompers shouted for "more." The labor movement and international communism were the natural responses to wage slavery. Neither would have come about without an industrial revolution dedicated to mass commodity production. As the industrial revolution nears the end of its natural course, both show a readiness to disappear.

The success of mass commodity output of basic goods and services was and is the main and only real stream of revolution for humankind in this millennium. Class warfare is no more than a guerilla skirmish at the periphery. The object is plenty for all. With knowledge of machines and materials pushed to present high levels, plenty is at hand if people will only perfect the technical and social systems through which it is created and distributed. Communism in the form of state owned production plants has certainly not been the answer. Capitalism moderated by popular democracy has done rather well by comparison, in spite of the many gaps and inequities of that system. Supply and demand is a crude mechanism for setting value that suits an emerging industrial economy well enough. But utility alone is not enough on which to build a system fully sensitive to the values of human beings. Utility only works equitably to meet human need when exactly the right amount of commodity production is supplied. Too much is waste; too little is a struggle for survival of the fittest.

The machines of mass production, originally built to satisfy demand with continually sufficient supply, no longer capture humankind's imagination. Abundance is taken for granted. If our need for basic commodities is not satisfied cheaply and consistently, the system lurches into malfunction until revised so that supply is again adequate. Western society expects and demands low-cost commodity goods and services. Presently, an internationalized economy stands ready to supply them. If private industry will not supply them because of cost pressure, the high expectations of the populace may force transfer of commodity output systems into government ownership. When that happens, though, the relationship of labor to their operation will be vastly different from today's arrangements, especially those that exist under communism. Ultimately, conscription of the young to operate our factories may become the moral equivalent of military service.

Utility is something to depend on. It is expected to supply the foundation of the good life. But utility is not sufficient as the sole basis on which to establish value. Efficiency sets a low price but offers little profit once plenty is taken for granted. Utility, even as modified by experience, cannot function alone in establishing value. There is another, more powerful fountainhead of economic worth. It is found in the power of human passion.

THE POWER OF HUMAN PASSION

Passion originally meant agony or suffering. It has come to denote any compelling or intense emotion. As the term is used here, it will mean any human action that is driven by emotional forces beyond mere utility. Utility in its rawest form is pure appetite; it is physiologically founded need that is distinguished by the absence of passion. Passion is the unreasonable, the idealistic, the materially unfounded purposes of humankind. Passion is stimulation and excitement, the fervor and ardor of life that has no simple explanation. Passion exists for no purpose other than its own sake.

Passion predated the industrial revolution. The great cathedrals of the old world were products of passion. They represented aspiration of the human spirit for expression beyond mere utility. The crusades to the holy land were passionate events driven by faith and hope, dependent on luck and providence. The ancient church inspired the passions of a Michelangelo to portray biblical stories pictorially on the ceiling of his church. Passion shaped Shakespeare's words. Passion drove Thomas More to sacrifice life for the integrity of his word and the law. None of these acts can be explained by utility.

The commercialism of the Christmas season is certainly utilitarian. But it is impossible to explain the need for elaborate seasonal decorations and the enduring myth of Santa Claus without passion. The seasonal spirit of giving is itself the gift of passion. Without passion, the utilitarian ritual of preparatory winter outfitting and storage would be occasion for fear and dread. With passion as its driving center, Christmas is a season of generosity and hope that looks confidently to the return of lengthened days of sunlight.

We may look for added quality and comfort in the utility of an automobile and expect to pay more than for the standard. A Rolls Royce or Lamborghini, though, is clearly overkill when measured in utilitarian terms alone. These machines are invested with passion, one for status and quality, the other for motoring excitement. The modern day armor of the brave and gallant knight is his automobile. It is invested with all the passionate symbols of knighthood and courage. It shines in the bright sun, purrs its guttural strength and leaps into pursuit of its quarry. Passion, indeed, permeates the entire Western marketplace creating magic where once there was only utility. Once the demands of utility are met, passion alone sells. Passion excites and stimulates by transforming the commonplace of mere utility into an expression of individuality.

The industrial revolution was itself an act of passion driven by invention and curiosity. Departing as it did from comfortable, human-scaled agricultural patterns of work and living, it required the militant dedication in its adherents. It was a holy war against pervasive human want. As the luster of commodity production line work fades, passion is first invested in improved quality of output. Quality is an investment in future performance, an act of faith. Quality reduces the market for mass commodity production by extending serviceable life. Initially, highest quality is contrary to utilitarian values. It is in the latter stages of industrial development that maximum quality becomes a utilitarian value because of its contribution to value. As a substitute for an earlier fervor for efficiency through industrial order, though, pursuit of quality is an act of passion.

Passion today is increasingly invested in uniqueness, customization, specialty. The availability of quality commodities is taken for granted. The excitement shifts to the unique, personalized product or service.

Passion comes easily in deep poverty and personal deprivation. With plenty, it comes with increasing difficulty. The human need for expression through passion is in no way diminished by plenty, though. As a result, goods and services are "marketed" by investing them with magic. Power, status, personal attraction, the thrill of risk and guarantee of instant sexual gratification are the newest commodities of the industrial revolution. With each passing year, autos become glitzier, clothes become more garishly styled, food becomes spicier, decorations in shop windows become more theatrical. The sale of nonutility—the sizzle of the steak—works better than the sale of its nutritional utility.

The nonutility of caffeine and nicotine sells more profitably than the utility of milk or orange juice. Cigarettes stimulate at the price of long-term health. Cola soft drinks stimulate at the risk of excess sugar consumption or uncertain effects of sugar substitutes. Neither is necessary in itself to human health or welfare. These chemical stimulants provide the momentary evocation of passion in a jolt of sensibility that becomes a habit. Manufacturers of products based on caffeine and nicotine are among the most profitable and powerful in the world.

Our passions are chemically activated to the maximum by the least useful substances imaginable—narcotic drugs. Cocaine, heroin and their derivative cousins are engines of pure passion, inspiring their users to incredibly bold acts of courage (and crime), creating insatiable appetites for yet more passion, destroying health, life and social order in their pursuit.

The utility and disutility of passion itself are demonstrated by narcotics. Under the influence of narcotic drugs a life can pass with the brilliance and brevity of a comet in the sky. Incredible energy and activity—often applied to outlaw pursuits—followed by severe lethargy, pain and even early death are the product of passion without purpose, stimulation without productivity. The efficiency with which passion itself is evoked finally describes the end station of mass commodity output. In the pursuit of efficiency, utility is first fulfilled by the industrial revolution, which obsoletes the passionate struggle for survival in a subsistence economy. When plenty has been supplied by the engines of industrial efficiency, passion is made available in superabundance through narcotic drugs.

Life's purposes are first trivialized by the industrial revolution and then transformed by it. Utility need no longer be the first requirement of production systems. Efficiency has been extended to its furthest limits. Passion must now be enlisted in the service of new aims. Utility without passion is hollow materialism that supports survival without object. Passion without utility is undisciplined appetite, infinite demand. The industrial revolution harnessed a passion for utility gained with maximum efficiency. Mastery of utility by efficiency produces malaise. Passion must now be found in other places. The locus of passion in postindustrial society must finally be addressed.

PASSION AND INTERNAL REVOLUTION

The shape of postindustrial society has yet to form. Its outline appears dimly visible on the horizon, but its details are not yet clear. Human passions can be acted out in war. But war has become so efficient a means of population reduction that it threatens extinction of humankind. The absence of passion in life under communism has driven its citizens to the edge of despair—they are ready to risk expression of long denied passions in open revolution against their governments. Centralized ownership and control of production under communism has lost its revolutionary passion. Hope is dead. Were war not more hopeless, it might be invoked to restimulate the passions of patriotism in the Communist citizenry. Nuclear war is unthinkable, but the demonstrated advantage of industrial efficiency in the West makes conventional war impractical for the leaders of communism. Containing the passions of internal revolution is safer.

Indeed, internal revolution has been recognized as the more cautions course and is under way within Western nations. Dissatisfaction—a disruptive and inefficient sentiment in mass society—is evidenced everywhere. Conformity under wise leadership is no longer assumed to be the safest route to mass survival. Individualism at the maximum, a widespread dash for total self-expression, self-actualization, self-knowledge, are the compulsions of the new age. They are undoubtedly the harbingers of postindustrial society.

Dissatisfaction is literally on the rise. Even in the decade of the 1960s, when dropping out of society came into fashion, dissatisfaction with work among the great middle class of America was seldom greater than 10% in national polls. Recently, it has climbed to 25% and more (see Figure 3–1). It is a classic paradox that at the height of human productive efficiency humankind cannot be satisfied—a paradox, that is, until the innate inability

Figure 3–1
Decline in Worker Satisfaction, 1963 to 1984

```
              % Satisfied with Work

              1963          1984

              90%           72%


         An 18% increase in 21 years

         Source: Gallup Poll, 1985.
```

of utility to satisfy is recognized. Once material plenty is ensured, satisfaction is a product of passion alone. Passion must be reckoned with.

PASSION AND INDIVIDUALITY

There is substantial risk that the freedom and plenty of postindustrial society will evoke maximum self-seeking in its citizenry. Self-interest when constrained by mutual respect can be a stabilizing force for the economy. Greed and self-aggrandizement, at the other pole, can approximate individual guerilla warfare against the interests of the greater number when carried to extremes. It is within the range of these polarities of individualism that the postindustrial economy must come to grips with human passion. Individualism with all its negatives and all its positives is fast becoming the foundation of human value. The passions of humankind will be, and presently are being, acted out through innumerable dramas of individual self-discovery.

Society is already departing from the norm of satisfaction that characterized the industrial revolution. When one is a wage slave, a mere cog in the industrial machine, it is necessary and even expected that one will look to owners of the machine for satisfaction. The wage bargain of the industrial revolution is that pay and benefits will satisfy workers' expectations of a decent livelihood. A job must offer minimum satisfaction. It is a satisfaction, however, that is based on the worker's judgment that his livelihood is neither better nor worse than that of his fellows. It is satisfaction that comes from acceptance of one's place in the economic order. The achievement of mass wealth based on efficient mass output pulls the floor out from under the very notion of an economic order. Satisfaction in postindustrial society arises out of the discovery and fulfillment of one's own, unique potential as a person.

Satisfaction was never an externally available commodity to begin with. Finding satisfaction outside oneself cannot be more than a mirrorlike illusion of seeming to find oneself and one's aspirations in the reflections of the surrounding world. Satisfaction is easy to achieve if aspirations are kept modest. As long as human passions can be enlisted in service of distant or future goals, sufficient satisfaction can be found in hope for a later reward. When the goal is achieved, though, and it is found to be little if any different from the products of the past, where do we then direct our passion?

In the absence of experience and social convention to assist, there will inevitably be random experimentation and readiness to seize quick payoff. Efficiency, though, is no longer a reliable guide to the best result. Egocentric greed, narcotic drugs, selfish, short-sighted competition are efficient routes to quick reward but are likely to carry a high long-term cost.

A PASSION FOR SKILL AND KNOWLEDGE

The future of humankind is to be found where passion is invested in the development of skill. Not just technical skill but skill with tools of all kinds is indispensable in this advanced technological economy, but social skill is equally important. An economy based on maximum individual expression means leveling of status and power differences across society and increased complexity of relationships between individuals. To succeed in a postindustrial society we must be prepared to relate individually with every member of that society. Success in a commercial and social sense will depend on getting to know suppliers, customers, friends and family in depth as unique individuals. That will demand a level of social skill far beyond anything imagined in today's mass society.

The future of humankind will also flow from a passion for knowledge. It will require not just formal knowledge of facts and definitions, formulas and places but a knowledge of how and why things work. A dynamic sense of system and structure are needed to deal with ever shifting uniqueness. Postindustrial people must learn to construct knowledge as they go along in order to solve the unique puzzles that emerge. Social and technological complexity will soon be (if it is not already) so vast that a lifetime will be inadequate to master it all. We can no longer expect to focus on detail in formal teaching and hope that the general rules are discovered. The industrial revolution rendered philosophy trivial and impractical. The postindustrial age will likely see a passionate renaissance of philosophical analysis and discourse.

Postindustrial economy will be highly individualized in character. Mass production of commodities by automated factories and farms, tended by a small fraction of the working population—10% or less—will ensure a foundation of plenty and affluence for mass society. The major mass service sectors of the economy—hospitals, banks, insurance, fast food, education—

must follow suit with rationalization, mechanization and pursuit of efficiency to provide commodity service in abundance. That process is already well advanced.

Ultimately, the largest part of the economy will be individualized and personal. Customized goods and services will dominate postindustrial economic exchange. Flexible equipment, skill and knowledge will be its foundation. Family centered cottage industry will again flourish. In many if not most ways, this will become an extended age of the project shop.

In many centers of our present day economy, already, efficiency doesn't count. Meeting the specialized, individual requirements of each customer, an inefficient but potentially highly satisfying experience to supplier and customer alike, is the emerging norm. Profitability is greater, quality is primary. There is no machine to shield worker from boss, customer from worker. Work and consumption are no longer divorced.

The passions of humankind are best expressed in the adventure of exploration, discovery and the pursuit, of personal growth. A system of learning that prepares the young to use the tools of society skillfully for its own and others' satisfaction is fundamental. Without mastery of language, machinery and social systems, individual participation in postindustrial society will be difficult if not impossible. Opportunity to compete and demonstrate mastery in their use will be necessary to test and validate ability. On that foundation, a society of skilled artisans can be built, each practicing his or her trade to satisfy the individual needs of customers who are artisans themselves. The opportunity then exists to master and serve in an ever changing, ever evolving economy where self-development and discovery are fundamental to success. That is a purpose to which our passions can be fully applied.

In preindustrial society, the absence of specialized skill and function left each person to find the correct discipline in which to work that supplied individual efficiency and satisfaction. Satisfaction and efficiency were competitors that required trade-offs. The strict, even passionate discipline of a Puritan culture, for instance, maximized physical welfare and survival as long as the urge to physical satisfaction was suppressed. In preindustrial society, pursuit of passion for its own sake was at risk of life.

The industrial revolution enlisted passion in the service of specialized labor and efficient production. The quality of physical life in the most basic of terms took a quantum leap—but only at the expense of a much increased narrowness of life. People, as a cog in the machine, improved the odds of survival and the chance at individual wealth. The waning of passion for pursuit of material wealth in commodities leaves us once more searching for the fullness of individual life. Material plenty is ensured. Even when temporarily demolished as it was in large parts of the earth by World War II, knowledge of the design of the system and its tools permits rapid reconstruction with assurance that plenty will flow from the newly restored productive system. Productivity depends on knowledge, and knowledge will not be stamped out as long as literacy prevails. The industrial revolution is preserved while a civilized humankind survives. Cheap, mass produced commodities depend only on the survival of civilization.

Postindustrial society requires a new discipline—the passionate self-discipline of skill and knowledge, attained in the early years of life, followed by a path of self-development, exploration and discovery focused on the potential of human life. It is a formula that simultaneously secures the benefits of civilization and of self-satisfaction. It is a design that creates maximum opportunity for uniqueness and individuality. In this coming era of passionate individualism, efficiency no longer counts. The passions of the coming era will consign efficiency to the history books.

4

CAPACITY STRATEGY AND MANAGEMENT OF BOTTLENECKS

"Managing a project shop starts with identifying the bottlenecks."

STRATEGIC CAPACITY DECISION MAKING

Bottlenecks arise out of insufficient capacity. Perhaps the most significant strategic decision that an operations manager can make is the capacity investment decision. In the absence of sufficient capacity, market share is at risk if the market grows. A large investment to increase capacity is almost a bet on increased market demand. If demand does not increase or, worse, if it falls, then significant, perhaps costly excess capacity is created and it becomes a losing bet. Sears, Roebuck's decision to expand locations aggressively after World War II paid off handsomely in profit and market share. Sewell Avery's choice at the same time to retrench Montgomery Ward essentially doomed it to the backwaters of retailing. W. T. Grant's decision to expand locations aggressively by borrowing heavily in the 1960s and early 1970s left it excessively leveraged with debt as interest rates skyrocketed and consumer buying suffered in an economic recession. Same business, same risk, but the winner takes all, and the loser can end up being put out of the game permanently.

The risk consequence of expansion is a direct function of the manner in which expansion is financed. If financed out of cash flow, added capacity can be added to the asset base and treated simply as an increase in retained earnings on the balance sheet. The only negative impact will be dilution of the ROI caused by the larger asset base that becomes the denominator of the ratio in its calculation. From the investor's perspective, though, this is capital gain and can, if the market permits, be reflected in the value of the stock. But when expansion is financed by debt, failure of the growth expectation means a shortage of cash to repay principal and interest on debt.

Figure 4–1
Financing with Cash Flow versus Financing with Debt

```
Assumptions:    $100,000,000 annual sales
                $  5,000,000 profit on sales
                $ 25,000,000 stockholder's equity

Proposed expansion:
                $ 10,000,000 added plant capacity
                   2,000,000 added profit potential
                   2,000,000 annual interest & principal

Year 1 yields no increase in sales or profit!

        Expansion financed with cash flow
        Equity increases by $10,000,000
```

$$ROE = \frac{\$\ 5,000,000}{35,000,000} = 14.3\%$$

```
        Expansion financed with debt
        Earnings reduce by 2,000,000 for debt service
```

$$ROE = \frac{\$\ 3,000,000}{25,000,000} = 12\%$$

```
Return on cash invested yields 19% better sales
performance.
```

Assets may have to be liquidated to cover debt and/or interest. Liquidation is typically accomplished at a discount of value for the asset. At best, earning potential is permanently diminished. At worst, the firm may be brought to the brink of bankruptcy as was W. T. Grant. Figure 4–1 illustrates these risks and their impact on corporate success.

Aside from the increased vulnerability of debt based expansion, a reduction in earnings on an existing equity base is more visible and dramatic than an increase in the equity base without any increase in earnings. Conservatively costed, the same ten million dollar expansion financed on cash flow results in almost 20% better earnings over debt financing if market growth fails to occur. A reduction in earnings from debt service against an unchanged equity base reduces earnings proportionately more.

The general rule that guides capacity decisions is the same rule that guides prudent speculation under all circumstances; *it is unwise to bet more than you can afford to lose.* Every capacity expansion decision has downside risk that is either tolerable or foolish. Therefore, any major increase in capacity deserves especially careful thought and analysis. A capacity expansion typically requires calculation of break-even points for existing and planned capacity. The elements of a break-even analysis are:

Figure 4–2
Consequences of Overoptimistic Investment through Incurring Heavy Downside Risk

```
Assumptions:              40% increase in capacity
                  95,000,000 current level of sales
                 100,000,000 is current capacity
                 140,000,000 sales potential after investment
                          5% annual market growth


                  70 million units is present breakeven
                  90 million units is expanded breakeven

                  Historically, sales have dropped as much as
                  12% in one year over the previous
                  year, and have typically remained depressed
                  for up to two years before rebounding.


Worst Case scenario with investment is

                  Sales drop to 83.6 million units
                  Breakeven increases to 90 million units
                  Two years of losses are incurred
```

$$BE = \frac{\text{Total Fixed Costs}}{(\text{Unit Price}) - (\text{Unit Variable Cost})}$$

The increase in fixed cost due to a higher break-even point should, as a matter of conservative policy, be easily covered by likely market growth under the worst case economic scenario. Going for expanded capacity that requires realization of the best case scenario of growth is a high risk gamble that will probably not pay off. When market position is already untenable, such risk may be justifiable on grounds that it is the only escape from business demise anyhow. Betting the company because it isn't big enough to satisfy personal ambition is irresponsible.

Probabilistic decision-making methods involving the calculation of the odds of a set of outcomes is often used as grounds for capacity decisions. Decision tree analyses, decision tables and calculation of the average expected value of an outcome can be used. The trap in such decision making lies in the seeming objectivity these methods convey. They appear to rely on unbiased numbers. In fact, probability estimates outside the play of cards are about as chancy and subjective as you can get. Only when worst case probabilities are used to support the decision to expand capacity should a decision based on formal, quantitative decision methodology be trusted. An example of the influence of optimism on a decision of this sort is shown in Figure 4–2. The argument in favor of committing to this investment is the 100 million unit output capacity ceiling that could be reached in one year. In the absence of new capacity, market share may be at risk. Worst case analysis for this expansion is a drop in sales to 83.6 million against a 90.0 million break-even situation. A seriously adverse market could produce major losses for this operation. Conservative planning would require that the expansion be recosted to yield a maximum 80.0 million to 82.0 million break-even situation.

In evaluating capacity expansion plans for custom, short-run project shop situations, it is essential to go even further to offset over optimistic growth projections based on either maximum possible growth projection or fear of lost market share. The folly of planning for full or even just very high capacity utilization in a project shop has already been argued. Capacities at 60% and less utilization of plant and equipment are necessary to a well-managed project shop. Costing capital investment on a full utilization basis is completely untenable. Return on capital investment that supports custom, short-run operations must take into account a longer payback period. Depreciation practices established for continuous flow operations will probably continue to be applied, which means that virtually all job shop investment depreciation will be on an "accelerated" basis. But return on investment will be stretched or phased out over a longer time base.

Plant and equipment for custom, short-run project shop operations must also be critically evaluated for its contribution to value of output. When it increases value sufficiently to increase price, a higher return may justify the investment or even make it a highly desirable business decision. Equipment that lends flexibility or improves productivity and service will often be sound investment for those reasons alone.

Increased capacity that reduces average capacity utilization has a potential for eliminating troublesome bottleneck situations and, overall, for improving customer service. Faster, more direct work flow in a nearly JIT mode through a project shop can increase quality in several ways. Improved quality and service can justify increased price. It was shown in chapter 1 that when price can be adjusted to reflect quality and service improvements inherent in low capacity equipment utilization, return on investment can be restored to a level that approximates full use. Capacity investment decisions that justify premium pricing can permit a high return on investment in spite of modest capacity utilization. It is appropriate to factor this into a capital investment decision that increases capacity.

Some project shop capital investment situations may justify acquisition of equipment that *must* be highly utilized to justify its cost. It may be argued that the equipment is sufficiently valuable to require everything else to be scheduled around it. The decision to buy equipment on these terms is essentially a decision to build a permanent bottleneck into the operation. If that is the nature of the choice, some means is required whereby the implications of building in a resident bottleneck can be examined. How many bottlenecks can a project shop tolerate before a policy of overall low capacity utilization is nullified? What is the tolerable level of capacity utilization in a bottleneck? What are the implications of a bottleneck for scheduling? To what extent can a bottleneck be neutralized with good scheduling?

Analysis of this kind of decision requires general expansion of understanding of the bottleneck phenomenon itself as well as scheduling principles, which are discussed in chapter 5. Strategic capacity decisions are often already complex enough in continuous process operations. The challenges of a project shop require that bottlenecks and bottleneck scheduling be fully taken into account when those decisions are made.

WHAT IS A BOTTLENECK?

The concept of a bottleneck is widely understood. It is a point of constriction of production, material or other traffic flow. Engineering of mass production requires that work and material flow be balanced so that bottlenecks are avoided or eliminated. Project shop, custom or short-run operations, though, exhibit inherently unbalanced work flow. Bottlenecks will happen. There is no way to avoid them.

A *bottleneck* is often defined as a point in work flow where demand exceeds capacity. This is not a complete definition until measures of both demand and capacity are specified. Furthermore, it overlooks the fact that demand is often determined by capacity at an earlier stage of flow. A more precise definition of a bottleneck requires that prior levels of capacity be used as estimates of demand on bottleneck capacity. A bottleneck then becomes a point in the system of work flow where capacity utilization is relatively and significantly higher than at any prior point. The appearance of a bottleneck, thus, depends on the existence of slack in capacity leading to a point of higher relative capacity utilization—the bottleneck. The flow of everything in the system past that point depends on the rate of work flow through the bottleneck.

A bottleneck can be "solved" by increasing capacity at the bottleneck, by decreasing demand on it or by scheduling to eliminate wasted capacity at the bottleneck. The easiest way to eliminate wasted capacity is simply to let a natural waiting line of buffer inventory build up in front of the bottleneck. R. B. Chase and N. J. Acquilano (1989) observed that a buffer inventory must be kept in front of a bottleneck to ensure that the full capacity of that workstation is always in use. Indeed, it would appear that bottlenecks and waiting lines of buffer inventory are inseparable. Buffer inventory at the bottleneck will grow indefinitely, however, unless production ahead of the bottleneck is reduced to match the rate of flow through the bottleneck. Matching capacity at the bottleneck is accomplished at the risk of underusing the bottleneck. A bottleneck dominates not only the rate of work flow for the entire system but its scheduling as well.

Despite the ubiquitous nature of the production bottleneck, there is a general lack of rigorous modeling of bottlenecks that might provide guidelines for either managing or avoiding them. A significant exception is found in the use of the critical path to identify *the* principal bottleneck in a project network so that a schedule may be accurately prepared and potential for delay managed throughout the project. Figure 4–3 illustrates a project network with a critical path. Limited labor or equipment is allocated on first priority to the critical path to prevent delay. The available slack along noncritical paths is then exploited to adjust allocation of scarce labor or equipment so that conflict with the requirements of the critical path is avoided. It is equally true of both a bottleneck and a critical path that an hour lost at a bottleneck (or on the critical path) is an hour lost to the total system (or project), and an hour saved at a nonbottleneck (or on a noncritical path) is a mirage (Fox, 1983; Goldratt, 1988).

Program evaluation and review (PERT) and control path method (CPM) analysis have potential as guides to managing bottlenecks in work flow. It is feasible, for instance, to treat production flow as a network analysis problem, subject to a PERT networking and critical path analysis. Indeed, when just-in-time production flow is to be implemented with work flow, it is probably essential to construct the flow network and identify the critical production flow path. Only then can potential bottlenecks be identified so that scarce manpower, machinery and material are properly allocated.

In a project shop setting, bottlenecks arise out of variations in the mix of work. Bottlenecks will occur as a result of high demand for a particular labor skill or machine. High capacity utilization can occur at any point and at any time in a project shop. It can, though, be managed where high utilization of skill or equipment is foreseen and planned. Management of bottlenecks is fundamental to successful on-time scheduling of project shop operations.

In the project shop setting, a variation on network analysis can be applied to both measurement of capacity utilization and to scheduling. If job flow is random, each job has its own unique flow network that must compete with other jobs and networks for available capacity. Analysis of the work mix to identify bottlenecks is more complex than with fixed sequence flow processes and more necessary too. All the flow networks for jobs currently in process must be juxtaposed upon one another. Figure 4–4 illustrates how work in either a random or fixed sequence flow could be loaded on available stations to estimate the locus of bottlenecks. When workstation work requirements are thus combined, it is possible to estimate the expected capacity utilization of existing, available manpower or machinery.

Computer based network models of project shop projects are also potentially useful for analysis and prediction of bottlenecks. Small to large scale simulations of production flow based on such models are widely used to study production flow (Solomon, 1983). Juxtaposition of project shop project networks requires only that jobs be carefully estimated and that available skill and machinery be accurately inventoried so that level of use

Figure 4–3
A Project Network Example

Steps to opening a new branch office

	Activity	Preceding Activities	Time (Weeks)
A	Choose Location(s)	–	1
B	Advertise for Workers	A	1
C	Interview and hire new workers	B	4
D	Train new workers	C,H	2
E	Order Furniture and equipment	A	1
F	Install Walls and partitions	A	5
G	Install Phones and electrical	F	3
H	Install furniture and equipment	G,E	2
I	Grand Opening	D	0

Schematic Network

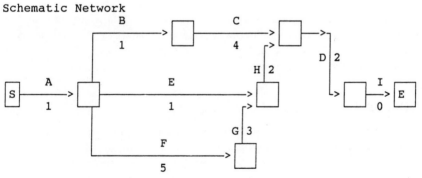

Path AFGHDI is 13 weeks long   The Critical
Path AEHDI is 6 weeks long   path is:
Path ABCDI is 8 weeks long   AFGHDI

Figure 4–4
Capacity Demand Model

```
40 hour work week assumed standard.
Estimates of job time on each station are
summed across all stations to ascertain
capacity utilization and identify
major bottlenecks.
```

Job #	Station 1	Station 2	Station 3	Station 4
		Required Station Time		
1	2 hr	3 hr	6 hr	4 hr
2	3	2	6	5
3	5	4	4	6
4	3	8	3	2
5	6	6	2	4
6	4	5	4	3
7	5	5	2	5
8	4	5	3	3
Total	32	38	30	32
% Cap Utiliz.:	80%	95%	75%	80%

over a given span of time can be assessed. What remains to be found if simulation models are to be made applicable to analysis of bottlenecks is the means whereby delay in the flow as a function of capacity constraint can be predicted and measured.

QUEUEING ANALYSIS OF BOTTLENECKS

A relatively clear and straightforward approach to measurement and prediction of capacity constraints is offered by queueing models and waiting line theory. Queue length and waiting time are a direct function of capacity utilization. Employing the simplest model of the queueing process, the single channel, single server model, it can be demonstrated that flow delay at any independent point in an unscheduled, unlinked work process rises exponentially with increases in capacity utilization. Assuming an infinite arrivals population, the length of the waiting line at maximum efficient (100%) capacity utilization itself becomes infinitely long. Figure 1–2 illustrates these functions. Bottlenecks, like critical paths, establish the maximum capacity level of the system. In the absence of production restraint ahead of the bottleneck, the waiting line at the bottleneck can stretch to infinity. Those elements of the flow system operating at less than bottleneck capacity must be adjusted to control the bottleneck queue.

When flow sequence is fixed rather than random, flow linkages can sometimes be managed to control bottlenecks. As in the mass production assembly line, equivalence of capacity utilization between linked workstations permits jobs to flow without delay. When capacity between workstations is equal and work flow is linked as in a continuous flow system, waiting time is absorbed by each prior workstation. Bottlenecks occur whenever a mismatch in capacity exists between elements of a production system. When all elements are balanced to the same level of unit flow capacity, as they are in a moving assembly line operation, delay is eliminated as long as there is no major breakdown in the system. Delay exists only at entry to the system when labor or materials are unavailable or at the output end whenever demand exceeds capacity. When it is not possible to schedule flow exactly because of unpredictable variations due to asymmetry in elements of the system, or when variety of work makes every job flow unique, delay due to existence of one or more bottlenecks becomes possible at every point in the system and is especially troublesome whenever relative capacity utilization is high. That is the dilemma of project shop custom and short-run operations.

BOTTLENECKS IN THE PROJECT SHOP

In a project shop, the seriousness of a bottleneck is a function of two variables: (1) average level of capacity utilization of all workstations and (2) the size of relative differences in the level of capacity utilization between workstations. Reference to Figure 1–2 and Table 1–1 reveals that very low levels of capacity utilization—10% to 40%, for instance—are characterized by very short waiting lines. Bottlenecks will be minimally troublesome. At capacity levels of 50% or 70%, there will typically be a short waiting line. The significance of the bottleneck will depend on how much higher than average capacity utilization at the bottleneck is. At capacity usage levels of 80% and above, lines will often be lengthy, and a few percentage points increase in demand in the 85% to 95% range will quickly double the length of the already lengthy queue to create horrendous bottlenecks.

When capacities are unequal, flow must be scheduled so that capacity is never wasted at the bottleneck. But scheduling is difficult in a project shop because both capacity utilization levels and job length may shift and vary unpredictably at every workstation. Project shop service time can be improved either by designing in excess capacity so that natural waiting line delay between jobs is minimal or by identifying bottlenecks accurately and scheduling to minimize their impact on production or service delay.

Typically, this means that when it is impractical to identify bottlenecks but delay is undesirable, overall capacity utilization below 50% must be acceptable. Sales personnel or automatic vending machines are usually scheduled to provide response at this level. When a small delay is acceptable and capacity is costly, use in the 50% to 70% range may be feasible. Airlines, for instance, cost their break-even points close to 60% to get the best trade-off between the high fixed costs of capacity investment and flexible customer service. At that level of capacity utilization even last minute travel can normally be accommodated on the first or second flight attempted. When capacity is too expensive to go unused, it must be scheduled in the 80% to 95% range with precise attention to the bottlenecks. Hospital operating rooms are staffed to handle just about all of a typical day's demand and are seldom empty while the staff is on hand. Operating room delays, though, are common enough to be expected and predictable.

Project shop work flow creates waiting lines. Unequal levels of capacity utilization in combination with unique network flows for every job means that some or all workstations will function independently of others in the flow. Unless they are linked together for continuous flow, a difficult or impractical solution in a project shop, each will have its own, independent waiting line. Thus in a project shop, overall level of capacity utilization interacts with bottlenecks to determine the length of waiting lines at bottlenecks. At average capacity utilization levels below 50%, bottlenecks may be inconsequential. The rate at which a waiting line forms is too slow to create concern. At higher capacity utilization rates, however, bottlenecks can create major delays in a project shop, just as they do in an assembly line. Because they are a function of variable work mix in a project shop, bottlenecks cannot easily be balanced by increasing workstation capacity or decreasing station capacity utilization. They must be identified and managed through creative scheduling that exploits earlier delays and capacity constraints to expedite work through the bottleneck.

Table 4–1 provides examples of the changes in flow time introduced by waiting lines in front of workstations. Average capacities of 80%, 50% and 30% are calculated for a three step operation. For the sake of example, capacity utilization at the middle step is then increased across these examples. In the absence of remedial scheduling, average processing time is increased by 50% or more in each case illustrated. Modest differences in capacity utilization brought about by variations in work mix would yield a similar result. Substantial increases in processing time and, hence, in delay of job completion will be encountered in the absence of recognition and management of the bottleneck. Because it contributes so greatly to reduced service, the bottleneck is the first priority for management and scheduling

Table 4–1
Queue Delay Increase as a Function of Bottlenecks with a Three Element Task
Requiring Six Days' Actual Working Time

80% Capacity with a 90% Capacity Bottleneck

Job Step	Working Time	Daily Arrival Rate	80% Ave. Capacity Service	Queue Length (days)	90% Ave. Capacity Bottleneck	Queue Length (days)
A	2 days	.5	.625	6.4	.625	6.4
B	2 days	.5	.625	6.4	.556	16.1
C	2 days	.5	.625	6.4	.625	6.4
Totals:	6 days			19.2		28.9

28.9/19.2 = 50% longer

50% Capacity with a 70% Capacity Bottleneck

Job Step	Working Time	Daily Arrival Rate	50% Ave. Capacity Service	Queue Length (days)	70% Ave. Capacity Bottleneck	Queue Length (days)
A	2 days	.5	1.0	1.0	1.0	1.0
B	2 days	.5	1.0	1.0	.714	2.5
C	2 days	.5	1.0	1.0	1.0	1.0
Totals:	6 days			3.0		4.5

4.5/3.0 = 50%longer

30% Capacity with a 50% Bottleneck

Job Step	Working Time	Daily Arrival Rate	30%Ave. Capacity Service	Queue Length (days)	50% Ave. Capacity Bottleneck	Queue Length (days)
A	2 days	.5	1.67	.26	1.67	.26
B	2 days	.5	1.67	.26	1.0	1.00
C	2 days	.5	1.67	.26	1.67	.26
Totals:	6 days			.78		1.52

1.52/.78 = 95% longer

attention in a project shop. In some cases, it may be the only point of attention needed.

Reduction of flow time where substantial variation in capacity utilization exists among workstations requires first that it be known where the bottlenecks exist. That is, relatively higher capacity utilization stations must be identified. A station loading estimate is probably the simplest way to identify bottlenecks for varying mixes of work. Simulations may also be useful. Once the bottlenecks are pinpointed, scheduling should focus on moving jobs through the stations before the bottleneck in such a manner that jobs get to the bottleneck in the shortest possible time and in the most efficient sequence possible. When, for instance, jobs can be scheduled through the bottleneck virtually on an appointment basis, there is no need for delay as long as any excess capacity exists, however small. It is a random, uncontrolled pattern of arrivals that creates the queue and the potential for delay. Good scheduling is the natural enemy of a waiting line.

When the bottleneck exists early in the work flow and there is no control over the time of arrival of jobs, it will be difficult or impossible to obtain control over work flow. The entry-point bottleneck will inevitably limit rate of flow and quality of service for the entire system. A bottleneck at the point of entry is virtually unmanageable. It is solvable only by increasing available capacity at that point. Bottlenecks late in the flow, however, offer opportunity to schedule work into them so that delay can be reduced or minimized.

Management of a bottleneck with improved scheduling downstream in the work flow is closely analogous to managing the slack in a project network. The job that can be put through the system and reach the bottleneck earliest must be expedited. That which cannot arrive until later need not be hurried. The object is to keep the bottleneck loaded by getting work to it quickly. Before reaching the bottleneck, flow is determined by the need to manage bottleneck capacity usage closely. The heuristic that underlies S. M. Johnson's rule (Johnson, 1954, discussed in chapter 5) can be applied here. To eliminate wasted capacity at the bottleneck, schedule those jobs that can reach the bottleneck quickly as early as possible. Among those jobs that will reach the bottleneck later, schedule any that require small amounts of bottleneck capacity last.

THE HOSPITAL EMERGENCY ROOM: AN EXAMPLE OF BOTTLENECK SCHEDULING

A hospital emergency room offers an example of how bottlenecks might be identified and managed.

Table 4–2 illustrates the average capacity constraints in an emergency room of a small hospital that is staffed with one admitting nurse, one doctor, and has the services of the hospital X-ray and laboratory departments. Average rate of emergency arrivals is thirty per day. The admitting nurse spends 45% of her time on emergency admissions and gives them first priority in her administrative duties. The doctor is busy 60% of the time with cases, the X-ray unit is used at 60% capacity at all times and the hospital lab is manned to 75% capacity around the clock. Applying waiting line theory to this situation, assuming that each of these work centers is a

Table 4–2
Hypothetical Emergency Room Work Flow

Work Station:	Emerg. Room Admitting	Attending Physician	X-Rays	Laboratory
Daily Arrival Rate	30*	30*	60**	90**
Daily Service Capacity	65	48	100	120
Percent Capacity Usage	46%	62%	60%	75%
Average Wait in Minutes	19	50	43	108

*Emergency Room Patients Only

**Emergency Room and Other Patients

single channel, single server workstation, the average delay can be calculated for each stage of the process. Life threatening emergencies that permit little or no delay are ignored for purposes of this analysis.

Average waits are calculated for the four stations. At admission, the wait is nineteen minutes, fifty minutes for the doctor, forty-three minutes for X-ray and one hour and forty-eight minutes for lab work. Lab work and X-rays are not required for every emergency patient; some require one or the other and a few need both. In a few situations, the admitting nurse can identify needed lab work or X-rays. In most cases, the doctor must specify what is required. X-rays are first come, first served, on the basis of arrival in the X-ray department, and lab work is first come, first served, on the basis of a telephone request for service.

For competitive reasons, which might mean another hospital emergency room in the area or a private clinic offering comparable service, this emergency room faces the prospect of losing patients because it has a reputation for slow service. Lost patients would simply mean higher per patient cost since both the admitting nurse and the doctor represent fixed, irreducible costs. Every effort must be made to speed up service.

The major bottleneck in this flow process is the laboratory because it requires more than an hour and three-quarters wait on the average. This situation exists because a trained lab technician must come to the emergency room with exactly the right equipment to do the needed tests. On rare occasions it is possible to combine patients and tests. Usually, a single patient must be served at the time of each visit.

If capacity utilization of the laboratory cannot be reduced, the solution to this problem is to alert the doctor to identify needed lab tests as quickly as possible in the examination of the patient so that a request for lab work can be made while the medical exam is still in progress. In those cases in which both X-rays and lab tests are required, always schedule X-rays to be taken during the waiting period for lab tests. If necessary, coordinate the lab tests to be done in the X-ray waiting area when delays are longer than usual there or if the lab technician is available earlier than normal.

A secondary bottleneck may sometimes exist in the X-ray area. When the physician is unusually busy, provision should exist for obviously needed X-rays to be done before the medical examination, even if this requires a brief preliminary exam by the doctor.

It is impossible to expedite either admitting—patients arrive on their own, random schedule—or the doctor—who is either available or busy as soon as the admitting process is finished. Bypassing the administrative process to use the physician's time would be poor practice administratively and could introduce offsetting inefficiencies into the process.

Clearly, the structure of the work flow determines what is or is not practical in this situation. However, calculation of capacity utilization and estimation of average waiting times points out the bottlenecks that may be subject to scheduling. In many situations, network analysis or simulation may be useful. The question to be addressed at all times in such analyses is: where is the bottleneck and how can capacity at the bottleneck be fully used through sound scheduling of work flow at earlier workstations?

By defining a bottleneck as a point of differentially high capacity utilization, it becomes possible to focus management and scheduling effort on solutions to the bottleneck. When task or service time is too variable to predict usefully, continuous attention at the point of highest capacity utilization—the bottleneck—may be the only practical way to improve service time. When differences in capacity utilization are unavoidable, specific attention at the bottleneck has the potential for large improvements in processing time. Queueing theory permits an estimate of likely delay at each workstation in the flow. Estimate of this delay may alternatively permit resolution of the capacity constraint or improvement in scheduling throughout the network. These are powerful models for improving the management of custom, project shop work flow and, perhaps also, for managing temporary bottlenecks in continuous flow, mass production operations.

MANAGING FLOW THROUGH BOTTLENECKS

The foregoing examples are intentionally simplified in form to illustrate the general principle of bottleneck management. Restated, that principle directs us to discover those points in work flow where relative capacity use is higher than the average of the system. When the point of constraint on flow is clear and easily identified, flow to that point is scheduled to ensure that the bottleneck is kept loaded with work. The object of scheduling is to prevent waiting lines at workstations ahead of the bottleneck from limiting flow of work through to the bottleneck, thereby wasting critical bottleneck capacity. If, for instance, the bottleneck is scheduled to operate at 80% capacity while the preceding stations are at 60%, the inherent delay in work flow through to the bottleneck could eat up 20% or more capacity even before the bottleneck gets to work. The net result is to exceed available capacity at the bottleneck. This produces the infinite waiting line potential predicted by queueing theory. As long as there is any excess capacity available in a bottleneck, creative scheduling should be capable of keeping the flow of work moving through it. Once capacity is exceeded, there is no way to solve the problem short of halting and rescheduling the entire flow process.

One bottleneck is straightforward to manage. Two or more have the potential to overwhelm the attempt to manage flow. Methods are needed, then, to deal with a multiple station flow of work where several bottlenecks may exist at various points through the flow. The first step would be to examine bottlenecks to see if extra capacity can be added to any of them. An increase in capacity available is the surest way to solve the bottleneck. Where flow sequence is fixed and there is no way to increase capacity, it can be feasible to identify bottlenecks that are close enough to one another to be linked in the flow process. This amounts to taking a page out of the book of balanced, continuous flow mass production. Nearly adjacent bottleneck stations along with any nonbottleneck stations between them can be scheduled as if they are a single production unit.

MANAGING CONTINUOUS, LINKED WORK FLOW THROUGH BOTTLENECKS

Table 4–3 illustrates limited versus unlimited work flow, demonstrating the net advantage of a linked flow solution. Fixed sequence work flow across nine workstations with variable capacity utilization is presented in this example. Waiting time for all nine stations sums to a little over twenty-four hours in the example. Stations 2, 3, 6 and 8, however, are bottlenecks. By treating stations 2 and 3 as a single unit for flow purposes, it is possible to reduce the average waiting time for these two combined stations to the waiting time required only for the higher of the set. The capacity utilization for the biggest bottleneck becomes the common capacity denominator for the set. Work can be scheduled through station 1 to ensure that capacity on the combined station 2 and 3 is heavily used. When the decision is made to combine workstations, work at station 3 is either cleared ahead of coming work—when possible—or the waiting line for station 3 is moved to station

Table 4–3
Savings in Delay Affected by Linked Work Flow

Station #	Capacity Usage	Average Waiting Line in Units	Unlinked Waiting Time in Hours	Linked Flow Waiting Time in Hours
1	60%	1	1.5	1.5
2	75%	2	3.0	4.0
3	80%	3	4.0	
4	60%	1	1.5	1.5
5	80%	3	1.5	1.5
6	60%	1	4.0	
7	60%	1	1.5	5.67
8	85%	5	5.67	
9	60%	1	1.5	1.5
Total Time			24.17	15.67

Arrival Rate = .6 to .85 per hour

Service Rate = 1 per hour

2. All work that goes through station 3 goes first to station 2 *even if there is no work assigned for station 2.* Thus while work is on station 2, which must flow through to station 3, no waiting line is permitted to form on station 3. The waiting line is kept entirely at station 2. Scheduling devices such as Johnson's rule that maximize use on the second bottleneck are then applied to all work queued at station 2. Jobs are scheduled past station 2 to keep station 3 busy.

The same methodology is employed at station 6 for the combined station 6, 7 and 8. Waiting lines at stations 7 and 8 are either cleared out ahead of new work or moved back in front of station 6.

Linking workstations to ensure direct flow-through as if the combined stations were a balanced line has the potential to cut delay time through the system by almost 40%, reducing it in this example from 24.17 to 14.67 average hours. In a subsequent discussion on setup of very short-run or one of a kind jobs, application of station linking will be used to obtain yet another improvement in work flow. Scheduling setup across linked workstations has general usefulness for simplifying problems of work flow through independent workstations.

As will be discussed more fully in chapter 5, the general rule for scheduling fixed sequence workstations is: that work goes through first which has either (1) the shortest processing time on an earlier workstation or (2) the longest processing time on a subsequent bottleneck. This serves to get work through to the bottleneck quickly and to keep the bottleneck fully loaded with work. With multiple bottleneck scheduling, work that will load stations 6, 7 and 8 most heavily must be expedited through combined station 2 and 3. Other devices for scheduling through to later bottlenecks are described in chapter 5.

MANAGING BOTTLENECKS WITH RANDOM SEQUENCED WORK FLOW

Fixed sequence work flow will, unfortunately, not be characteristic of many project shops. A more common project shop situation will require that random sequence flow be accommodated. When sequence of flow is random, bottlenecks migrate with changes in the mix of work. Any change in mix will inevitably change the pattern of bottlenecks and the adjustments required to manage them. Weekly, perhaps even daily and, in rare cases, hourly, revisions may be required to accommodate the shifting mix. Indeed, acceptance of major new project work should perhaps routinely be preceded with a station loading estimate or Monte Carlo simulation of the effect of the new project on existing capacity and work flow. Work that even temporarily exacerbates already difficult bottlenecks may not be worth taking on because of the difficulties it creates. Work that exceeds capacity at any point in the flow is certain to create monumental headaches, up to and including complete work stoppage in parts of the operation.

As long as some slack capacity exists on all workstations, careful management employing the tools provided here or in chapter 5 or 6 will probably permit acceptance of new projects. Any overall increase in capacity utilization will probably require a stretch-out in promise dates for the work. Surges in demand for goods or services through the project shop mean added delay regardless. If customers understand and accept delay, demand surges that push up capacity utilization can be managed. If they do not, it may be better to turn away work and gain a reputation for quality and service in preference to increasing revenue by pushing up capacity usage.

DEALING WITH INSUFFICIENT CAPACITY

The classic answers to insufficient capacity are to subcontract work out or to use overtime to cover the excess. When overtime is employed, the psychological and physiological concomitants of repetition and fatigue must be taken into account. An extended discussion of these issues is provided in chapter 6. It is appropriate only to note that if the problem is truly transient and can be fully solved by a small amount of overtime, scheduling overtime may be a viable solution. If capacity and scheduling are out of control, the problem is likely to be chronic. Solving chronic problems of capacity with overtime is almost always counterproductive. Productivity generally drops when overtime is used as a crutch to meet today's priorities without solving the underlying problems. Workers can easily defend themselves from the excessive pressure of chronic overscheduling by slowing down.

Subcontracting is equally complex. The availability of a subcontractor to supply additional capacity for overflow work implies the existence of excess skill or equipment capacity in the industry. When industry capacity in general is stretched, the danger is that customers will opt for substitute goods or services. Measures that increase capacity are the only viable solution. The opportunity to consider subcontracting when industry capacity is plentiful must occur in those situations in which the contractor shop is so well managed that it takes in more than its share of work or a shift toward big projects has occurred in-house that are easier to manage at higher levels of capacity utilization (work can be efficiently grouped, some continuous flow is possible, etc.). It is worth while looking at the implications of these opportunities.

Large, longer run projects are always the cream of the project shop's business. If this kind of business appears stable and consistent, the operation will probably reshape around it. But competition is likely to be stiff in this kind of business, and pricing and profits will come under severe, continuous pressure from the customer. If the business gets big enough to merit a shop committed to it, it will probably transform into continuous flow organization of work. Being at the boundary between continuous flow and project shop organization is not a particularly desirable operating niche. Methods for managing a project versus a continuous flow operation are qualitatively different in many fundamental respects. Attempting to blend them both in a single operation is not likely to be successful or profitable. The discipline and responsiveness required of a project shop operation should not be diluted. Output approaching long run proportions should not be mixed with custom short-run work.

If business flows into the project shop that is well managed while surplus capacity exists within the industry, there is opportunity to exploit the management skill itself for added profit. But any project or part of a project that is subcontracted out must be controlled for schedule and quality by the contractor. The subcontractor becomes a new workstation in the work flow managed by the contractor. Capacity utilization must be specifically managed for that workstation. The most reliable approach to managing a new workstation is to qualify it as a work specialty. The best subcontractors will be top specialists in the project areas they handle. The opportunity emerges for the primary contractor to manage work flow centrally, using independent specialists to handle the things they do best. In a project shop economy, independent ownership of equipment is likely to be common, and subcontracting arrangements of this sort may become routine. Project shops with the best customer development skills and management capability can become the scheduling nexus of a more or less loose association of independent, highly specialized project shops.

In handling subcontracting this way, some of the advantages of intensive specialization enjoyed by the continuous flow shop are made available to the project shop. To ensure that they are fully available, however, the legal contract between contractor and subcontractor or customer must be carefully drawn. Due dates set for the subcontractor must be firm—a contract penalty or real chance of loss of future business must exist to prevent broken promises. A further, completely new class of risk exists, however, that needs to be addressed in the contract. The subcontractor or the customer may decide to eliminate the middleman in this arrangement to increase profits or save costs. When a subcontractor becomes a significant workstation in a large number of the project shop's jobs, it may be necessary to write a reasonable fee arrangement into the contract when the subcontractor or customer bypasses you. Otherwise it may be necessary to keep each one completely ignorant of the identity of the other.

In the dawning age of the project shop, sales and management skill will be important assets in the conduct of business. Many subcontracts will become recurrent and routine, though still custom or short run. The management skill required to coordinate and control this kind of operation will contribute major value to the product or service. Retaining reasonable control at the nexus of the operations process will be essential.

When capacity industrywide is tight, the advantage obtained in strong project shop management will arise out of the ability to expand capacity quickly and efficiently without loss of quality or service. The temptation will inevitably exist to use surplus capacity to fill demand at the expense of service. If 60% capacity is normal to provide superior service, capacity usage will be ratcheted upwards toward 70% or 80% to gain the available, added revenue from sales. This will occasion a test of the value of service. Depending on the goods or service offered, customers may accept a decrement in service or fight it. In a project shop economy the opportunity to sacrifice service for revenue will become a major strategic issue. The business that meets increased demand with the least loss in quality of service will enjoy a distinct competitive edge.

Capacity is likely to be the most critical strategic call a business has to make. The Federal Reserve Board (Bulletin G–3402) attempts to measure capacity utilization across the economy as a whole on a continuing basis. Low capacity utilization is typically interpreted as a sign of weakness in the economy. Nationwide, low utilization means something around 70%. Utilization that reaches 90% is widely believed to draw on marginal capacity, which means it has the potential of raising costs. In fact, the added confusion and loss of customer service that goes with something close to 90% capacity nationwide is enough to explain the inefficiencies associated with approaching that level. Normal maximum capacity in conventional economic terms approximates something like 85%.

Capacity is measured, however, in terms of maximum planned output for hours of work currently scheduled and is premised on the assumption that cost efficiency of operations demands the highest possible capacity utilization. It does not include second or third shifts that could be worked but aren't. It does not include weekends or holidays that won't be scheduled because of conventional work preferences. It leaves out machines that are in storage or are surplus. Capacity utilization as measured thus includes only equipment or workstations that are available but not manned.

Obviously, there is immense additional capacity already available in some economic sectors if it can be administered effectively and manned by adequately trained people. The economy as it is presently structured does not begin to use available potential capacity. In all likelihood, much of that potential *is* marginal and cost ineffective. It is there, nonetheless. It's existence illustrates the power and inevitability of excess capacity. The attempt to use capacity at levels approaching 100% will usually be defeated by an imposing array of counterforces. The marginality of the capacity itself; the introduction of multiple, major new bottlenecks; fatigue and disinterest on the part of workers, all mitigate against the success of maximum, high capacity utilization. Maximized efficiency of the plant and equipment is a prohibitively expensive ideal in the postindustrial age. It not only doesn't count, it doesn't work.

5

SCHEDULING RULES

"Now we'll discover why expediting is so often fruitless."

Scheduling in a project shop presents a special challenge. Planning is made difficult by the unpredictability of job arrival and job size. It is common in managing a project shop to run large jobs first so that efficiency can be gained and cash flow maximized. When setup time is substantial, the queue is typically scoured to expedite the large jobs that can be used to maximize output efficiency and generate large, early billings.

JOB AND CASH FLOW CONSIDERATIONS

The appearance of increased productivity and earnings when large jobs get first preference is an illusion. A project shop must include setup time in the job estimate. Setup is an integral element of cost for a custom or short-run project. Separating it out and treating it as a independent cost is wholly inappropriate, even for short, multiple runs of an item. No efficiency is gained by doing so. Indeed, it will even be demonstrated in a later chapter that it is often more cost effective to hold setups in place until the entire custom/short run is finished, just in the event that the job must be run again. In the examples that are employed in this chapter, setup time is consistently included as part of the normal processing time.

Beyond the error of separating out setup time from job run time, any advantage assumed to be available from using either short or long processing time to improve average run and billing turnaround time may be illusory. Prioritizing jobs by size on a one-station project does not guarantee improved scheduling. Table 5–1 illustrates this point by comparing both longest and shortest run time priority scheduling on a single workstation over one month.

Table 5-1

Average Job Flow Time with Longest and Shortest Job Time Prioritizing and Effect of Priority on Cash Flow Measured by Net Present Value of Billings

Thirty (30) working days
Average job is 3 days in length
Range of task time is 1 to 5 working days
All jobs are on hand on day 1
Billings are at $1000 per day
Normal Collection cycle is 30 days

Job #	Run Time In Days*	Largest Jobs First			Smallest Jobs First		
		Priority Ranking	Completion in Days	Discounted Net Present Cash Value**	Priority Ranking	Completion in Days	Discounted Net Present Cash Value**
1	4.5	2	9.3	4486.05	9	25.2	4462.20
2	3.8	4	17.1	3778.34	7	16.7	3778.85
3	1.4	9	28.8	1386.56	2	2.6	1398.79
4	2.3	7	25.7	2280.30	4	6.6	2294.94
5	4.8	1	4.8	4792.32	10	30.0	4752.00
6	1.2	10	30.0	1188.00	1	1.2	1199.52
7	1.7	8	27.4	1684.47	3	4.3	1697.56
8	2.9	6	23.4	2877.38	5	9.5	2890.82
9	4.0	3	13.3	3982.27	8	20.7	3972.40
10	3.4	5	20.5	3376.77	6	12.9	3385.38
Total	30.0		200.3	29,832.45		129.7	29,832.45
Means	3.0		20.03			12.97	

*Randomly generated with 9 degrees of freedom to total 30 days.
**New Present cash value of billing at 12% interest rate at end of 30th day.
Billings are mailed immediately on completion of each job.

Figure 5–1
Net Present Value of Billings at the End of the Thirtieth Workday If Mailed
Immediately on Completion of Each Job (12% Interest Rate Is Assumed)

$$\text{Sum of Jobs} \left[1 - \left[\begin{array}{c} \text{Completion} \\ \text{Days} \end{array} \times \frac{.01}{30} \right] \right] \times \left[\begin{array}{c} \text{Task Time} \\ \text{in Days} \times \\ \$1000. \end{array} \right]$$

Run times for this and all other simulation frames employed in this chapter
are randomly generated within the constraints specified for the example. Run
times on these ten jobs average 3.0 days totaling to 30.0 continuous days of
work. Jobs are first prioritized by longest run time on the presumption that
this will generate early large billings and thereby improve cash flow return for
work done. The completion time in total days from "day one" is determined
for each job in the priority list, and the average number of days to completion
for these ten jobs is calculated to be 20.03 days. For each job and in the same
priority sequence, the discounted net present value of the billing on the job
completion date is calculated to the thirtieth day of work and summed over
all ten jobs. (See Figure 5.1 for method of calculation here.) For the longest
job, first priority, the net present value of 30.0 continuous days of work, at
12% interest and billed at $1,000 per day, is $29,832.46.

Prioritizing the same ten jobs by the shortest processing time yields an average run time of 12.97 days and a net present value for billings at the end of
the thirtieth day of $29,832.46. Shortest processing time prioritizing cuts the
average run time by a little more than one-third but results in *no* improvement
in cash flow. As long as jobs are billed at a uniform hourly rate, cash flow is
uninfluenced by priority or their order. Cash flow can be improved in a job
shop *only* by scheduling to avoid slack in work flow, thereby releasing some
billings earlier than they would otherwise be mailed.

This simple example illustrates the basic problems that are faced in scheduling a project shop. As long as jobs are costed comparably, there is no advantage available from using *any* prioritizing system to improve cash flow. This
result obtains because run time and billing size are correlated. Short runs generate earlier but smaller billings, whereas long runs produce later, larger billings. When averaged out as a composite of net present values, there is no
difference in financial performance with either of these (or any other) prioritizing rules as long as no slack is permitted in the schedule.

Shortest processing time, though, clearly produces a shorter average run
time. Notice, however, that exactly the same number of jobs are completed in
a fixed period. All work is finished at the end of the thirtieth day regardless of
which job is scheduled first or last. On first impression, indeed, one might reasonably conclude that the difference in average run time between shortest and
longest processing time is purely an artifact of scalar measurement.

It is likely, though, that customers will experience quicker service with shortest processing time (SPT) prioritizing of work. Using SPT, six jobs move out of the project shop before the end of the fifteenth workday. With longest processing time prioritizing, only three jobs leave the operation in fewer than fifteen days. Larger jobs pay the price under SPT scheduling by running consistently longer to completion.

There is, perhaps, a psychological advantage in keeping the larger number of customers happier by employing SPT project shop prioritizing. Customers with large jobs may reasonably expect their work to require more time to completion. If the psychic superiority of SPT scheduling is accepted, it will become the dominant scheduling heuristic of the project shop. It might even be declared to represent the more efficient prioritizing rule. There is, however, no inherent cost or time saving available to the shop in using shortest processing time prioritizing. Like the express line in a supermarket, it merely keeps the largest number of customers happy. The preferred solution to improved service continues to be that of minimizing waiting lines through reduction of equipment capacity utilization.

A single work station or operation simplifies processing sequence and cash flow analyses for the sake of illustration, but offers no real scheduling challenge. Projects that require processing over multiple workstations can yield an improvement in both run time and billing cycle (as long as time and cost are correlated, there is no difference between them) if jobs are scheduled correctly. More often than not this result will be obtained by consistently running first that project with the shortest processing time for the station it is presently queued on. This is a principle that has been demonstrated through extensive computer simulation. It is a robust and consistent rule. Indeed, in any project shop, overriding the rule of shortest processing time first will almost always increase average job run time. Thus the most widely employed general rule for scheduling custom, short-run work is to select that work which requires the least (shortest) processing time through the workstation at which it is now waiting. We may well be skeptical, though, that doing so will produce anything other than a psychic result in operating efficiency. Much of the effect of shorter average throughput time with SPT is psychic. Scheduling is more complex than merely achieving improved average job flow time.

ELEMENTS OF SCHEDULING

An understanding of scheduling requires beginning at the basics. Fundamentally, scheduling is a question of the sequence in which work in-house or in a work queue is done. An appointment system, as for dental work or similar personal service, establishes the sequence in which clients or jobs will be handled by the system. The existence of an appointment implies the absence of waiting upon arrival at the dentist's office as long as the patient is on time and the schedule is realistic. Depending on the tightness or looseness with which appointments are scheduled, one may still end up waiting in a queue, even with an appointment. There is nevertheless some limitation on the length of the wait imposed by the total number of clients scheduled in an appointment system. Arrivals by appointment are not randomized in that any number of patients or clients could walk through the door simultaneously. But an emergency appointment or an especially difficult job/client might throw the schedule off. Patients are still normally seen in the order of their appointment, and each suffers about the same wait when scheduling fails. Appointments are queues that are restrained so that waiting does not require holding one's place in line more than a brief period immediately in advance of the actual work.

Dealing with unplanned, random arrivals, as with patients in an emergency room of a hospital or customer assignments for a public relations firm, permits, even requires, application of some kind of sequencing rule. The most common such rule is first-come, first-served (FCFS). Service is offered in the sequence of customer or client arrival at the point of entry for service. First-come, first-served is a fair, conventional sequencing rule for service but is not necessarily always desirable or preferable, especially in those settings where good scheduling can improve the speed of job flow-through or can reduce delay inherent in waiting lines at bottlenecks. As has previously been demonstrated, faster average service may be offered by taking smaller jobs in the queue ahead of larger ones—that is, by applying the shortest processing time sequencing rule.

Scheduling is a matter of sequence—an ordering of events in time. Continuous flow operations are sequenced logically through balanced work modules to permit maximum efficient use of production capacity. Some project shop work sequences are fixed; some are discretionary. The lug bolts cannot be put on the wheel of a new car until the rim on which the tire is mounted has been installed. This sequence is fixed. It is probably faster to install the tire on the rim before attaching the rim on the wheel, but it is conceivable that tire installation could be affected after rim and wheel are joined. This sequence may be fixed by virtue of cost efficiency or it may be discretionary. But is makes no difference whether the rim goes on the wheel before or after the body is dropped onto the chassis. That sequence is entirely discretionary.

Sequence requirements change as a function of changes in tools. When one is writing with a conventional typewriter, it is necessary to correct spelling and grammar on the document in advance of keying in the copy. A word processor, however, permits exceptionally efficient correction of spelling errors and easy revision of grammar *after* all copy is keyed into memory. Both sequences are now made discretionary. Spelling, indeed, is more efficiently checked with the assistance of a computerized system. That sequence may be considered to have been revised and refixed by the advance in available tooling.

FIXED VERSUS RANDOM SEQUENCE WORK FLOW

In scheduling work, the constraints of fixed sequence and station capacity must always be taken into account. A continuous flow operation is designed to manage both constraints as efficiently as possible. Fixed sequences establish the broad outline of the continuous flow system. Efficiency of capacity utilization determines how everything else is fitted around fixed sequences. The ideal end result is a system of continuous flow in which everything moves forward in sequential, lock step. The waiting line for the job currently in progress is the job in progress on the immediately prior workstation in the continuous flow sequence.

Project shop operations may or may not be constrained by fixed sequences. An auto repair shop *must* remove the rim and wheel before replacing the brakes. In some cases, the sequence of operations may be fixed by convention even though it is discretionary. The maintenance service cleans rest rooms and hallways first because they are the most visible to the largest number of users. Office areas are handled last. In other situations, the sequence may be wholly discretionary or, if fixed by project design, unique to that one project. The typical project shop operation is a rich mixture of fixed sequence and discretionary sequence with tasks of variable size. This introduces high variety and complexity into the scheduling of project shop operations.

Indeed, with this kind of variety to deal with, a project shop manager can be faced with a bewildering range of scheduling requirements. In some ways, it may seem that the notion of project shop scheduling may well be an oxymoron—an inherent contradiction in terms. How is it possible to schedule in the face of randomness of flow sequence or job arrival? The answer is not necessarily as difficult as it seems; random job arrival can be modeled with queueing theory. When two or more jobs are waiting in the queue to be processed, one of several rules of choice can be applied in deciding which will go first. Scheduling in a project shop is the art of deciding which jobs go first when there is a queue of work in front of a workstation or series of stations.

The length of queues in the system is above all a function of the level of capacity utilization at each station. High capacity utilization creates lengthy waiting lines at the station because it is in heavy use. Individual jobs may be resequenced in the flow at a bottleneck. As capacity utilization is relaxed, queues disappear at workstations. At bottlenecks, they reappear. The rules for resequencing individual tasks must be clearly established wherever queues appear.

For purposes of task sequencing, it is always necessary to differentiate between project shops that have a fixed sequence of stations versus those that permit random work sequences through the shop. With a fixed sequence flow of tasks, it is possible to attempt a balance of workstation utilization and thereby approximate a continuous flow system. Law offices, hospital emergency rooms, advertising agencies, print shops or municipal administrative offices typify this kind of scheduling requirement. The only inevitable waiting line is at the point of entry into the flow. But other queues will appear wherever a bottleneck exists in the flow. The emergence of a growing queue of work offers an opportunity to manage the schedule by resequencing tasks. A fixed sequence flow can be managed either by struggling to balance flow or by making the most of queues at bottlenecks to opportunistically resequence the flow of tasks.

The decision to balance or to resequence tasks with fixed sequence flow turns largely upon the variance in average task or run time between jobs. When task time is too variable to even attempt balanced flow, reduction in capacity utilization combined with task resequencing at bottlenecks is the most likely solution to improved work flow.

The absence of any fixed sequence of work flow offers a very different set of opportunities. Many projects arrive on a random schedule, proceed randomly to the first point of action and then flow randomly through the system. This kind of job is typical of modern day project shop operations requirements. It includes businesses like auto repair shops, retail stores, X-ray laboratories, clerical services offices, and maintenance services. In operations of this kind, the work load may be predictable in the aggregate, while arrivals for processing are entirely random. Jobs may go to any workstation first, call on any number of other workstations in random sequence, and vary widely in task size by station. Work of this kind lends to exceptional variability of both task time and capacity utilization on individual workstations. Commonly, some stations are empty while others are crowded to excess. Scheduling is an exceedingly complex task in this setting.

SIMULATION OF WORK FLOW

For a variety of reasons, this kind of operation lends nicely to the Monte Carlo simulation technique. Monte Carlo requires randomized task times and sequences that are computer generated and iterated a large number of times to test differences in system performance. Given this extent of unpredictability, the two major factors in system performance are capacity utilization and choice of which sequencing rule to use in scheduling. Given the prevailing assumption of maximized capacity utilization, most simulators test sequencing in a high capacity utilization setting. Indeed, at capacity usage below 50%, queues are so rare that sequencing is seldom necessary or possible. In a well-managed project shop, queues may be so rare that sequencing is possible only at bottlenecks. Scheduling simulations have typically been applied on what amounts to a series of bottleneck operations. A number of useful lessons can be found in them, nonetheless, and a set of simple hand-drawn simulations will satisfy most of the need for scheduling simulation in the average project shop. These simulations are employed in the discussion that follows.

SIMULATION RESEARCH ON SCHEDULE SEQUENCING

"Job Shop Simulators" have been in use for more than twenty years. The foundation statement on job shop scheduling was made by R. W. Conway, W. L. Maxwell and L. W. Miller in their *Theory of Scheduling* (1967). In this study, a Monte Carlo simulation was employed to examine the effect of various prioritizing rules on a hypothetical job shop with nine machines (workstations), all at or about 90% capacity utilization. Task time for each workstation was randomly assigned and order of flow of jobs through the stations was randomized. This was a dynamic simulation in that the simulation was "run-in" before measures of performance were gathered, and data gathering ceased before it was "run-out." The net result of a dynamic measure is to assess operation of system flow at full, ongoing flow capacity.

Work on the project (job) shop sequencing study by Conway and associates was sponsored by diverse agencies such as the Office of Naval Research, the National Science Foundation, General Electric, Western Electric and Touche Ross. It represents a systematic attempt to deal with the problems of job shop work flow. Monte Carlo simulation permitted testing of a variety of sequencing rules. Waiting lines like those that might be found in a typical project shop operation were represented. Job routings inputted to the system were independent of the state of the system, and inputs were characterized by exponential and Poisson distributions.

The Conway, Maxwell and Miller studies assumed that high levels of capacity utilization are normal and unavoidable. Setting their average capacity utilization rates at approximately the 90% level ensured the presence of lengthy waiting lines at all workstations. The major scheduling rules tested included first-come, first-served; last-come, first-served; least work remaining to be done; most work remaining to be done; nearest due date; randomized assignment; empty queue available and shortest processing time.

The most significant, persistent and robust finding from these simulations was the superiority of the least (shortest) processing time (SPT) sequencing rule. The SPT was found to cut flow time anywhere from one-half to one-fourth the time required by first-come, first-served and other sequencing rules when applied to prioritizing of work in a random sequence, high capacity flow system. In Table 5–1, it was demonstrated that this result is mathematically inevitable. Average flow time is consistently reduced when shortest processing time prioritizing is applied to queues of waiting work. This result is independent of the actual working time applied to the sum of jobs. Most customers will see quicker turnaround in their work when the SPT is the prevailing prioritizing rule, but this does not necessarily mean that the operation is run more efficiently or that cash flow is improved. Improvement may rest entirely on the psychic value of perceived faster service alone.

Conway and associates observed that several intuitively appealing sequencing rules had only very limited effect in reducing work flow time. Putting work at the head of the queue, for instance, which had the least processing time remaining, or which would go to a workstation with the shortest current queue, produced a small, sometimes statistically significant effect on average rate of job flow but paled in importance when contrasted with the effect of the shortest processing time job sequencing. In light of the dominance of SPT math on average completion time, the discovery of any effect whatever from other processing rules probably deserves closer examination. A useful beginning point for better understanding of how the SPT may interact with other prioritizing rules is offered by Johnson's rule.

JOHNSON'S RULE: SPT AND DOWNSTREAM SLACK

It is appropriate to reflect carefully on the contribution of the SPT to improved work flow. It is not so much that shortest processing time is not a useful scheduling rule—it is. The concern that must be raised is that it often does make complete sense to push work through a current station when the station immediately beyond (for the task) is empty. A widely employed two station scheduling heuristic, Johnson's rule (1952) blends the shortest processing time priority selection on the first workstation with a maximum early task load rule on the second. The rule prescribes that the shortest available job is scheduled first if on station 1 but last if on station 2. The net effect of Johnson's rule is to move short jobs quickly through station 1 so that run-in time slack is minimized on station 2 and to sequence larger jobs preferentially onto station 2 early in the work sequence to keep it loaded with work. Table 5–2 and Figure 5–2 illustrate the operation of Johnson's Rule.

Prioritizing with Johnson's rule presumes that task times on successive workstations are independent and variable. Thus the odds are that a relatively short task on station 1 will be followed by a longer task on station 2. The result is to move short jobs off station 1 quickly, thereby minimizing run-in slack time on station 2 and building a queue of work on station 2, especially if short jobs on station 2 are specifically deferred to last. This keeps station 2 running as nearly continuously as possible. One or two jobs are continuously queued up waiting in line on station 2.

Observe that this rule consistently yields the desired result only when work can be organized in two steps. All jobs are waiting in the queue at station 1 as scheduling begins, and station 2 must wait for jobs to move through station 1. Work flowing on from station 2 to further processing would not necessarily queue up tightly at the next processing point. To

Table 5–2
Johnson's Rule: Two Station Fixed Sequence Job Allocation
Monte Carlo Simulation

Table of Task Time Hours

Jobs Average four hours, with range from 1 to 7 hours
and are randomly timed with 9 degrees of freedom.

Job #:	1	2	3	4	5	6	7	8	9	10
Station #1 hours	6.5	2.0	7.0	5.5	1.5	2.0	6.0	6.0	2.5	1.0
Station #2 hours	4.0	5.0	6.5	3.5	4.0	4.0	5.5	1.5	1.5	4.5
Johnson's Rule Priority Assignment Rank	7	3	6	8	2	4	5	9	10	1

simulate outflow from a workstation that is already tightly scheduled using Johnson's rule and permits no choice of job sequence, reverse priority assignment by Johnson's rule is also illustrated in Figure 5–2. Immediately, large gaps of slack open up in the early schedule for station 2. Whereas the work flow to station 2 using Johnson's rule permits work to be finished with only an hour of work beyond the end of the fifth day, the extensive slack generated by reverse priority assignment requires more than two days more of work (overtime?). Under reverse priority assignment the first queue longer than one job on station 2 occurs when jobs 6 and 2 arrive while job 7 is still in progress. At this point it no longer matters which job goes first *unless* there is an opportunity to push one of these jobs through onto an empty workstation and thereby close system slack. When work must flow through three or more high capacity workstations, SPT alone is more likely to keep the work flowing by quickly building queues of work at the bottlenecks. Improving on SPT requires a close look at the existence and effects of slack in the system.

REFOCUSING ON SYSTEM SLACK

From this simple simulation of work flow with Johnson's rule, it is possible to see the power of shortest processing time in eliminating slack on a subsequent workstation by rapidly building a queue of work on the later station. As work moves through the system, large gaps of slack can develop following logjams that occur in high capacity utilization workstations—bottlenecks. When SPT makes a contribution beyond the psychic level to improving work flow, it will be in the form of reduced system slack. Reduction of

Figure 5–2
Johnson's Rule: Two Station Fixed Sequence Job Allocation from Table 5–2

Jobs average four hours, with range from 1 to 7 hours
with job time randomly assigned within 9 degrees of freedom.

Work Flow Chart for Assignment by Johnson's Rule

Work Flow Chart for Assignment by Reverse Johnson's Rule Priority

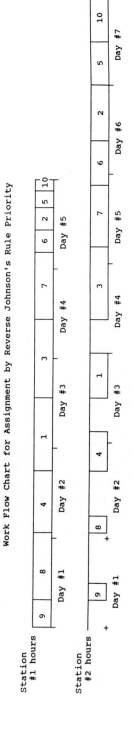

system slack has the potential to accelerate billings and improve cash flow. Average job completion time, thus, is neither the only nor even the most significant measure of project shop scheduling performance. Indeed, as various approaches to project shop scheduling are examined here, it will become apparent that management of system slack is of major significance to scheduling success. When SPT scheduling succeeds with multiple workstation flow, it is because it effectively fills station slack. When some other sequence exists that would serve more effectively to close system slack, that sequence may be more effective in improving cash flow and system slack. Simulations are needed that examine the impact of scheduling on slack and on the net present value of accelerated billings.

Given the intuitive simplicity and appeal of Johnson's rule, it might be easily presumed that some combination of shortest processing time and Johnson's rule prioritizing would make a difference in some situation. In fact, Conway and associates did find that average job flow time was improved marginally by moving jobs to the head of the queue when they served to fill an empty workstation following *if* applied in weighted combination with shortest processing time prioritizing. They also found that giving first priority to jobs moving through to stations with a high proportion of slack in their schedules served to improve average flow time.

At least three prioritizing principles with which to reduce average job completion time are suggested by the available evidence. These rules suggest that a project shop manager should prioritize first on the basis of shortest processing time on the current workstation. This keeps work moving through the system rapidly and keeps queues at the bottlenecks. It also expedites small jobs through the system quickly, creating a reputation for rapid service. Select next those jobs that will keep potentially underused workstations loaded and working longer. Finally, select as a first priority those jobs that will fill anticipated slack capacity downstream. The common theme across these three rules has to do with avoiding or reducing gaps in the flow schedule. Project shop scheduling should use natural slack capacity in the system to avoid added, unnecessary slack due to those logjams where one project's progress is blocked by another's unavoidable delay. It is in reduction of system slack that SPT makes its real contribution, and it is straightforward minimization of slack that makes departure from SPT desirable.

SIMULATING SEQUENCE RULE APPLICATION

Three factors are at the root of logjams in work flow; first is large natural variation in the size of tasks. A mixture of small and large task times at workstations offers an opportunity for blockage. Second is the number of workstations in a line of flow. The more stations in a logical sequence, the more snarls and gaps in the schedule downstream. A long sequence of tasks amplifies problems in the flow at later workstations. The third factor is the existence of bottlenecks in the flow. Relative constriction on work flow at any point in the system will result in reduced use of capacity downstream with resulting larger and larger gaps in the flow. Improved scheduling in a project shop must begin with an examination of these three sources of delay.

Monte Carlo simulation can be used to illustrate how delay is created. Though on a much less complex level, the simulations used in chapter 1 and those that follow are parallel to those of Conway and associates. The Monte Carlo simulations used here, however, are static, single frame simulations that permit easy tabular and graphic display of the work flow and scheduling process. All of the present simulations are generated with a hand calculator, and a mix of fixed flow and random flow simulation frames is employed.

For purposes of an introductory demonstration, a clerical service office with random sequence flow and high capacity utilization is simulated in Table 5–3 and Figures 5–3A and 5–3B. Five workstations are defined: typing, proofing, copy, graphics and fax. This is a random flow shop. There is no fixed sequence to flow of work. The sequence of station arrival is random, the number of subsequent workstations is randomly determined, and the task time on each station is randomized around a mean service time of 2.0 hours within a range of 0.4 to 3.6 hours per task. A single job may go to a minimum of two and a maximum of four workstations. The number of stations per job is randomized around a mean of three with a maximum of four and a minimum of two. To further match this simulation to the data of Conway and associates, the level of that capacity utilization of stations is set at 93% plus or minus 5%. This effectively makes every station a bottleneck.

This is a simulation, created exactly as Monte Carlo simulations typically are but limited to only a static single frame. As such, it is a rough analog of the studies of Conway and associates. A full scale simulation would generate several hundred "pictures" of work flow within these statistical parameters for each of the prioritizing rules under test, average the flow time and system slack across these large samples and compare the averages to assess which one is superior. The example presented here is only one frame from such a series of simulations, modified slightly to permit the mechanics of work flow to be observed more easily.

Two prioritizing rules are applied; first-come, first-served is used because it is such a conventionally common rule in usage and because it approximates a random arrival sequence. For practical purposes, FCFS generates a randomized or unscheduled flow of work in which logjams do their worst to the flow. The second rule is shortest processing time. The SPT calls for the job with shortest expected processing time on its work station to be moved

Table 5-3
High Capacity Utilization Random Job Flow Sequence under Conditions of High Capacity Utilization, Single Frame Static Monte Carlo Simulation Based on an Eight-Hour Day

Number in parentheses indicates sequence of job flow.
Task Times are in tenths of hours.

| | Hours of Task Time | | | | | COMPLETION TIME | |
Job #	Station #1 TYPE	Station #2 PROOF	Station #3 COPY	Station #4 GRAPHICS	Station #5 FAX	FCFS*	SPT
1		(3) .6	(2) 1.4	(1) 2.2		6.0	8.2
2			(1) 1.4	(2) 3.4		5.6	7.4
3	(1) 1.6	(2) 1.8	(3) 1.6			7.0	7.6
4	(3) 1.4	(2) 1.6			(1) 1.0	5.0	5.6
5			(1) 0.8		(2) 2.4	4.8	4.8
6	(2) 1.6	(3) 1.6	(1) 0.4		(4) 2.0	11.2	7.8
7	(3) 0.4	(2) 0.4	(4) 0.4		(1) 1.4	7.4	4.4
8			(1) 1.0		(2) 1.0	5.8	5.8
9	(1) 2.0	(3) 0.6		(2) 1.4		7.8	9.4
10	(2) 0.6	(3) 1.2	(1) 0.4			7.2	4.2
	7.6	7.8	7.4	7.0	7.8	67.8	65.2

% Capacity

| Utilization | 95% | 98% | 93% | 88% | 98% | | |

Sequence of job flow is indicated by numbers in parentheses
* First Come First Served job sequencing

88

Figure 5-3A
Random Job Flow Sequence with High Capacity Utilization Work Flow Graph from Table 5-3 Based on an Eight-Hour Day (task times are in hours and tenths)

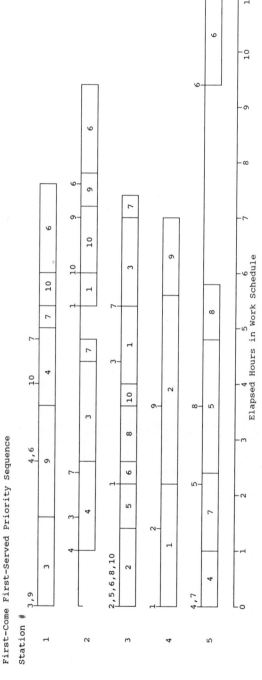

Arrival times of tasks at subsequent stations are indicated above task flow bars.

89

Figure 5–3B
Random Task Flow Sequence with High Capacity Utilization Work Flow Graph from Table 5–3 Based
on an Eight-Hour Day (task times are in hours and tenths)

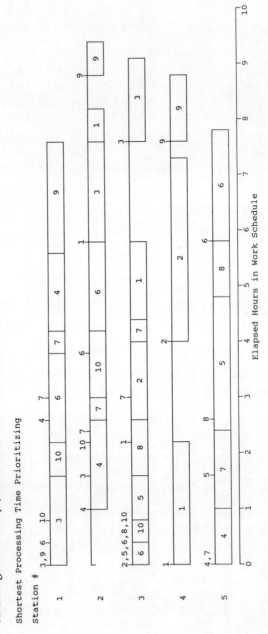

Shortest Processing Time Prioritizing

Elapsed Hours in Work Schedule

Arrival times of tasks at subsequent stations are indicated above task flow bars.

to the head of the queue. Average flow time is compared by job in Table 5–3 for these two sequencing rules. It is also graphically visualized in Figures 5–3A and 5–3B.

Because this is a static simulation, work flow begins and ends within the bounds of the simulation. If jobs were coming in constantly and being assigned to the appropriate queue upon arrival, it would become a dynamic simulation. For this clerical shop, the effect of the simulation condition is to schedule work one day at a time. Work that comes in today is estimated and put on the schedule for completion the following day. All work begins at the beginning of the day and ends at the end of the day. This simplifies the example for purposes of interpretation of the result.

The outcome of the simulation is that SPT prioritizing is slightly quicker (65.2 versus 67.8) on the average and represents approximately a 4% improvement in flow time over FCFS sequencing. The major important difference is one very large gap in capacity utilization which occurs at the end of the day's schedule on station 6. Job 6 stretches out well beyond the end of the work day on both stations 2 and 5 when prioritized by FCFS. Considerable overtime will be required to finish these jobs in this workday. If they are not finished, they will become a burden on tomorrow's capacity, which could create bottlenecks on these two workstations and disrupt scheduling on the remaining stations. This illustrates the fundamental cause of breakdown in project system work flow; when capacity on any workstation is poorly used to the point where 100% capacity is exceeded, a major bottleneck is created. Once in existence, that bottleneck disrupts scheduling and flow in all remaining workstations that follow.

The advantage of applying SPT to this set of jobs is to reduce the overtime required (or the capacity burden carried forward) from 5.2 hours to 3.2 hours. If the average number of stations in the line of flow were increased from three to five, the advantage of SPT prioritizing probably would increase further. As will be discussed under the topic of labor scheduling in chapter 6, if cross-skill training permits one person to carry out tasks on more than one station in the overtime work beyond eight hours, the overtime requirement in this example could be reduced from 3.6 hours on FCFS scheduling to 2.5 hours under SPT. When costs like these accumulate day after day, the difference between FCFS and SPT can be of great importance.

The reduced flow time of SPT prioritizing has been illustrated conclusively with parallel simulations by Conway, Maxwell and Miller (1967). The present example is not a statistically acceptable test of the flow time superiority of SPT over FCFS. The present purpose is to demonstrate how and why SPT makes the degree of difference that it does. The SPT is an apparent winner here because the capacity utilization assigned at each workstation is high enough to make every single workstation a bottleneck in its own right and because there are large differences in the time size of tasks.

These two conditions in combination are sufficient to bring out the natural efficacy of SPT in reducing flow time. The SPT fills more of the natural slack gaps in the work flow. It should be noted that even at the very high levels of capacity utilization, three workstations in the FCFS model, 1, 3 and 4, have no slack in them other than at the end of the workday. With SPT, two workstations, 1 and 5, run continuously through the day with no slack until the end of the day when the natural slack in capacity—the difference between 100% full and 95% employed capacity on station 1, for instance—finally appears.

It was earlier proposed in chapter 1 that project shop management must break out of the grip of capacity maximization as the assumed necessary foundation of operations effectiveness. The demonstration just offered may be taken either as justification of continued use of high capacity utilization or as an illustration of why service is inevitably slow in a high capacity operation. The conclusion drawn will probably be a function of the value base it is founded on. Efficiency demands maximum use of plant and equipment. Service demands moderate to low use of those same resources to achieve better service. When service wins over efficiency, and capacity is provided in abundance, scheduling may become irrelevant. Large amounts of natural slack with suboptimized use will largely eliminate scheduling problems. Or will it?

The demand driven nature of a project shop in combination with an expectation for exceptional service response will most likely drive down the average level of equipment capacity utilization to moderate service levels. But the unpredictability of work flow has the potential to create bottlenecks at any point in the flow. Logjams are still possible, though now they will only tarnish the service reputation of the project shop. System breakdowns due to chronic excess demand on available capacity will be much less a concern than in continuous flow operations. The problem will become one of anticipating and scheduling around bottlenecks to maintain high levels of service. The question that arises is how to prioritize and schedule in the low capacity utilization project shop where bottlenecks can occur at any time.

SCHEDULING FIXED SEQUENCE OPERATIONS

With the basic scheduling and prioritizing rules illustrated, it is useful to continue by exploring ways to improve on SPT as a prioritizing rule for fixed sequence project shop work flow. Fixed sequence simplifies the simulation process for demonstration purposes.

The first example is a tax consulting office that handles both individual and business tax questions (see Table 5–4). The sequence of flow is fixed. Documentation is first reviewed. Customers whose accounting has been handled by this office do not need documentation review since this has

Scheduling Rules • 93

Table 5–4
Fixed Sequence Work Flow in a Tax Preparation Office Scheduled at Moderate
Capacity Utilization Levels: A Single Frame Static Monte Carlo Simulation
(Estimated Task Time Is in Hours)

```
35 hour work week is standard
Station tasks range from 1 to 4.5 hours
and are randomly established
```

Job #	Station #1 Document Review	Station #2 Business Taxes	Station #3 Personal Taxes	Station #4 Prepare Forms	Job Completion Time When Assigned by:	
					FCFS	SPT
1	1.5	2.5	3.0		18	10.5
2	3.0		3.5	4.5	15.5	18.5
3	1.0		3.5	2.5	20.0	7.0
4		3.5	3.0	4.0	11.0	10.5
5	2.0	3.0		2.5	22.5	14.0
6	4.5			2.0	15.5	20.5
7		1.5		2.0	7.0	3.5
8	3.0	3.5	3.0		22.5	17.0
9		4.5	2.5		16.0	24.0
10	3.0	3.0	2.0	4.5	29.0	25.0
TOTAL Hours	18	21.5	20.5	22.0	177	150.5
Capacity Utilized	51%	61%	59%	63%		

```
Average Job Completion Time in hours          17.7      15.0
```

already been accomplished throughout the tax year. Then business tax issues
are examined if there are any. Since business tax decisions impact on personal taxes more than the other way around, personal tax matters are always
handled after business taxes when both are involved. Finally, forms are
prepared. Some clients prefer to do their own forms after the data have
been examined and recommendations made. Therefore, not all jobs require
preparation of the final forms. The normal work week is thirty-five hours.
Task size varies around a mean of three hours with a minimum of one and
a maximum of five hours. Capacity utilization is held near 60% on average.

Figures 5–4A and 5–4B illustrate what happens in these circumstances.
A small amount of slack time opens up in the schedule on stations 2

Figure 5–4A
Job Flow Graphed by First-Come, First-Served, and Shortest Processing Time
Priorities from Table 5–4

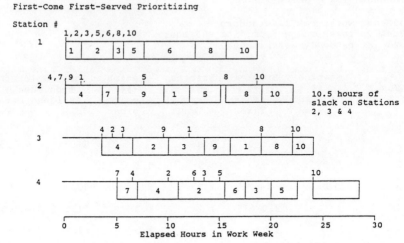

Arrival times of tasks at subsequent stations are indicated above task flow bars.

and 4 (business taxes and forms preparation) when the sequence is strictly first-come, first-served. Shifting to a shortest processing time priority sequence redistributes slack, starts work earlier on stations 3 and 4, shortens the workweek on station 4 but lengthens it on station 3. Ten and a half hours of slack with the FCFS is reduced to eight and a half hours with the SPT. This amounts to a one-fifth reduction in slack within the active work sequence.

The SPT reduces flow time from an average of 17.7 hours per job under FCFS prioritizing to 15.0 hours. Less time is lost to slack under SPT also. Flow of work under FCFS, however, is smoother. Workers on stations 3 and 4 could start work later in the week and encounter fewer gaps due to scheduling slack with FCFS. The SPT introduces slack in new places. If all workers work from the same beginning point in the week, SPT saves two hours of unapplied time in scheduling slack. Customers are serviced more quickly with SPT. But how the schedule is evaluated depends on the broader purposes on the scheduler. That workers are on a reduced workweek can be ignored. Workstations are covered, and workers take a long weekend or else do fill-in work that requires no scheduling pressure. Visual inspection of the work flow graphs shows that the differences between FCFS and SPT are small and of a qualitative nature that goes beyond mere reduction of

Figure 5–4B
Job Flow Graphed by First-Come, First-Served, and Shortest Processing Time Priorities from Table 5–4

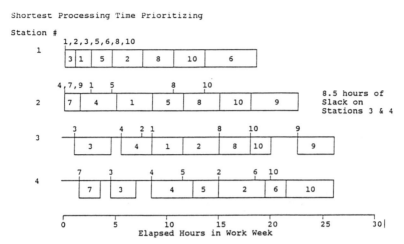

Arrival times of tasks at subsequent stations are indicated above task flow bars.

average job flow time. Each prioritizing rule introduces its own pattern of slack.

Table 5–5 with Figures 5–5A, 5–5B and 5–5C present a variation on the same work situation. Now all workstations have increased capacity utilization to near 90%, and all forms are prepared for customers by the service. These are the bigger tax jobs that come later in the tax season. High variation in task size is combined with a high level of capacity utilization. Average total job time is increased from 12.0 hours to 16.5 hours. The number of jobs remains the same (ten). Task distribution across stations 1, 2 and 3 remains the same (seven of ten) for each station. To adjust the simulation to these constraints, task time on stations 1, 2 and 3 varies randomly from 2.5 hours to 6.5 hours around a mean of 4.5 hours. Similarly, task time on station 4 varies from 1.0 to 5.0 hours around a mean of 3.0 hours.

The first observation is that considerably more slack appears in workstations downstream and that SPT still outperforms FCFS in average flow time. There is an increase in flow time for SPT from 15.0 hours at 60% utilization in Table 5–4 up to 26.45 hours at 90% capacity in Table 5–5. This amounts to slightly more than a 75% increase in flow time against an average capacity increase of about 50%. Increasing capacity utilization accounts for about a third of the total increase in flow time.

The availability of added slack in the system suggests an opportunity for improved sequencing. Under all three prioritizing rules illustrated, work-

Table 5–5

Fixed Sequence Work Flow in a Tax Office Scheduled at High Capacity
Utilization: A Single Frame Static Monte Carlo Simulation

A 35 hour work week is standard.

Job #	Station #1 Document Review	Station #2 Business Taxes	Station #3 Personal Taxes	Station #4 Forms Prep	Prioritized by: FCFS	SPT	SPT Sum
1	4.0	5.5	3.0	3.5	40	29.5	25.5
2	6.5		7.0	5.0	22.5	43.5	40.0
3	6.0		2.0	4.5	33.0	38.0	17.0
4		2.5	4.0	1.0	11.0	8.0	11.5
5	4.5	5.5		4.0	36.5	33.5	35.0
6	3.0			1.5	28	7.0	4.5
7		4.0		3.0	10.0	11.5	8.0
8	2.5	5.5	6.5	2.0	42.0	20.5	44.0
9		6.5	5.5	3.5	26.5	47.0	22.0
10	3.0	3.5	2.5	5.0	47.0	26.0	30.5
Total	29.5	33.0	30.5	33.5			
Capacity Usage:	84%	94%	87%	96%			
Sum of hours:					296.5	264.5	238.0
Average Completion Time:					29.65	26.45	23.8

stations 1 and 2 complete work within the thirty-five-hour workweek, but
tasks on 3 and 4 extend well into the weekend. In spite of the decreased
average flow time with SPT compared to FCFS, there is little reduction in
slack on stations 3 and 4. The flow schedule comparing FCFS with SPT
shows only a rearrangement of jobs around still large gaps of slack. This
illustrates a quality of SPT that is not always made clear with simulations
of project shop flow; SPT moves jobs that are consistently smaller through
workstations with dispatch, but overall small jobs that include one large
task can become stalled at an intermediary station and lose the advantage
of early completion. Early completion now *does* carry with it the advantage
of earlier billing and improved cash flow. It is, therefore, worthwhile to get
large jobs through to completion as quickly as possible.

In a fixed sequence flow at high capacity utilization, a possible variation
is to make use of the total task time summed up to the final station to
schedule shortest processing time. By summing the total processing time
across stations 1, 2 and 3, and giving priority to those jobs with the shortest
total processing time to station 4, average processing time is reduced even
more, and a noticeable reduction in slack time on stations 3 and 4 is brought
about. This is illustrated in Figure 5–5C. It is apparent that when capacity

Figure 5–5A
Graphic Display of Tax Office Work Flow from Table 5–5

A 35 hour work week is standard.

First-Come First-Served Priority Flow:

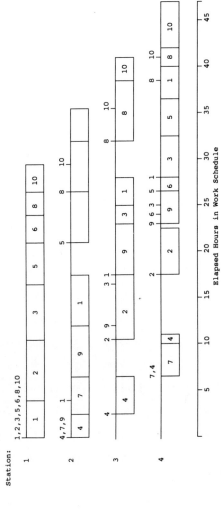

Arrival times of tasks at subsequent stations are indicated above the task flow bars.

Figure 5-5B
Graphic Display of Tax Office Work Flow from Table 5-5

A 35 hour work week is standard.

Shortest Processing Time Priority applied at each station:

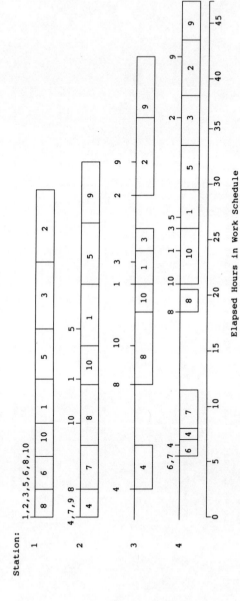

Elapsed Hours in Work Schedule

Arrival times of tasks at subsequent stations are indicated above the task flow flow bars.

Figure 5–5C
Graphic Display of Tax Office Work Flow from Table 5-5

A 35 hour work week is standard.

Shortest Processing Time to Last Work Station priority assignment
Work time required across the first three stations is summed:

Station: 1,2,3,5,6,8,10

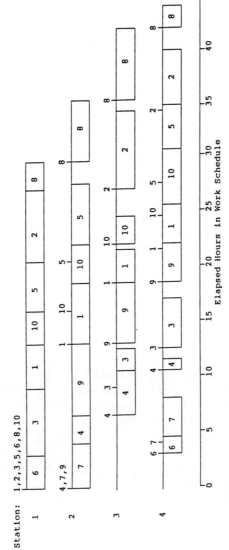

Elapsed Hours in Work Schedule

Arrival times of tasks at subsequent stations are indicated above the task flow bars.

Table 5–6
Fixed Sequence Work Flow at High Capacity Utilization in a Tax Preparation Office Beginning with a Bottleneck Station: A Single Frame Static Monte Carlo Simulation

A 35 hour work week is standard.

Job#	Station Document Review	Station Business Taxes	Station Personal Taxes	Station Tax Forms Prep	FCFS	SPT	SPT to work
1	5.5	1.5	4.0		11.0	42.5	41.0
2	4.0		5.0	6.0	22	27	27.5
3	4.5		4.0	2.0	26.5	36.0	29.5
4	1.5	1.0	5.0	6.0	35.0	13.5	13.5
5	2.0	6.0		2.5	29.0	16.0	21.5
6	1.5			2.5	24.5	30.0	37.5
7	4.0	3.0		3.0	38.0	30.0	32.5
8	3.5	6.5	3.5		35.5	24.5	30.5
9	5.0	3.5	5.5		41.0	38.5	37.0
10	3.5	6.0	4.0	4.0	50.5	34.0	19.0
Total Hours:	35	27.5	31.0	26.0			
Capacity Utilized:	100%	79%	89%	75%			
Mean Job Time to Completion					31.3	25.0	29.0

utilization is high over a group or set of workstations and there is considerable variation in task time overall, it may be worthwhile to schedule the earlier stations as a unit for the purpose of applying SPT prioritizing to reduce slack and flow time through the entire sequence.

Table 5–6 and Figures 5–6A, 5–6B and 5–6C illustrate the effect of a bottleneck on subsequent work by showing how work flows out of the bottleneck in a fixed flow situation. Task hours on station 1 are randomized from 1.5 to 5.5 hours with a mean of 3.5 hours and 9 degrees of freedom. This produces 100% capacity utilization. Task times on stations 2, 3 and 4 are randomized between 0.5 and 6.5 hours with a mean of 3.5 hours. Slack on subsequent workstations varies from 11% to 25% with a maximum of seven jobs on each station to permit the number of workstations following the bottleneck to vary.

In figure 5–6A, the FCFS, which approximates a random priority, tends to spread the work out broadly over the subsequent workstation schedules. Tasks on the fourth workstation stretch to the fifty hour mark. The SPT, shown in Figure 5–6B, tightens the package of flow up considerably over

Figure 5-6A
Fixed Sequence Work Flow Out of a First Station Bottleneck in a Tax
Preparation Office Based on Table 5-6

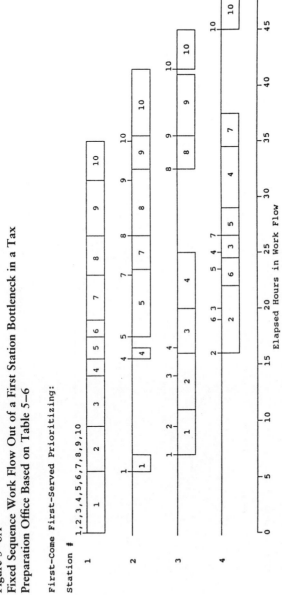

First-Come First-Served Prioritizing:

Station #   1,2,3,4,5,6,7,8,9,10

Elapsed Hours in Work Flow

Arrival times of tasks at subsequent stations are indicated above task flow bars.

Figure 5-6B
Fixed Sequence Work Flow Out of a First Station Bottleneck in a Tax
Preparation Office Based on Table 5-6

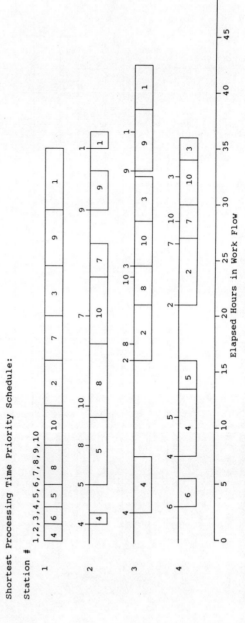

Shortest Processing Time Priority Schedule:

Station #   1,2,3,4,5,6,7,8,9,10

Arrival times of tasks at subsequent stations are indicated above task flow bars.

Figure 5-6C
Fixed Sequence Work Flow Out of a First Station Bottleneck in a Tax
Preparation Office Based on Table 5-6

Shortest Processing Time with first priority to number of work stations ahead:

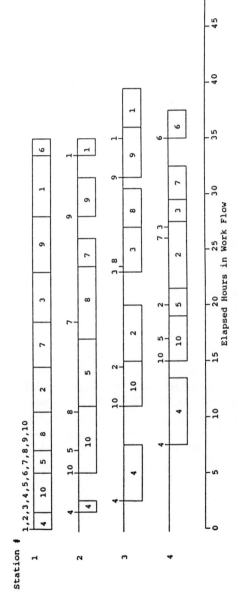

Arrival times of tasks at subsequent stations are indicated above task flow bars.

the subsequent workstations, mostly by exploiting the early slack on those stations. Small jobs are pulled through to begin work earlier. There is still a gap of slack between the few consistently small jobs that sail through and the rest of the pack.

Figure 5–6C illustrates a mixed priority rule application. Jobs are prioritized by shortest processing time giving first priority to jobs with the largest number of workstations following the bottleneck on which the job must be processed. This serves to spread out the slack on station 3 and tightens up the work flow considerably at workstation 4. Comparing the three prioritizing rules for effect on average job completion time shows that SPT again has an advantage in this respect. But prioritizing by work remaining to be done is only a 16% increase in average flow time and closes up some of the worst gaps of slack in the flow. The preferred prioritizing rule will depend on the scheduling objective sought.

SCHEDULING RANDOM FLOW AT MODERATE CAPACITY WITH ONE BOTTLENECK

When capacity utilization of workstations in the flow is kept at modest levels (60% and below), flow time is dominated by capacity. In a dynamic flow system, there will seldom be a queue longer than one or two waiting jobs. Whenever there is more than one job in a queue, shortest processing time can be used to push the jobs through to fill downstream slack. Short jobs will negotiate the path more quickly, and all jobs will finish rapidly. At high levels of capacity utilization in fixed sequence flow, processing time summed over two or more stations to a common conclusion point can improve flow time and reduce system slack.

But when overall capacity utilization is low and there is either a clear bottleneck (point of relatively high capacity utilization) or a random flow sequence through workstations, what happens then? Bottlenecks in fixed sequence flow are fairly straightforward to manage. The occurrence of a bottleneck in a fixed work flow because of random occurrences of heavy station loading will be signaled by the buildup of a work queue at that station point. Shortest processing time prioritizing will usually move work through the bottleneck with the shortest average completion time. Where a series of bottlenecks exists, shortest processing time prioritizing of work up to the last bottleneck can be employed to speed up the flow and close some of the slack. These principles work reasonably well to solve bottlenecks in a low capacity, fixed sequence work flow.

Random flow project systems present a special challenge for scheduling. Whether they can be generalized to random work flow remains to be examined. The earlier example of a clerical service with five workstations can be used as an illustration of the problems and opportunities for scheduling low capacity random sequence flow with one bottleneck.

Table 5–7
Clerical Services Shop Work Flow Is Randomly Sequenced. Capacity Utilization
Is Moderate: A Single Frame Static Monte Carlo Simulation

```
Number in Parenthesis is Sequence in Flow.
An 8 Hour Day is Standard.
Task Times are in Hours or Tenths of Hours.
```

	Station TYPING		Station PROOF		Station COPYING		Station GRAPHICS		Station FAX		Priority Assigned by:		
Job											FCFS	SPT	SPT Thru Bottleneck
1					(1)	0.8	(2)	1.0			1.8	1.8	4.4
2			(1)	0.6	(2)	0.6					3.4	1.4	2.6
3					(2)	1.0			(1)	0.8	4.4	3.4	5.2
4	1(1)	0.6	(2)	1.0					(3)	0.6	4.8	4.6	6.6
5			(3)	0.8	(1)	1.0			(2)	1.4	7.4	4.8	4.0
6	(2)	1.6			(1)	1.0	(4)	1.0	(3)	1.2	8.4	9.0	7.0
7							(2)	1.2	(1)	1.6	3.6	7.6	6.0
8									(1)	0.8	3.2	0.8	7.4
9			(4)	1.4	(3)	0.8	(1)	0.8	(2)	1.0	6.6	6.2	5.6
10	(1)	0.4	(2)	1.2							2.8	1.6	2.8
Total Hours		3.5		5.2		5.2		4.0		7.4	46.4	41.2	51.6
%Capacity Utilized:		44%		65%		65%		50%		93%			
Mean Job Time to Completion in Hours:											4.64	4.12	5.16

The five workstations are typing, proofing, copying, graphics and fax.
For the simulation presented in Table 5–7, station capacity varies around
the 60% level for all stations except fax, which on this particular day is
pushed near capacity. Station task times and number of tasks assigned are
randomly varied to fit the capacity levels illustrated. All stations range in
task time from 0.4 to 1.6 around a mean of 1.0 hour. Tasks assigned range
from three to seven per station.

Three prioritizing approaches are presented in Figures 5–7A, 5–7B and
5–7C, first-come, first-served, shortest processing time and SPT, with first
priority to jobs that must pass through the bottleneck to completion. In
terms of average job completion time, SPT is best with an average of just
over 4.0 hours, FCFS is second at 4.6 hours and priority to passage through
the bottleneck is last with an average of a little over 5.0 hours.

Figure 5–7A illustrates how first-come, first-served prioritizing loads station 5 fully, ensuring full use of bottleneck capacity. But it generates overtime
work for station 4 because the last job of the day on station 5 must be

Figure 5–7A
Graphic Display of Clerical Services Shop Work Flow Based on Table 5–7

First-Come First-Served Priority Flow Assignment:

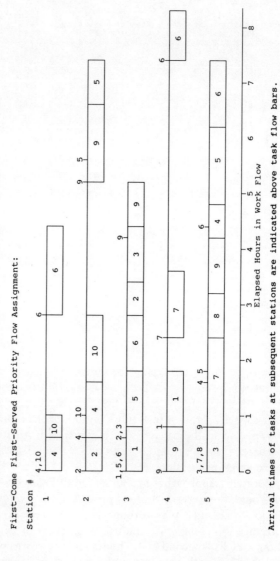

Arrival times of tasks at subsequent stations are indicated above task flow bars.

Figure 5–7B
Graphic Display of a Clerical Service Shop Work Flow Based on Table 5–7

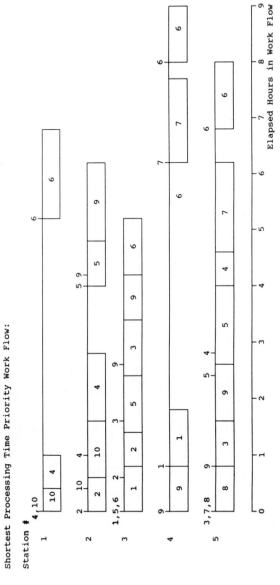

Shortest Processing Time Priority Work Flow:

Arrival times of tasks at subsequent stations are indicated above task flow bars.

Figure 5-7C
Graphic Display of Clerical Service Shop Work Flow Based on Table 5-7

First priority goes to work remaining beyond the bottleneck (Station #5).
(Work remaining beyond bottleneck is indicated by underlining of job numbers
before and at the bottleneck station – #5, FAX).
Shortest Processing Time priority prevails otherwise.

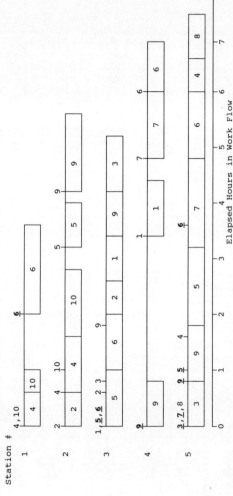

Arrival times of tasks at subsequent stations are indicated above task flow bars.

finished on 4. Shortest processing time, shown in Figure 5–7B, even though it yields an average flow time less than FCFS, still pushes job 6 into even more overtime on station 4, thereby slightly increasing the overtime needed to finish the day's work beyond the FCFS schedule requirement. Both FCFS and SPT exhibit large gaps of slack in the schedule that will waste labor capacity if five workers are assigned.

The bottleneck priority graph for Figure 5–7C was produced by first assigning priority to any work that had to get through the bottleneck and then giving priority to competing first priority jobs by giving precedence to the shortest processing time. Competing nonpriority jobs were also prioritized using SPT.

Giving first priority to work that must get past the bottleneck produces a distinctly new result in work flow; the average flow time of work increases slightly, from four hours with SPT prioritizing to over five hours. This is a 20% increase. It is, however, largely accounted for by the fact that jobs, like job 8, that would race through to completion under a strict SPT priority schedule now are deferred in preference to work that must get past the bottleneck. Assigning a priority to work going beyond the bottleneck increases average flow time but decreases slack in the flow system and reduces the potential for overtime at the same time. With this simulation frame, SPT actually introduces additional slack into the bottleneck station to get minimum average flow time. Assigning priority to jobs through the bottleneck serves both to get jobs to the bottleneck as fast as possible to keep it loaded with work and to push jobs through the bottleneck to minimize delay at stations on the other side. But it does so at the expense of average flow time.

The effect of these prioritizing variations is to illustrate the interaction of the shortest processing time with the available alternative priority rules. Combining SPT with alternative rules serves to push work quickly through a bottleneck to load subsequent workstations more fully, especially with a random workstation flow situation. In any project shop where bottlenecks migrate from place to place as a function of the mix of work, SPT often will not be the best policy for keeping stations loaded or for minimizing the overtime necessary to clear out the shop at the end of the day or week. The SPT can sometimes introduce large amounts of slack into the low capacity utilization flow situation. In working to reduce overall average job completion time, SPT may sometimes create undesired results. Average job completion time is not the only criterion of scheduling effectiveness in the moderate capacity project shop. Scheduling in the project shop requires an appreciation of the effects of different prioritizing rules.

SUMMARY

Opportunity to schedule by resequencing jobs exists whenever a queue of work is lined up in front of a workstation. But existence of the queue is also an indication that a bottleneck exists in the process flow at that point. The most direct way to solve a bottleneck is to increase capacity. If that is not possible, the bottleneck must be kept loaded so that available capacity at the bottleneck will not be wasted. In the absence of other information, the safest approach to managing bottlenecks is to resequence jobs by the shortest processing time. Scheduling jobs from an early bottleneck to a later one is sometimes improved when the total processing time in advance of the later bottleneck is summed and priority sequence assigned at earlier stations by summed SPT. Giving priority to jobs through a bottleneck that fill empty capacity downstream or that have large amounts of work remaining to be accomplished on them beyond the bottleneck can also be useful.

The manner of scheduling work through a bottleneck can either increase or decrease the slack on stations following. A decrease in slack will sometimes, though not always, reduce average job flow time. In a project system that is characterized by low capacity utilization policies, though, improved flow time is likely to be unimportant. The greater priority will be to schedule available labor as efficiently as possible. Depending on the range and flexibility of the available labor pool, it may sometimes be desirable to close slack so that minimal worker time is wasted or to open slack so that workers may be effectively cross-assigned from station to station to cover the work flow. It will be shown in chapter 6 that when labor utilization is taken into account, there is no one best way to schedule work flow in the project shop. Circumstance and a degree of trial and error will determine the best approach to scheduling equipment and labor together. Approaches to simultaneous scheduling of work flow and labor will be explored more fully in chapter 6.

Scheduling the project shop is a highly complex process. No single scheduling rule or policy will do the job. The SPT is a useful option when no information is available as to the existence of bottlenecks or for slack in the schedule. It can improve billing time and cash flow when it reduces system slack, and it is easy to apply. The SPT requires only that the amount of work on the present workstation be determined (or estimated) and that the shortest job in the queue consistently be given priority over all remaining work in that queue. The biggest hurdle to overcome in applying SPT will often be the strong intuitive fear of not getting large jobs through the queue at all. An alternative is to establish a maximum time for a job to remain in the queue before it is given first priority. Although this is an appealing compromise, it is seldom really necessary. The result is all too likely to be creation of a logjam with a number of small jobs behind the large ones on the station, inflicting proportionately greater delay on them than would have been imposed on the large jobs waiting.

The better approach will be to identify potential bottlenecks by loading work on available workstations and following work flow through the system with some form of simulation. Once bottlenecks are identified, apply variable prioritizing rules to observe the effect on both average processing time and system slack. Simulation can take the form of manually graphed preplanning, such as that illustrated in this chapter, or may be a custom computer program designed for the purpose. The objective of simulation is to permit creative management of slack in work flow and labor allocation. As we will discover in an examination of scheduling labor, there will be times when more, rather than less, slack in the system will be the key to efficient allocation of existing manpower and skill. Efficiency in the loading of workstations will in many (if not most) cases be secondary to efficiency in the use of manpower. Ultimately, indeed, we may conclude that in sequencing work on equipment or workstations we will follow the same rule called for in allocating capacity; efficiency doesn't count. It is of greater importance for a project shop operations manager to understand how various prioritizing rules can be used to influence work flow and slack in the flow system. An understanding of the effects of scheduling rules will be indispensable, though, when it is time to reconcile the often conflicting demands of equipment versus labor efficiency. The effective project shop scheduler must appreciate the variable effects of different prioritizing rules and use them intelligently to achieve the desired scheduling objective.

6

SCHEDULING AND MOTIVATING WORKERS

"Flextime you say? You ain't seen nothin' yet."

In a mass commodity output operation machines are kept busy continually by applying narrowly specialized human skill. This does not necessarily mean that less is paid to the worker. On the contrary, the absence of intrinsic work interest may require that compensation be set high enough to make up for the dullness of the work. The net effect is that worker capacity for higher levels of skill capability is wasted to keep machine capacity loaded.

In the project shop low levels of capacity utilization result in a high proportion of machine idleness. Workers, though, must stay busy. Continuous assignment to useful project shop work will mean increased variety in application of skills and work assignments. Workers are now paid for the range and flexibility of their skill repertoire. Higher pay goes to those who are most versatile.

Consideration of necessary revisions of the compensation system to ensure proper payment of project shop workers will come in chapter 10. In this chapter, methods for achieving fullest application of available labor capacity are examined. Although the project shop requires suboptimization of equipment capacity and workstations in use, labor must be maximally, if not optimally, applied to achieve lowest cost. Within limits, as will become apparent, efficiency *does* count in scheduling labor.

KEEP WORKERS APPLIED AT FULL CAPACITY

It is not a new principle. Shigeo Shingo, the Japanese production expert, observed that "in Japan, even if our machines sit idle for a certain period of time, we make every effort to have human beings work at their full capacity" (Shingo, 1988). Flexibly skilled workers can be kept busy more easily than narrowly specialized ones. Low level, limited skill is more difficult to use flexibly. Keeping the narrowly specialized employee continuously occupied with work generally means keeping him working continuously at the same machine. Scheduling equipment and scheduling labor are, in the mass output operation, the same activity.

In the project shop, scheduling people and scheduling equipment are related but different activities. The first priority is to keep workers busy. If workers must move from station to station with the flow of work, waiting lines in front of heavily used equipment will waste labor skill and time in long queues of waiting work. The primary cost control objective of project shop scheduling is to avoid needlessly wasted labor skill and time.

WAITING TIME AND SLACK

It was shown in chapter 5 how different approaches to prioritizing the work waiting in queues can reduce average work flow time and shrink out or increase slack in the equipment loading schedule. It has also been observed that the key to management of flow time and slack in the system is in how work is managed through a bottleneck. The same basic rules apply to labor scheduling. Equipment bottlenecks, whether temporary or chronic, require special attention since waiting lines at these points have the potential to create wasted capacity that cannot be recovered. Any time equipment capacity utilization level plus slack exceeds 100%, real delays behind a crisis queue are unavoidable and real increases in cost are incurred.

Equipment scheduling in the project shop is best solved by the existence of surplus equipment capacity. This is a solution that substantially eliminates queues and schedules. At 50% capacity utilization the typical machine is empty and ready 50% of the time when a job arrives. When waiting time is intolerable, work can be assigned by priority or equipment can be dedicated to the worker. Worker skill that is unusually valuable or in critically short supply may justify dedication of equipment to the individual worker. The master mechanic or surgeon is fully equipped with all of the necessary tools for the task for maximum personal efficiency of use. Jobs requiring costly or sophisticated equipment will share tools for the sake of cost effectiveness. The project shop is a resource center of tools and talent. It is in the effective scheduling of their use to achieve economies of scale, time and cost that it makes its economic contribution.

Multimillion dollar medical diagnostic devices, giant high speed printing presses, mainframe supercomputers, transport jet aircraft, ambulance-helicopters and similar equipment are clearly found within this class of use. Too rare, expensive or valuable to be dedicated to any one worker's application, they are held in common availability by loose associations of coworkers who share them at 20% to 50% capacity application. A variety of systems for scheduling such equipment may be employed. At capacity usage in the 30% range, first-come, first-served, is satisfactory as long as some variation in timing of arrival of jobs is ensured. At most, a minimal appointment system is devised to keep everything from jamming up around overly popular times of the day or week. The major scheduling concern with equipment of this sort is to predict bottlenecks as early as possible.

Scheduling rules alone contribute only limited control over work flow. Prioritizing by shortest processing time does consistently reduce average job flow time. Frequently, this is no more than an artifact of the numbers. Short jobs flow through first at the expense of long jobs. The time from beginning of the first job to the end of the last can be identical whether short jobs or long jobs are pushed through first.

Shortest processing time prioritizing sometimes closes slack, sometimes increases it. When reduction in system slack is the object of scheduling, it is more likely to be achieved by pushing through bottlenecks those jobs that have the most work left to be done on them beyond the bottleneck. As with Johnson's rule, slack at a bottleneck can sometimes be managed best by following an early SPT priority until the bottleneck is loaded with work and then shifting to some other prioritizing rule. There is, thus, no single priority rule that meets all the needs of project shop work flow scheduling, whether it be of equipment or labor.

MANAGE BOTTLENECKS

It is clear, though, that scheduling high relative capacity skill or equipment usage must be handled differently from scheduling low capacity utilization. Bottlenecks require special attention. Critical path (CP) management requires that priority in assigning resources be given first to jobs on the critical path. Eliyahu Goldratt's (1988) approach to computerized shop floor scheduling resolves down pragmatically to scheduling bottlenecks forward first and then scheduling everything else backward from the bottlenecks to support the need of the bottlenecks. In "push" and "pull" terms, it is necessary to push work through bottlenecks but to pull work in the right sequence and timing into bottlenecks if they are to be kept fully loaded.

In the project shop, the general rule is first to schedule bottlenecks fully and then to fill in ahead of them with lower capacity utilization work. This rule holds for both skill and equipment. This is the equivalent of finding the critical path in a PERT network, applying resources to the critical path first and then scheduling the remaining paths and branches around the availability of skill and equipment. Flow of work over any given period must be examined for both its demand on skill and on equipment. Probable bottlenecks must be identified for each. Bottlenecks are ranked by level of seriousness so that the more critical can be scheduled first. To complicate matters, priority of assignment should also favor continuity of worker assignment to a given job in order to enhance quality performance of the job. This requires construction of a comprehensive (possibly computerized) shop model through which flow of jobs and assignment of skill can be simulated.

FLEXIBLE SCHEDULES AND NATURAL ENERGY CYCLES

Before labor assignment in a flow model can be accomplished, though, a new set of working-schedule principles must be formulated to guide the labor scheduling process. For the most part these principles will bypass the traditional eight-hour workday, five-day workweek scheduling in favor of vastly more flexible timetables.

It has been established that on a fixed eight-hour, five-day schedule, both productivity and quality tend to be low on Monday morning, rise to their best levels near midweek and then decline toward a Friday afternoon low. Human beings have metabolic cycles that seem to go around approximately every month. The natural length of the metabolic day seems to be about twenty-five hours. These daily and monthly cycles, though, are subject to self-management with simple drugs like caffeine or nicotine. They are naturally managed by exciting the flow of adrenaline in the body. Some jobs are inherently exciting, even risky. High interest and energy are generated that override natural cycles of energy. The simple expedient of vigorous exercise—through the work itself or as an adjunct to it—also stimulates and energizes to adjust the metabolic cycle.

Routine jobs on an exact routine schedule depress physical and emotional response. Lack of interest in one's work permits the natural metabolic cycle to determine the energy available for application to the job. Depression arising out of job routine may then amplify the downswings of energy creating severe lows at inopportune times in the work schedule.

A large part of the question of how to motivate workers on their jobs has to do with finding ways to avoid severe lows of physical and emotional energy that depress performance. Coffee and coke machines are among the simpler devices for generating an energy jolt. Introduction of risk and threat can raise adrenalin levels to produce a natural energy high. Interest in the work itself is the most comfortable way to keep energy high. There is one device for keeping interest and energy high that is inherently ruled out by the routine, fixed hour work schedule of the mass output system: schedule work flexibly and variably in accordance with customer need and demand. Adjust the work schedule so that it is responsive to the customer's schedule. Work long days, short days, no days, as the market dictates. In the shadow of mass production's dominance, this device has almost been forgotten.

Work that must be done on schedule under penalty of loss of customer confidence, which varies in daily schedule to accommodate order backlog and which permits semivoluntary diversion to routine work only when there is no backlog, is work that is customer responsive and that drives a natural schedule. A natural schedule includes periods of intense output, periods of no output and a lot of in-between fluctuations from short to "normal" days. This is the natural schedule of a project shop. It is flex time taken to its natural limit where the schedule is driven fundamentally by the customers' needs, limited only by the energy and health of the worker. The threat of lost business, the challenge of job and task variety, the absence of dulling routine, all combine to raise energy and performance under this kind of work schedule. "Motivation" is built in to it.

The routine forty-hour workweek is a severe burden on society. Transport and roadways are clogged by rush hour traffic Mondays through Fridays. Restaurants, schools, banks and stores are staffed to handle the evening and weekend crush. Telephone and power utility capacity is pushed to the limit for a few hours and then grossly underused for the majority of the day. Routine work requires strict enforcement of discipline to keep workers from sliding into energy and productivity slumps. The majority of disciplinary action is for tardiness and absence, not work ineffectiveness. The pattern of boss–employee relationships downgrades to one of workers putting out the minimum necessary to keep the boss off their backs, while the boss warily patrols the standards perimeter to catch slackers. Workers take the maximum time off possible, produce the minimum quantity and quality required to keep their jobs, and are paid the minimum going rate for their production and quality. The job contract produced by the work routine of mass commodity production, the eight hour day, five day week, depresses work performance to the minimum. It is not so much a matter of poor motivation as it is a set of very bad habits that naturally arise out of the stale routine of working in a rigid schedule during the standard workweek. It is not all bad worker habits either; a good part of the problem is the direct result of outmoded management habits of scheduling work to maximize efficient use of capital equipment.

Workaholism has its good and bad sides. It results directly from worker self-flagellation to avoid the downside depression that comes when there is no excitement, no threat, no interest, in the job. The workaholic takes on increasingly more responsibility and accountability just to keep the challenge of work high, the threat and excitement maximum. At its worst, workaholism crosses over into stimulant drug abuse, favoring drugs that generate major highs. The workaholic drug addict, strangely and tragically, is compulsively driven by the imperative of high payoff for maximum productivity and quality in his or her work routine. The workaholic easily goes to extremes with energizing, exciting drugs.

A healthy work schedule is a variable work schedule that allows for periods of stress and relaxation. Relaxation may or may not be work related depending on business need and the individual's personal preferences. But it is an essential element of effective performance under stress. Extremely high stress occupations like professional football offer long periods of relaxation that allow for physical and emotional recovery. During the season some days are long, some short, but days off are rare. Off-season, the sole requirement is to stay in physical shape and keep learning the game. It is a work schedule that naturally supports the stress of the game.

MAXIMUM WORK OUTPUT SCHEDULES

Much of the error of management thinking about scheduling arises out of the assumption that hours equals productivity. This assumption is closely tied to the expectation that efficiency depends on maximum use of available equipment time. "Time is money" is the maxim of efficiency maximizers. It is a truism only if the skill or machinery that supports production is in short supply. This is an age in which skill is in short supply long before equipment is. The route to wealth now is through the better idea, not through running the factory harder. Today, "information is money."

Time as an element of productivity and work scheduling must be rethought. Frederick Winslow Taylor (1911) demonstrated that human energy applied to work was more efficient when sufficient rest was permitted around brief maximum output work periods. An extremely intense term of work produces higher output when there are regular breaks or diversions from the work focus. High intensity work output is typically limited to a span of about three hours. This is the optimum length of a sporting event. Sports provide the best measure of optimum human physical and emotional capacity available since they demand "maximum" output from participants during the period of play. Football, which calls for bursts of maximum strength, employs an average play length of about twelve seconds, interrupted by a planning/regrouping period about twice that time. The entire game concludes in about three hours and includes a twenty minute half time for rest and reassessment of strategy.

Baseball is approximately a three-hour game. Double headers are occasionally (but not routinely) played to make up for rained out games, but the same pitcher never starts both games, and other changes in the lineup may be made to keep the team fresh. Pitching represents the limits of physical/emotional capacity best. The physical intensity of the pitching task is so demanding that several days of rest are virtually mandatory before undertaking another game. Relief pitchers who play only an inning or two may pitch more frequently. It is unrealistic, though, to try to be both a starting pitcher and a relief pitcher because of the different cycles of energy output demanded by these different roles.

The track and field athlete can compete several times a week with bursts of short performance through a two- or three-hour event. The marathoner, though, will put everything he has into the three to four hours of continuous, grueling competition required by the event and must then rest for several weeks to recover from the physical and emotional stress of the run.

In all of these athletic contests, energy and adaptation allow performance to be measured out over approximately three hours by the physically well-trained, disciplined athlete. This is matched by many other established patterns of work scheduling. Sea duty on shipboard is generally scheduled on a four hours on, four hours off basis. Provision is often made for brief rest or diversion midwatch. Eight-hour shop work schedules are usually divided into four periods of approximately two hours' work each by the conventions of rest and lunch periods. Whether this is the most efficient or effective scheduling of work is subject to question. Part time workers on a five-hour workday with a short rest period midday have produced the same amount and quality of work as workers on the eight-hour workday schedule (Bassett, 1980).

Productivity has risen consistently in the twentieth century. In its first thirty years, from 1899 to 1929, the average manufacturing workweek shrank from 53.5 hours to 44.2 hours, a reduction of 17.4%. During the same time, the National Bureau of Economic Research (NBER) index of manufacturing labor input rose by 75.0% (Kendric, 1961). The NBER labor index holds services per manhour constant in terms of real income, which permits it to be directly compared to hours of work. This makes it reasonable to suggest that although the workweek shrank through 1929 by more than one hour for every six worked in 1899, absolute weekly productivity came close to doubling. These changes are typical of nonagricultural productivity in general during this period.

E. F. Denison (1974) suggested that part of this improvement is the result of reduced fatigue on the job. There are probably other important factors at work in this equation. Production output can vary widely in different circumstances. Experienced production managers, for instance, know that overtime without exact controls on output results in a relative loss of productivity or quality. Experience with part time work period schedules suggests that productivity increases that depend principally on high worker energy and motivation may come about more easily if the workday is shortened than if it is lengthened (Bassett, 1980).

LONG WORKDAYS AND EXTRA LEISURE

If, for instance, work is scheduled in two and a half hour modules, a full day's output may be available from two work sessions. It has been experimentally shown that workers will work faster to achieve set work goals when pay is equivalent and the payoff is extra personal leisure time (Bassett, 1979). Polls and interviews of production workers frequently reveal a preference for more leisure time over increased pay. Workers often take time off without pay in spite of the threat of disciplinary retaliation. Shorter, higher output work periods may be an important solution to increased worker productivity and job satisfaction.

At the other extreme of scheduling, energetic, highly motivated workers can often work extended hours without serious loss of effectiveness. Long work days generally require variety in the pattern of daily activity. Executive twelve and fourteen hour days seldom are spent solely on the same decision or exclusively at a single administrative task. A variety of issues and activities often require movement from place to place and a modicum of travel will make up the typical, long executive workday. Observed closely, most such days are a series of three to four hour work sessions requiring very different physical and mental activities and strung together so that each subsequent period is a refreshment and diversion from the former. Yet those same executives expect lower echelon workers to stay at the same workstation performing the identical task for eight, ten or twelve hours without relief.

Under the right conditions, a continuously tasked twelve or more hour workday is feasible. Factory output of critical war material during World War II sometimes demanded double shifts of work. Worker commitment to the need, extra pay and generous recognition of accomplishment were sufficient to produce truly extraordinary output.

But when the same task is performed from beginning to end of the day under routine conditions, breaks and diversions must be liberally supplied. If not available, support in the form of extra emotional bolstering up, physical assists in the form of coffee and high energy snacks brought to the workstation and recognition of exceptional performance are all necessary. It is essential to know when the pace is too much. Soldiers on forced march or in an extended firefight become unpredictable when pushed beyond their physical and emotional limits. They can explode in anger at the enemy, dissolve in retreat or begin shooting one another. There are limits to human capacity. The maximum working time in a day, week or month should be limited, perhaps even by law, to a realistic level that reflects recent work schedules, average good health, the physical or mental strain of the work and the age of the employee. Work schedules beyond sixty hours a week should perhaps require supervision of a health professional. Work schedules under fifteen or twenty hours a week, on the other hand, should allow maximum worker choice in setting hours. For each individual, the limit may be different. As soon as any member of the team starts to fade in performance, it is time to let them all off the hook.

Long work sessions are feasible but demand closer management. A series of long work sessions must normally be followed by an extended rest. Workers can condition themselves physically and mentally to endure long workdays without loss of effectiveness, especially when they know there will almost certainly be a payoff in extended leisure when the big push is finished. In the project shop environment, considerable variety of work focus may also be possible as a refreshment and diversion to the long workday. Work scheduling in a project shop requires and allows a new perspective on patterns of working time for workers and managers alike.

PRODUCTIVITY AND FLEXIBLE WORK SCHEDULES

The body of evidence and experience that deals with work hours and work schedules lends to several radical conclusions about productivity and work schedules. Schedules that meet the real and obvious needs of the work, market and customer can be highly flexible. Short workdays often produce proportionately more work output than routine standard eight-hour days. Long workdays followed by short days or even an extended period of leisure can sustain high productivity over long periods. Task variety through the long workday in combination with strong personal/emotional support removes the stress of workdays and makes them easier to endure.

The standard project shop workweek may turn out to be two twelve-hour days and three five-hour days, or just about any other imaginable pattern between. Three twelve-hour days may come to be considered as a standard workweek. Alternatively, seven five-hour days may constitute an acceptable standard. A day's work schedule may commence anywhere from 5:00 A.M. to 6:00 P.M. and extend a dozen hours or up to midnight. Routine, fill-in work now used to complete the standard eight-hour day will in some cases become a perquisite assigned to longer service or more skilled or time-flexible workers. The need for such flexibility is obvious from the examples offered in chapter 5. Logical sequencing of project jobs and tasks may one time require compacting the slack and getting as much work done in a continuous term of work as possible. Another time it will call for short periods of closely timed work to meet bottleneck schedules. The schedule may require five hours in the morning or five hours in the evening. Outside the schedule, though, the worker is free to use the time as he or she wishes. But the schedule must be flexibly responsive to the customer's needs. That will most likely become the fundamental scheduling standard of the project shop.

In motivational terms, departure from the routine eight-hour, five-day week offers major benefits. It focuses on work to be accomplished rather than on hours to be applied at the workplace. When work can be done in five hours, it will be stretched out over eight if that is the normal workday. The major impediment to motivating more effective use of time and higher productivity on compressed work schedules will be equivalence of pay for the work accomplished. An effective program of higher pay for higher skill and experience will go a long way to offset this concern. The variation in length of workdays alone, though, can take the emphasis off hourly pay rate and place it on work to be accomplished. Workers who are in no hurry to finish can be assigned fussier jobs. Those who want more leisure time can hurry to finish. The risk of the former approach to work (workers in no hurry) is that work will be stretched out. The risk of the former is that quality will be slighted to cut time. Both variations in work pace preference can be managed as quality opportunities. Workers who take their time can be assigned tighter quality specs and be expected to do their own quality checks. Those who work fast to have time off can be teamed with more deliberate, detail oriented workers to audit quality. Differences in worker temperament and style that can impact on quality will be directly managed in this fashion.

Workers who prefer routine can be assigned to steady work on high capacity utilization equipment or at bottleneck stations. The variety of work needs that characterize a project shop can be fitted, within limits of the needs of the work, to the temperaments and preferences of workers. Accommodating worker differences in some reasonable measure is a strong stimulus to work effectiveness.

THE EMPHASIS IS ON THE CUSTOMER

The most significant change in worker perspective, though, will arise out of the primacy of emphasis on accomplishing work. The flexibility of the project shop work schedule serves customer needs first. Workers must be available to work when the work is available. Work no longer waits in the queue for the scheduling convenience of the worker. The schedule is adjusted to fit the work that needs to be done. Long workdays need no longer be seen as working overtime to catch up; they are now normal, necessary hours required to keep on top of the work. Premium (overtime) is not offered to make up for the inconvenience of the longer day or week; it is the necessary additional pay to reestablish equity after fringe benefits have been fully paid off by hours already worked. In many instances, there is no longer any need for paid personal time or holidays—a costly benefit at best that can and should be added to base pay. When there is work to do, work is scheduled. The Fourth of July, Labor Day, Thanksgiving and Christmas may continue to be sacrosanct days off in many businesses, but in the project shop they will simply not be scheduled for work. Leisure time will be in sort supply only when business is good. Old habits of taking time off regardless of business need can be challenged by the flexible work schedules of the project shop. Pay for time not worked, a questionable practice at best, will disappear. Its passing will go virtually unnoticed in a world in which work and leisure time are naturally regulated.

The project shop offers opportunity for a revolution in work schedule patterns and worker attitudes toward working schedules. The history of wage labor begins with long hours—sixty and more a week—at highly repetitive, routine work for bare minimum but consistent wages. It moves forward to shorter workweeks of largely routine work at consistent and conservative midrange wages. With the passage of time, the motivational power of a stable paycheck is all but lost. Reduced hours offer leisure time that itself becomes routinized. Some workers voluntarily "moonlight" at a second job to build up a large enough financial stake to escape the routine and go into business for themselves. The opportunity to build skill, work flexible hours, earn more when business is good, take more leisure when it is poor, is needed to attract the best talent into the project shop. It is time to abandon the artificial security of a fixed workweek and paycheck in favor of fitting work to customer need on a flexible schedule.

SCHEDULING LABOR IN THE PROJECT SHOP

Labor scheduling in the project shop will require an appreciation of the value of leisure time to workers, the energizing effect of mixing long and short workdays, the desirability of some minimal predictability of the schedule and the basic courtesy of a minimum pay for reporting to work.

Leisure time needs can be accommodated in the form of starting late or quitting early on a short workday or an extended series of full days off work. Variety of work schedule in terms of starting and quitting times, or length of workday, is refreshing and stimulating in itself. Work schedules and hours should be announced at least a day, preferably a week, in advance whenever possible. This should not prevent adjustment by an hour or two to account for improvements or delays in working time on the actual day of work. Most workers want only to know that they can sleep in, plan the afternoon or evening for special need or have the whole day off. Otherwise, the needs of the customer's work come first.

The practical side of project shop scheduling calls for work schedules that vary within an acceptable range of hours to provide sufficient earnings and confer the benefits of leisure time opportunities. Schedules must be laid out and broken up in terms of workdays of varying length. Individual workdays can be adjusted by pushing work forward (starting later) to bypass slack (wasted time) in the schedule. Meals or breaks can be scheduled around some slack periods. As much work as possible will be accomplished at the beginning of the week to permit adjustment at the conclusion of the week when needed. To demonstrate how labor scheduling interacts with equipment scheduling, examples offered earlier in tables and figures from chapter 5 are extended here to illustrate the practical mechanics of project shop labor scheduling.

SOME ILLUSTRATIONS OF GOOD LABOR SCHEDULING

Figure 5–4 based on Table 5–4 in chapter 5 illustrates the options that are available when the equipment schedule is relatively slack free. In this tax office, a computer terminal is provided at each workstation. Each terminal is connected to a central data base and can be used for any of the four tasks. The sequence of work is fixed requiring a straight line flow of work through the four stations. For this tax preparation firm, available work in this workweek requires about half a normal forty-hour week.

Slack in Figure 5–4 begins to appear downstream in a fixed sequence schedule. Slack can be shrunk out of the fixed schedule merely by pushing work forward to cover gaps in the schedule. This is the equivalent of starting as late as schedule allows in a project network. Late starts can be scheduled on stations 3 and 4, for instance, to minimize slack labor time in the schedule.

Once the emphasis shifts away from maximum equipment utilization toward efficiency of labor hours scheduled, processing time is clearly much less important than full use of available labor and predictability of work flow. Figures 6–1A and 6–1B show how the original SPT work schedule can now be modified to permit two workers to complete all of the work in almost a normal workweek with only a single hour of overtime. Since all work on stations 3 and 4 follows that on stations 1 and 2, and some jobs skip one of the middle stations, it is feasible for the worker on the first station to move immediately to waiting work on station 4 when the first station work is completed and work a forty-hour week at both stations. The worker assigned to station 2 moves directly to station 3 and works forty-one hours. All work is accomplished within the span of a near standard workweek.

Work on stations 3 and 4, now, can be scheduled independent of the flow from the two earlier stations. This permits a revised schedule that expedites work through station 3 to station 4 so that station 4 need not be dependent on station 3 for work at the end of the week.

Three options are possible with this work schedule. First is to work four people, one on each station until the work is finished in the shortest possible time. Slack on later stations in Figure 5–4 can be closed by moving work forward to close slack. Second, work two people, each forty or more hours and each covering two stations as illustrated in Figure 6–1A. A third option is to schedule three workers, each twenty-seven or more hours. Figure 6–1B illustrates how the schedule is to be adjusted to accommodate three workers. The schedule adopted will depend on number of workers who should be kept busy and the flexibility of skill transfer from task to task. Since this is relatively highly skilled work, the frequency of transfer should probably be held to a minimum.

The illustration of Figure 5–4 station schedules is based on moderate capacity utilization of workstations and equipment. The average across the four stations is approximately 60%. A somewhat different problem is encountered when capacity utilization is increased to the range of 90%. Figures 5–5A, 5–5B and 5–5C are based on this level of capacity utilization. For all three prioritizing rules applied to Table 5–5, large amounts of slack begin to appear early in the schedule on later stations, and large gaps open up between some jobs. If this schedule is held to, labor utilization will be poor. Within limits, slack on stations 3 and 4 can be closed by pushing tasks forward to close the gaps. Work that is thus advanced has the potential to push other jobs ahead on later stations, thereby increasing flow time. Su-

Figure 6–1A
Two Worker Schedule Rescheduling of Tax Office Work Flow to Eliminate Slack in Workers' Schedules Based on Table 5–4 and Figures 5–4A, 5–4B, and 5–4C

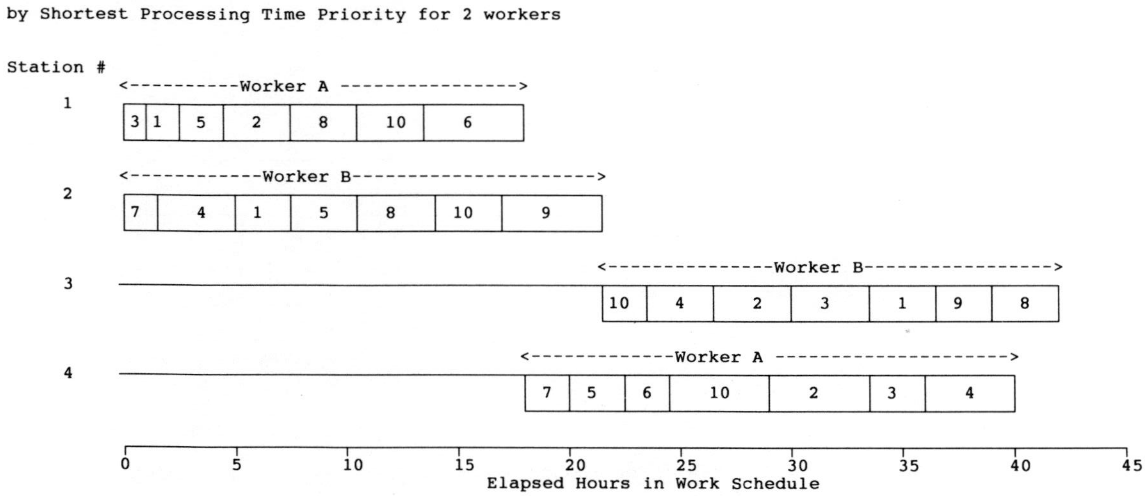

by Shortest Processing Time Priority for 2 workers

Station #

1 <------- Worker A ------->
| 3 | 1 | 5 | 2 | 8 | 10 | 6 |

2 <------- Worker B ------->
| 7 | 4 | 1 | 5 | 8 | 10 | 9 |

3 <------------------- Worker B ------------------->
| 10 | 4 | 2 | 3 | 1 | 9 | 8 |

4 <--------------- Worker A --------------->
| 7 | 5 | 6 | 10 | 2 | 3 | 4 |

0   5   10   15   20   25   30   35   40   45
Elapsed Hours in Work Schedule

Figure 6–1B
Three Worker Schedule Rescheduling of Tax Office Work Flow to Eliminate Slack in Workers'
Schedules Based on Table 5–4 and Figures 5–4A, 5–4B, and 5–4C

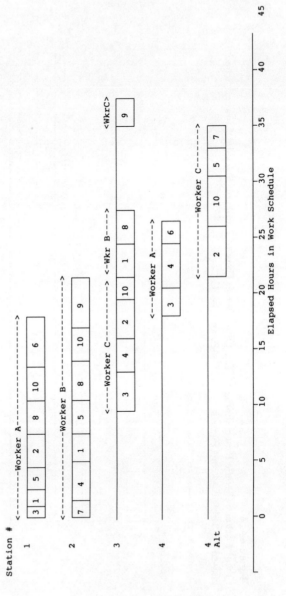

perimposing the labor schedule on an equipment schedule complicates matters by introducing added delay. Obtaining high efficiency in the use of labor, though, is the higher priority.

Figure 6–2 illustrates how work from Table 5–5 can be rescheduled to accommodate labor constraints. A maximum twelve-hour day with no more than two twelve-hour days in sequence is assumed. To whatever extent possible, gaps between days are used to close gaps in the schedule. Work days can start late if necessary as long as no more than a two-hour delay is introduced with a twelve-hour schedule. A six-hour day might start as much as eight hours later than normal.

In Figure 6–2, work on stations 1 and 2 flows normally and expeditiously through to finish on the third day, which is also a briefer day for both stations. Work on stations 3 and 4 begins on the second workday and is finished on the fourth workday. Each worker gets four days off in the week, and all work is finished within the week. Work on station 4 begins late on the first workday (day 2) and the third workday (day 4) to close small gaps when jobs ten and nine transfer off station 3. Labor is scheduled as efficiently as possible.

If the same work flow were to be scheduled in eight-hour modules, the work would require five days on each station and begin on the third day of the week for stations 3 and 4. A six-hour, six-day schedule is also feasible but results in work flowing over into the following week. When work flow is continuous, and the fixed sequence of flow represents a built-in downstream delay, this may be acceptable.

The choice of working schedule turns on the preferences of workers and the demands of customers. Several long workdays with added leisure are likely to be preferred when workers do not fatigue rapidly from the work itself. Work variety, health and stamina play a part in this choice. Exceptional customer need may occasionally require a schedule of this kind. A twelve-hour day can and should include brief breaks. Lunch and dinner periods as well as substantial work variety are desirable in a long workday. When work must be done under high pressure, a series of shorter work days that supply more leisure on a day by day basis will be the better option. When maximum work output is sought, the logical range of a week's work within the typical worker's stamina and motivational capacity would appear to be something like from three twelve-hour days a week up to six, six-hour days in a week.

Compared to a fixed sequence schedule, random sequence flow operation is more difficult to schedule at higher levels of capacity utilization and less difficult at low to moderate levels. Random sequence flow distributes gaps due to slack in the schedule over all workstations randomly. Moving work forward to take up slack on any station has the potential to disrupt the schedule of another, follow-on station. Bottlenecks will appear randomly and migrate from station to station as a function of the mix of work.

Figure 6–2
Tax Preparation Office Work Flow Day by Day Schedule of Workers to Maximize Labor Efficiency:
Modified SPT with Twelve-Hour Workday Maximum Based on Table 5–5 and Figures 5–5A, 5–5B,
and 5–5C

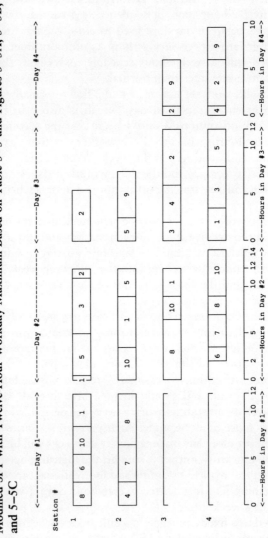

Bottlenecks will create still larger gaps in workstations that follow. Scheduling labor effectively requires that the gaps and bottlenecks be exploited to permit shifting of labor from a skill area not currently needed to another that is.

Figures 5–7A, 5–7B and 5–7C, all based on Table 5–7, illustrate this kind of scheduling problem. Station 5, Fax, is a potential bottleneck. Poor scheduling here will waste capacity and force needless overtime on other stations. The remaining stations are at much lower levels of capacity utilization. The size and extent of internal schedule gaps are approximately a function of the level of capacity utilization; lower utilization is associated with more and larger gaps.

Labor time required for this standard eight-hour day schedule in total is 25.3 hours, or just slightly more than three person days. Three full time workers with flexible skills working a small amount of overtime could cover the requirement. Three full timers and one part timer will more than cover the schedule. Unless workers are all narrowly specialized in the skill of a single workstation, it should be possible to salvage at least one full day of labor through careful scheduling.

Figure 6–3 offers a solution to the three full timers plus an overtime solution to the schedule. The major changes here compared to the SPT with priority through the bottleneck sequence of Figures 5–7A, 5–7B and 5–7C are on jobs 9, 7, 1. Job 9 is moved forward to accumulate better a block of continuous work late in the day on station 4. Job 7 is pulled forward to keep station 5, the bottleneck, continuously busy. The sequence of job 1 is switched with job 2 on station 3 to spread overtime more evenly. Blocks of work on stations 2, 3 and 4 are now adjusted around one another and keyed on station 1. Worker A begins on station 1, typing, finishes that work and moves to station 4, graphics. Briefly near the end of the day, worker A shifts to station 3, copying, and then back to finish on station 4. In doing so, worker A lends continuity to job 1. Worker B begins on station 3, copying, does two early jobs that feed the bottleneck and then switches to station 2, proofreading. Toward the end of the day, worker B briefly moves to station 3, copying, and then back to station 2, lending continuity to the completion of job 9. Worker C stays occupied on the bottleneck, station 5, until all work there is completed and then moves to station 3, copying, to finish out the work on that station. Small gaps occur between jobs 10 and 6 on station 1 and then again between job 8 on station 5 and job 2 on station 3. In both cases, the gap can be closed by starting slightly later on the day's work without creating problems on another work station.

THE OBJECT IS EFFICIENT SCHEDULING OF LABOR

These illustrations effectively demonstrate the extent of the change in operating practices required of the effective project shop. The first priority

Figure 6–3
Clerical Service Office: Three Workers Scheduled Continuously on Five Stations for Maximum Labor
Utilization Based on Table 5–7 and Figures 5–7A, 5–7B, and 5–7C

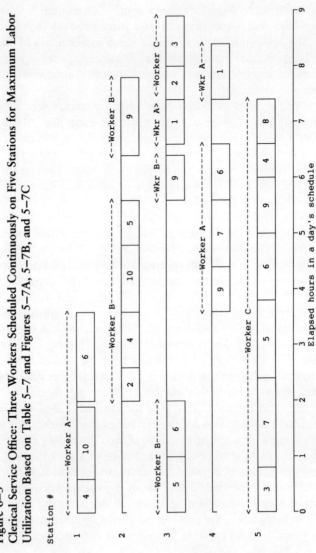

in a project shop must *not* be capacity utilization of equipment. Attending exclusively to problems and priorities of equipment utilization keeps workers busy full time *only* if capacity utilization is high. High equipment capacity utilization results in slow service. Attempting to improve service through use of priority sequencing rules can improve actual flow time only when it closes gaps of slack in the schedule. Pushing shorter jobs through first may give the appearance of faster service to some customers. Unless slack is reduced in the schedule, though, it is illusion, not substance, that is produced by simple priority sequencing of work.

Only a real reduction in equipment capacity utilization has the potential for substantially reducing job flow time and improving customer service in the project shop. When work flow sequence is fixed, labor scheduling can be accomplished by completing enough work on early stations to permit moving workers onto later stations. Later slack on stations early in the flow sequence is balanced against earlier slack on stations late in the flow. Blocks of work are accumulated over time to achieve this balance. Ultimately, this is a form of balanced, sequential production flow on a grand scale in which workers continually follow the work onto different work stations while equipment is allowed to stand idle. Low capacity utilization allows high labor utilization.

When job flow is random, workers flow to where the work must be done. Low capacity opens gaps randomly and produces bottlenecks randomly. It is now necessary to predict task time and the appearance of bottlenecks from the mix of work in-house. Otherwise, labor scheduling is impossible. Bottlenecks are scheduled first to ensure that they are fully used. Gaps on other workstations are exploited by shifting work ahead so that when workers finish on one workstation, they can be quickly shifted over into the gaps that await them on others. This process is closely analogous to identifying the critical path in a project, allocating resources first along the critical path and then adjusting remaining resources on paths that contain slack so that limited resources are scheduled without overlap. The major difference between project shop scheduling of equipment and labor skill versus PERT/CP scheduling arises out of constraints on the sets of stations and workers in combination with the random flow of work from station to station. Otherwise, there are many similarities.

Prioritizing rules used with labor scheduling are principally a lever for opening up slack in various ways. If one prioritizing rule is hard to schedule, another may be easier. Slack may be minimized to accommodate labor scheduling as the situation may require. Average job completion time is kept low by keeping equipment and station capacity utilization levels moderate. Average job completion time, indeed, is no longer important as a measure of scheduling efficiency. In its place, maximum application of available labor time becomes the criterion of scheduling effectiveness.

SIMULATION OF WORK FLOW AND THE SKILLS BANK

Two critical methods must be added to the standard set of operations devices to meet the needs of project shop equipment/labor schedules. A device must be provided for estimating station sequencing and loading requirements for work in-house. Bottlenecks and gaps of slack in the schedule must be predicted. Either an interactive system of schedule adjustment must be provided with this device, or powerful scheduling algorithms must be built into it. This essentially calls for some form of simulation system that models the flow and schedule and permits adjustment to maximize labor use around emergent equipment bottlenecks.

The second critical requirement is a data bank of available worker skills and experience. A project shop requires not only that available labor time be allocated to work to be done; the allocated time must also be fully skilled and experienced to fit the task assignment. Wholly new systems and scheduling algorithms must be developed to fit these requirements.

The concept of a skills bank is not new. As computer technology advanced in the fifties and sixties, the notion of maintaining comprehensive data banks on employee skills and experience was widely and popularly proposed. Some companys attempted to build such banks. Extensive coding systems and categories were developed to permit rapid computer search for the desired skill or experience. The most successful banks were developed on technical and scientific personnel working in what were essentially scientific project shops. Until the notion of matrix organization was introduced, prevailing organizational forms severely limited the flexibility of skill reassignment even in these settings. Matrix organization structure introduces the project (or product) dimension into formal structure cutting across the traditional hierarchical chain of command. Matrix dual lines of organizational authority permit greater flexibility of skill and experience application to project needs.

Most projects pursued under matrix structure are large scale. Assignment of workers to these projects is more often accomplished by having the project manager seek out qualified personnel and then negotiate with their direct manager for participation in the project. Looking for qualified people to man large projects is often little different from advertising to fill a job opening. In large project organizations typical of the technological go-go spirit that prevailed through the fifties and sixties, the skill and experience data bank was little more than an automated resume system. Rudimentary skill categories were included as part of the system to permit ease of screening, but the decision maker looked at the full resume of skill and experience as the basis of his or her selection for inclusion on the project team. Government contractors also found automated resumes handy as descriptions of available skill and experience in support of contract proposals.

The skills data bank notion has since largely disappeared from the popular management literature. The expense of building and maintaining such data banks was usually prohibitive compared to the ease with which an informal search could be mounted. Few project managers were willing to take a worker's unsupported word on a critical skill. Most relied on their own direct experience or the direct experience of trusted coworkers for assurance of worker ability. A matrix organization project manager's stock in trade became his or her broad knowledge of the abilities of scientists and technicians available for assignment to the project. With very little fanfare, computerized resume systems have begun to reappear in recent years, usually limited to trained, high-tech entry-level personnel. A growing surplus of cheap computer capacity promises to extend the practice of an increasingly wider range of jobs.

The coming age of the project shop will require rediscovery of skill and experience data banks. The qualification tests required for advancement in pay class will be the primary assurance of skill capability. When it comes down to either the computer simulator or a production control manager assigning workers sight unseen to their tasks in the schedule, that assurance must be substantial and reliable. Effective scheduling in a project shop is built around low equipment capacity utilization and broad worker skill flexibility. A viable skill/experience data bank *must* support the simulator that schedules labor.

The number and levels of skill or experience included in the data bank will depend largely on the criticality of the work. A skilled typist may be a fast copy typist or an experienced format typist. The medical technologist may understand operation of the equipment but be unable to interpret results. The experienced lathe operator may handle simple or complex set-ups. The number and levels of skill or experience required by different jobs will be determined by the special needs of each business. Once identified, skill and experience must be verified and coded into the data bank. Care must be taken to limit categories realistically since excessive numbers of categories will reduce opportunity for cross-assignment needlessly and reduce flexibility of the system. Attention to skill level and verification of skill capability will be a major concern of management in the project shop. Small differences in ability that impact on work performance will be critical. Large differences that do not make a difference will be unimportant. Deciding which is which will be fundamental to cost and scheduling effectiveness.

The skills bank itself need not be any more complex than operator identification and coding of verified skills that he or she can apply to work. From there on it is entirely a problem of artful scheduling that matches jobs and skills with minimum lost labor time. The simulator/scheduler employed must identify available skill for application to work in the shop and adjust around slack time to eliminate lost labor cost.

SCHEDULING EQUIPMENT VERSUS SCHEDULING PEOPLE

An understanding of the equipment scheduling process is invaluable for purposes of scheduling equipment and labor to ensure maximum labor utilization. Prioritizing rules that apply to equipment scheduling are of significance to the full scale scheduling problem only to the extent that they make apparent how effectively one rule moves work through to a bottleneck or another rule opens up added slack. Bottlenecks must be kept loaded. Excessive delay at a bottleneck is irreparable. Capacity is irrecoverable when pushed by slack beyond 100%. But slack offers opportunity. Slack can be closed up to reduce lost labor time or opened up to permit greater flexibility in labor scheduling. Different prioritizing rules create different patterns of slack and different locations of logjams. Which is easier and more efficient to schedule around will often be a problem of iteration or trial and error. The bases on which equipment scheduling is accomplished are important only to the extent that they offer different scheduling alternatives. Alternatively, the schedule may be determined by first-come, first-served (usually the equivalent of random sequencing), shortest processing time, longest processing time, most work remaining past the bottleneck or any other of dozens of possibilities. If a good labor schedule cannot be founded on one priority system, another can be attempted. As long as equipment capacity utilization is kept low to moderate, job flow time will not be a significant consideration in the final schedule. That pattern which allows available labor time and skill to be effectively scheduled at minimum labor slack is the right one. A soundly conceived skills inventory will be a valuable adjunct to this scheduling system.

The effectiveness of labor utilization in the project shop largely rests on response to real customer need, availability of flexibility in worker skill and on efficient scheduling of labor hours. Efficiency continues to count peripherally in the application of paid labor time to projects in-house. But it is the renewed power of worker commitment to the customer, expanded breadth of worker skill and management understanding of scheduling principles that give real strength to project shop operations scheduling. Labor scheduling and worker motivation work in tandem in the project shop. They work together supplying powerful new incentives to high productivity. They are the backbone of the effective project shop.

7

PUTTING QUALITY FIRST

"High quality comes naturally in a well-managed project shop."

Competitively, there is no better strategic business position than to be known for consistent high quality at moderate cost. McDonald's, for instance, maintains standards of cleanliness, freshness and consistency that are awesome, especially so in view of the popular commodity prices charged. Not everyone has a taste for McDonald's kind of food, but those who do know exactly where to get quality and price satisfaction with every purchase.

Lincoln Electric Co. manufactures the highest quality arc welding equipment in the world, pays its labor nearly double the going rate and consistently undercuts its competition in price. Customers who are willing to wait in line for delivery (Lincoln's capacity and market share are exactly targeted) know they will have the best tool at the lowest cost.

Japanese auto and electronics manufacturers have established a worldwide reputation based on consistent high quality. From a post–World War II reputation as a producer of cheap copies the Japanese vaulted into a position of global industrial leadership, largely through emphasis on quality. It would seem that quality is the royal road to business success. Why doesn't every business focus first on quality? The answer is probably that quality is many things and always, ultimately, is in the eye of the beholder.

QUALITY IS VALUE

Quality is offered in many product and service lines at a premium cost. A Rolls Royce or Mercedes is reputed to offer reliable, trouble free driving comfort for almost as many years as you want to drive a car. But you can drive ten different Fords or Chevys until they wear out at the same price. There is often a positive relationship between price and durability. But an exceptionally durable product may be superseded by a better performing one long before the first one has worn out. Products or services that are subject to rapid technological change may best be selected for their moderate cost and interim utility. The best available medical procedure today may be supplanted by safer, simpler, lower cost methods next year. Chasing the leading edge of technological progress can become an exercise in chasing your tail.

Rapid scientific discovery and technological change suggest a consumer strategy of near-term use, cost effective purchases. Premature entry into a new technology can turn into a dead end as an alternative technology leapfrogs the existing position onto higher ground. The pursuit of quality without concern for the pace of change can suddenly mutate to waste. The appearance of quality can be an illusion that fades in light of morning.

It is essential to define quality in order to achieve it. For an automobile, quality is a blend of durability, ease of maintenance, operating reliability, comfort, safety and style. Whether or not it has a built-in TV or wet bar is not so much a measure of quality as of luxury. Luxury is generally expected to reflect high quality but high quality is not necessarily luxurious. Confusion of luxury with quality is common. They must be differentiated.

Luxury increases comfort, convenience and status. It often requires marginal or extravagant use of resources. American car makers adopted a pattern after World II of selling luxurious styling and comfort. Monstrous gas guzzlers with huge fins and yards of flashing chrome announced that the age of elegant abundance had arrived. Quality in terms of engineering design, materials testing and the thoroughness with which production problems were solved was allowed to suffer. Japanese auto companies entered the market with low-cost cars that, although they lacked styling and comfort, were at least as mechanically reliable as American cars. From the base of equivalent quality and low cost, the Japanese escalated the competition by improving quality and then introducing styling, convenience and comfort. Detroit was almost lost in the dust. At equivalent quality, it is a matter of preference whether the choice is based on low cost or on styling and comfort. But styling and comfort with less than expected quality is an anomaly. Luxury makes no sense if it is not built on a foundation of the highest quality. It is a contradiction in terms. For a brief time, luxury may create an illusion of high quality, but eventually the deception will be found out.

UNDERSTANDING THE QUALITY FUNCTION

Contradictory as it may sound at first, the foundation of genuine quality is cost effectiveness. Figure 7–1 illustrates how optimum quality is found

Figure 7–1
Quality as a Function of Value

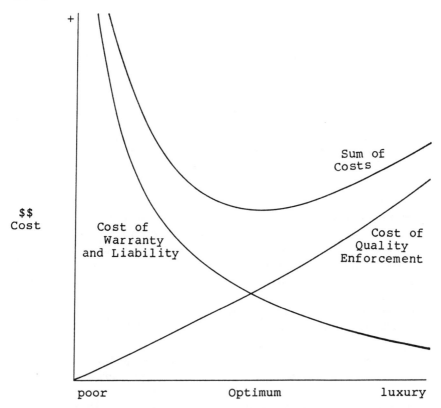

at the point of trade-off between the higher cost of a low quality product or service and the increased cost of luxurious quality. The simplest terms of the model are employed to make the model easy to grasp. The cost of poor product quality is calculated as a cost of warranty repair. Warranty is a means of guaranteeing customer satisfaction with quality. The cost of higher quality arises out of the cost of increased quality inspections and rework to enforce high quality. Low quality increases warranty cost while increased inspection and rework raise quality enforcement cost.

At a given level of engineering and materials technology an optimum cost trade-off exists at the point where the sum of the two costs is minimum (optimum). A less expensive, less durable, less reliable product or service can be delivered at lower cost under a shorter warranty for customers who seek minimum near-term cost. The customer accepts reduced performance at lower cost. Quality is low because overall cost effectiveness of the bargain is less than what is available at optimum. At the other end of the curve a more expensive, more durable, more reliable product or service is available at higher cost and longer warranty for customers who want luxury. The customer gets improved performance at premium cost. Quality is low because overall cost effectiveness of the deal is beyond the optimum point.

Quality is a function of prevailing design and materials technology in combination with the current level of worker skill and conscientiousness. High quality is obtained when these factors are blended to produce the optimum overall cost of the product or service delivered. Lower quality at lower price is a cheap position. Higher quality at higher price is a luxury position. Cheap and luxury output alike deliver less value than quality output delivers.

Japanese automakers drove up the point of optimum quality trade-off by mounting an assault on four factors of quality. Investment in improved design and materials raised quality without a proportionate increase in cost. A collateral investment to improve worker skill and conscientiousness was successfully undertaken. On the foundation of those investments, autos with greater durability and reliability were produced without a proportionate increase in price. The competitive advantage obtained by the Japanese through earlier, wiser investment in quality was a major one that American automakers will be hard pressed to catch up with.

Quality is anchored on the prevailing customer expectation for value. Luxury may point the way to future standards of quality but is a lower value in quality terms. Luxury is economically wasteful. But, then, cheapness is also wasteful. Quality demands the right balance.

The issue of performance is addressed technologically by the rule of maximum practical performance. This is a variant on the Pareto principle, sometimes called the 80/20 rule. Figure 7–2 illustrates this concept. Engineers know that the last 5% of performance capability in system design will typically cost as much to obtain as the first 95%. New products are seldom cost effective above 95% performance. Improved performance requires redesign. Redesign requires better understanding of the product and the customer's need. Increases in design and material technology as well as in worker skill and conscientiousness are required to raise quality significantly.

LEVERS TO INCREASED QUALITY

Quality strategy, a current popular buzzword, demands the right investments. The critical difference between American and Japanese automakers was in willingness to risk investment in higher quality. Americans sold styling and comfort and milked existing production systems for high profit. The Japanese plowed money into improved quality and captured the market.

Figure 7–2
The Pareto (80/20) Principle Graphically Displayed

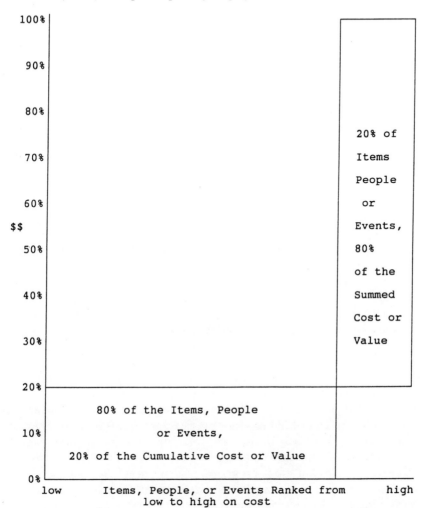

It is important to note one other strategic difference between Japanese and American car makers; the Japanese abandoned the assumption that profit was inevitably tied to high volume, capacity maximized output. American car makers bet on costly, increased production capacity to ensure their market share. The Japanese looked for flexibilities that would permit adjustment to changing market demand. American car makers are plagued with gluts of expensive inventory that require price cutting to move. The Japanese stop manufacturing when market demand wanes or disappears. A blend of flexibility in the face of market demand combined with a high quality product have produced an awesome result. Japan has very nearly converted mass commodity production into custom and short-run output.

American habits of driving production at near maximum capacity are as much to blame for the difference as anything. American managers are bold optimists. They expect a poor market to improve and will aggressively build inventory to be ready for it. They have to be ready because their systems are too rigid and inflexible to be quickly adapted to market change. Considerable lead time is required to gear up for an increase in sales. If the competition holds more inventory, it has already beat you to the punch in America. The Japanese gear up faster. Their moving assembly lines are tools to be adapted quickly to changing market requirements. Workers are more broadly skilled, more deeply involved in solving the problems of changeover and quality deficiency. Americans are laid off. Japanese are redeployed. The point is not the superiority of the Japanese. It is that they have discovered the weaknesses of the mass commodity production system and have moved toward project shop style operations in organizing and managing them.

One of the most serious problems of a mass output system is the basic quality strategy that characterizes it. Mass output depends on capacity maximization and continuous flow. Performance is above all measured by quantity of shipments. Quality is *always* secondary in a capacity maximized, efficient, commodity production operation. Quality receives lip service, sometimes with a bullhorn. Exhortation of workers to higher planes of conscientiousness is common. Quality is often the subject of ideologically flavored tirades from management. But it is nonetheless *always* secondary. Stopping the production line to remedy a quality problem instantaneously idles machinery and labor, thereby reducing capacity utilization of both. Giving workers the authority to stop the line to fix quality problems, such as is standard practice for some Japanese manufacturers, is still controversial and rare in the United States. The American practice is to give continuity of production flow clear priority over quality problems at the individual workstation and maintain "high quality awareness" through various educational or communications programs. Management accepts as normal an irreducible minimum of rework and rejection that it is the responsibility of quality inspectors to identify and repair.

In many continuous output processes, workers do not have the time to take notice of quality problems. Even if they know something has gone wrong, they must let it pass and hope that inspectors will later spot it. Quality problems that are too subtle to catch with the naked eye are ruled out of the worker's job automatically. Everything else is crowded out by the pace of production and the unmistakable urgency to keep the line moving. In highly specialized, high volume commodity output production, capacity utilization is dominant. Quality is, literally, incidental. Workers are expected to concentrate on quantity of production at *minimum sacrifice* of quality. Whether today's production goal has or has not been made is immediately visible. The pace of the process provides an automatic count. Whether today's quality is or is not within an acceptable range will be reported to the worker tomorrow or the next day. The boss nags about insufficient output here and now with immediate effect. He berates everyone about inadequate quality later after its causes have been forgotten. Research on the bases of productivity (Bassett, 1979), for instance, demonstrates that even when the task requires inspecting for errors in the work of others—a clear quality emphasis—setting quantity goals for output overwhelms worker attention to improved quality.

High capacity utilization demands explicit goals for quantity output. Quality is inevitably handicapped when efficiency of capacity utilization is the primary lever on cost reduction. Quality of work or product cannot advance to first priority until efficiency of capacity utilization is downgraded in importance.

THE POWER OF QUEUELESS WORK FLOW

The queuelessness of the tightly scheduled, low capacity utilization project shop quickly highlights quality problems. Sufficient time must be planned into the schedule to achieve quality because rework will usually be much more costly than doing it right the first time. Rework lengthens queues and spotlights quality problems by disrupting work flow. The worker who cannot get the job done right cannot hide; the growing queue of waiting work points to him or her. The worker who is afraid of running out of work can take his time to do it right. Queuelessness also leads naturally to vertical job enlargement and operating flexibility. Workers who run out of work move to other workstations where they can learn new skills. Rework reduces job variety and skill development opportunity. The worker who seeks variety and growth can use efficient methods to clear out the queue and go on to other activities.

In a project shop, introduction of low capacity utilization and queueless workstations impacts directly on worker motivation. Queuelessness transforms the worker's experience of his or her job. Initially, the lack of backed-up work waiting to be done is a shock. The certainty of a long WIP queue formerly has been management's principal motivational device for keeping workers steadily at their stations working lest they bring the system to a costly stop by their absence or laggardness. But those same, long WIP queues at each worker's station have also depressed initiative and obscured quality problems. They have even come to be associated spuriously with job security for legions of workers. As a motivating device, the long WIP queue has left more than a little to be desired. The search for good alternatives is long overdue.

The JIT, the rubric that is most prominent in the Japanese industrial revolution, is primarily a return to rigorous, continuous flow discipline on the assembly line first used by Henry Ford. Properly scheduled and managed, mass commodity flow processes need have no bottlenecks, no pileups of work-in-process inventory. The JIT dissolves the queues before workstations. Almost incidentally, the JIT also reduces inventory and the related holding cost, but that, too, was a natural by-product of the queues. Queues of WIP on a continuous mass output line are a corruption of the assembly line concept. They are, however, made necessary by the imperatives of keeping the line and its workers continuously occupied in the performance of their specialties so that capacity utilization is maximized. Those same queues hide the poor quality that results from requiring that quantity output goals be achieved above all else.

WORKER CONTRIBUTIONS TO QUALITY

Making quality a first priority on a moving assembly line requires that the line be stopped whenever there are quality problems. Solving chronic quality problems on a moving assembly line may also require extensive redesign of the line or of jobs on the line. Japanese workers have the authority to stop the line and are given the training to implement simple changes. Japanese engineers work closely with the line in working out solutions to problems and needed improvements. But the Japanese have a much briefer history using mass commodity production systems. They have seen the error of capacity maximization policy and relegating quality to a back seat. They made the changes that were necessary to make assembly lines work as they are intended to work. Queuelessness of work flow is the key to cost reduction as well as to significant quality improvement.

ELEMENTS OF QUALITY: DESIGN, MATERIALS, SKILL AND CONSCIENTIOUSNESS

Quality in any work setting is founded on design and materials technology blended with worker skill and conscientiousness. American industry has been slow to invest in improved design and materials. Narrow skill specialties continue to prevail. It is a cliche of work life that management endlessly exhorts workers to higher levels of quality consciousness. But deeply ingrained habits continue to demand full use of equipment and to reward high quantity output. The message the system gives to the worker is "keep the machine running, let someone else worry about quality." "Efficiency above all" is the watchword. But efficiency in capacity usage defeats high quality. Exhortations for greater care and conscientiousness are just a rhetorical device to lay the blame on workers. It is all a horrible, gigantic lie.

The project shop can and must be liberated from this malignant body of tradition. The technology of design is central to the project shop, be it an auto repair shop or a medical laboratory. Continual search for better tools and methods is a competitive necessity in raising quality. Choice of the best material to suture and dress a wound or build a cabinet makes materials technology a major contributor to quality. Worker skill directly levers the degree of quality in the job. Care and conscientiousness are the polish that makes quality glow. Each is indispensable to the success of the project shop.

Quality begins with sound design. Every project shop job is a problem in design. It may be design of the product itself or it may be design of the process through which a product or service is created. Design cannot be borrowed from habit or custom. It must be fitted to the special task at hand. Everyone must think in terms of good design and be ready to begin redesign whenever problems arise. Only those designs that have been fully tested in use are worthy of full trust. Every adaptation of an existing design, every new design, requires thorough testing.

TESTING THE DESIGN

Quality of design is ensured by the quality of the testing process. The test must be comprehensive, representative and realistic. It will often be impossible to test every aspect of the design. A new piece of computer software, for instance, will offer so many possibilities for test that it will be cost prohibitive to attempt them all. Only a random or representative sample of possible tests will be feasible. Sampling is a familiar and effective tool of quality assurance, but sampling from the universe of possible use sequences in new software is very different from sampling a barrel of actual parts. Any one individual user will favor certain sequences over others. Sampling may require a random sample from the universe of possible users. Alternatively, all possible sequences (or levels) of use can be modeled with the Monte Carlo technique and used with the new software to determine their effect.

Traditionally, design has been a competitive trial and error process. A new product or process is proposed by designers, sold in, implemented, revised and reimplemented. In some rare instances a prototype operation may be set up to test the design. More often testing is bypassed in favor of a full scale commitment to the new idea. Success generally requires extensive revision and redesign, often at high expense. Management reputations ascend and crash on the viability of the design or the success of the fixes required. Often the competitive success of an entire company turns on the quality and success of the product or process design under test.

There are arguments in favor of real life trial and error test of designs. The totality of commitment demanded improves the likelihood of success and overcomes fear of risk in members of the implementation team. Directly implementing the design saves time and money *if* it is successful. In the competitive race for a market share, time is always critical. The sell-in of every new design is routinely founded on overassurance of success, which means that it always appears wasteful to delay for additional tests. It is a bold and envigorating strategy that sweeps everyone along before it like a gigantic tidal wave. More often than not, it is a failure in all ways except as a learning opportunity for those involved.

When products and processes were simpler, the costs of failure were lower. The opportunity for redesign and repair of a new process or product was also significantly better. Competitive trial and error was tolerable. The level of competition has escalated. Competitive trial and error is fast becoming a prohibitive cost. It is now rational to expect that the inevitable complexities of design and use of a new product, procedure or service will defeat informal judgment and testing. The test of a design requires rigor and discipline. The merging operations discipline of "design of experiments" addresses the difficulties inherent in testing the quality of a product or process design configuration. A long and technically complicated sequence of operations required in producing a new computer chip, a new surgical procedure or a new operations audit procedure requires new techniques for test and validation of the procedure. Multivariate statistical procedures such as those offered by Analysis of Variance of Orthogonal Arrays (Taguchi's methodology) will become frequent elements of design quality assurance. At a minimum, ongoing analysis of operating data with sound quantitative techniques will be commonplace.

Quality of design in the project shop requires a completely new set of attitudes, expectations, knowledge and skill. Designs must be intensively reviewed by a committee of two or more that includes one trained and specifically designated Devil's Advocate. Any campaign to generate emotional mass commitment must be instantly recognized and stopped. When the committee is sufficiently satisfied, a simulation or prototype may be attempted. A random or representative sample of all new sequences, methods and usages should be drawn and tested as measure of the quality of judgment applied to the new design. If surprises exceed a set standard, the entire idea must go back to review with new members added to the committee. A tougher, more extensive simulation or prototype test may also be formulated.

One-of-a-kind designs may bypass some of these rigorous steps *if* they are simple enough and the cost of failure can be built into the price. Some competitive trial and error may still be cost effective when the risk and cost of failure are not excessive. But competitive trial and error as a way of life and habit of management must be replaced with wholly new methods if the quality of designs is to be improved.

QUALITY OF MATERIALS

Materials have achieved a level of complexity and risk equivalent to design. Systems of materials evaluation and tests that parallel the design test must be adopted in the project shop if materials quality is to be ensured. The major difference is in the availability of extensive listings of materials specifications that may be available for reference. But references cannot deal with all possible qualities of material. Some must be tested. Samples of material must be obtained whenever there is no prior direct experience with the material. Reference specifications alone can never be trusted to tell the entire story. Material samples must be subjected to tests that are representative of the proposed use. Every new material and every new design must be expected to yield surprises in application. The quality of the material or the design will be a direct function of the skill with which tests are devised and applied. Entirely new approaches to sampling methodology and product testing technology will be brought into play to achieve higher materials quality in the project shop.

In the project shop, traditional, error tolerant materials sampling methodologies such as the acceptable quality level (AQL) and statistical process control (SPC) will recede into the background of quality assurance work. The AQL and SPC belong to the era of capacity maximized output. The AQL assumes the inevitability of unacceptable quality and attempts only to contain it at an "acceptable" level. It is the antithesis of "zero defects" and "total quality" ideologies that purport to improve quality performance. But it can produce the best available value. If the quality of design and materials when conjoined with worker skill and care do not produce total quality, what they did produce *must* be acceptable because anything better is luxury bought at high cost. The output available at concurrent levels of capability for design, materials, worker skill and conscientiousness always represents the best available value. The AQL is a way station on the road of operations progress that can help.

Statistical process control deals with quality at the level of individual discrete operations and processes. The SPC requires a single measurement of quality that is usually an indicator of the precision of the process or operation. The SPC is feasible only because the level of precision expected by the customer has increased with improvements in tools, materials and designs. A specific quality dimension that once would have been measured with an AQL yardstick by a quality inspector is now sampled and charted at each step of the operation by the machine operator. The SPC is basically an ongoing audit of machine or operator precision, applied to repetitive operations. Because it occurs earlier in the process flow, it provides more timely feedback of quality problems.

The SPC requires that out-of-tolerance work lead to immediate cessation of work to correct the source of the problem. As a quality improvement method, the SPC supersedes capacity maximization policies by supplying something like real time feedback of quality performance and giving the worker authority to stop production to maintain quality. The SPC can be a powerful measure for improving quality performance. As expectations for increasing quality rise with escalation of the point of optimum value trade-off on the quality curve (Figure 7–1), manual sampling with SPC will eventually be replaced with 100% automated inspection, which will display an ongoing, real time measure of precision on a CRT screen complete with bells, whistles and rockets to signal the approach of quality problems. The SPC has yet to be taken to its logical limit.

WORKER SKILL AND CONSCIENTIOUSNESS

The sources of quality that remain to be exploited after design and materials technology have been nailed down are worker skill and conscientiousness. Entire texts are currently available on the subject of worker motivation. The difficulty with most treatises on the subject is the failure to address the conflict between motivation to keep production running and maximize capacity utilization versus motivation to solve quality problems. The ever present demand for efficient use of equipment and manpower through specialized, mass repetitive output is in conflict with the demand for quality. The amount and pace of output are immediately visible to everyone. Achieving expected quantity of output, thus, is easy to manage. Quality is less visible, sometimes invisible to the inexperienced. Quality takes a back seat. No amount of motivational theory or exhortation can change that fact.

Indeed, exhortation in the United States is widely and correctly interpreted as a substitute for effective action. Talk is cheap. Pompous exhortation is easily discounted as mere rhetoric. Talk solves only those classes of problem that arise out of inability to respond effectively with real action. Politicians make empty or ambiguous promises to their constituents when they know that their choice, if they do not abstain, will be to cast a single vote yea or nay. When he knows a bill will lose anyway, the politician can vote yea and thereby keep the public campaign promise to support the position that he has privately promised to defeat. Strong talk supplies the appearance of effective effort in the presence of actual failure.

Managers and supervisors put the pressure on for increased quality with florid oratory but require that output quotas be met. They invest in quality training programs but refuse to let workers stop production flow when quality problems are apparent. It is safer for a worker to appear productive and efficient while making scrap than to appear idle trying to solve a quality problem. Efficiency and capacity maximization are absolute values in the mass output operation. Quality is a relative value. Talk is useful substitute for real action when action is painful or impossible.

Because quality is more difficult to observe and measure than is quantity of output, a special effort must be applied to getting quality. Feedback must be in real time. It makes no sense to inspect work done last week if quality is truly the first priority. The work just accomplished must be inspected. If it fails to meet quality standards, everything done since the last inspection is suspect and must be 100% inspected. Eventually, automated, 100% quality checks will become routine in many industries. The automated checkpoint will supply a measure of quantity and quality simultaneously. Feedback of information on both dimensions of performance will be parallel. Worker motivation to deliver high quality will then become effective.

Ultimately and inevitably, workers must become partners in the achievement and maintenance of quality, as well as in managing all of the elements of cost control and customer service. Workers who are seen as "hands," as mere robot extensions of the master mind who runs the business and makes all the decisions, can never produce quality because they must stay busy and look efficient in order to satisfy the boss. The boss "knows" what must be done because that is the standard role of the boss in American industry. Anything less is wimpy and indecisive. A good boss must be coldly decisive and efficient. Sacrificing quality to make shipment quotas and getting away with it is a measure of the boss's boldness and skill. It is the efficient way to do the job. These are the long standing habits and assumptions that are at the core of the mass commodity production system. They are also practices that effectively and consistently work to defeat quality.

WORKER PARTICIPATION: HOW FAR, HOW FAST?

For almost a half century, theorists and visionaries have proposed that major revisions to the culture of work are required if worker motivation and productivity are to be improved. The most common recommendations have to do with enlargement of jobs and worker involvement (participation) in decision making. The consistency with which these ideas are put forth as answers to the problems of worker motivation requires that they be examined and either confirmed as a necessary element of the solution or soundly rejected.

It has already been demonstrated that an increased level and range of skill are indispensable elements of the project shop. It would appear that greater exercise of judgment and discretion is also fundamental to project shop work. Job enlargement and worker involvement, on the face of it, are likely to have a central place in the evolving scheme of the project shop.

It is inherently uneconomic to break up custom and small quantity jobs into small, specialized work fragments. In a project shop setting, the greater efficiency comes from breaking the job up into as few stages as possible. A custom blow-mold die, for instance, will be produced on a dozen different pieces of equipment. Moves from station to station will determine the maximum number of task elements. Repair of an automobile, preparing a legal contract, construction of a dental prosthesis, will all be accomplished in logical, equipment associated steps, each of which is a minimum task element. Any of these projects might also be handled from beginning to end by the same worker. Indeed, there is significant potential efficiency and quality improvement in assigning the full job to one individual for completion. Project shop jobs lend naturally to job enlargement up to and including having the whole job done by the same operator.

Major projects must typically be overseen by a single project supervisor. Becoming fully conversant with the specifications and requirements of the project is a relatively large investment. Requiring a series of individuals in sequence to familiarize with the same job is the equivalent of adding additional setups to it. Every time the job is refamiliarized, there is an opportunity for error and misunderstanding. But a single project director can be held solely accountable for the end product or service.

Once a project director has been appointed, each worker in sequence receives work direction directly from him or her. Every time directions are given there is, again, an opportunity for error and misunderstanding. The safest method, then, is to combine tasks and assign project supervisor and worker roles to the same person. This is a clear move in the direction of job enrichment and enlargement.

REAL JOB ENLARGEMENT: APPLYING LOWER AND HIGHER LEVELS OF SKILL TO THE JOB

Existing habits of mass output thinking are likely to reject this solution because it underuses the higher levels of skill while the one person project supervisor/worker is performing low skilled tasks. But for many one-of-a-kind or small quantity tasks, it can take longer to instruct and inspect the lesser skilled work than to do it. For the engineer who has computer aided design on a personal computer, for instance, it is usually faster and more cost effective to enter directly the general outline of a design in draft form on a desk terminal. Describing the design or roughing it out in long hand to a draftsperson significantly increases the labor content of a simple task. For some computer oriented technicians, it may also be simpler to finish the design and generate the final copy on a desk plotter. Alternatively, the computer stored draft might be messaged to a data center to be edited, copied, filed and distributed as needed.

The TV news cameraman is often the best person to edit fast breaking footage for broadcast because he knows what has been shot and can mentally plan the final product without a complete preview before editing. Cameraman and producer can become one and the same when this happens.

Habits of specialization and, especially, old concerns for staying at the higher level of status by delegating less skilled work can easily interfere with simple efficiencies of labor such as letting one person carry the job through multiple stages or even through to completion. Yet both the cost and quality of the final job can be improved by enriching work to include a variety of simple to complex tasks.

Job enlargement as it is currently conceived is often a matter of greater variety of work on the same or next higher level of work skill. Lower status work not currently encompassed by the job is seldom added. The expectation more often is for a shot at higher skilled work. But a variety of barriers work to prevent expansion of any specialized job upward or downward. Expanding a job into a higher skill range, for instance, is an investment in training cost. Lost productivity in application of currently lesser possessed skill, as well as increased costly scrap and error are inevitable. Skill upgrading at the employer's cost is rarely undertaken unless it is an economic necessity. When the labor market for a skill is tight or when skill upgrading will raise morale and hold workers with other, needed skills, training in a new, higher skill can happen. Upgrading the skill of workers whose present skills are in widespread supply just to prevent the possibility of boredom is an unnecessary and unlikely expense. Expanding downward to a lesser skill, on the other hand, is likely to be seen as a loss of higher paid skill capacity.

In the project shop, increased skill adds flexibility. Workers will be paid according to their highest skill with the expectation that other skill at lower levels is still applicable as needed to meet customer need. Increased skill mastery is on a shared cost basis—workers seeking upgrade will normally practice on their own time. Low risk tasks and simulation projects will be employed for learning.

Once a higher skill is mastered, assigning an entire job to one worker has the potential to reduce costs and improve quality, even when lower level skills are called on for its completion. If not one person alone, then certainly fewer people will work on the job applying a wider range of skills. Communication of job requirements and frequency of job audit will be reduced. Opportunity for error and misunderstanding is reduced. For quality purposes, the highest quality and lowest cost can be expected when one person carries through from start to finish and then "signs off" and guarantees the job. Job enlargement for these purposes makes complete sense. Skill upgrading that reduces cost and improves quality is a good investment. Skill downgrading that avoids needless change of hands to complete the work is cost effective. Job enlargement applied in these terms has the potential for improving quality and productivity in the project shop.

UNINTERRUPTED WORK FLOW: BAN THE QUEUES!

The more direct and uninterrupted the flow of work in the project shop, the higher the potential quality. Direct, uninterrupted work flow requires low equipment capacity utilization and an absolute minimum of job queues. Quality problems due to damage are less likely. Continual or near continual attention to each job reduces the opportunity for error or confusion in handling the job. Expediters, project supervisors and others assigned accountability for following jobs will need to keep fewer jobs in mind. They can refresh specifications and process requirements more quickly and accurately when they must put aside and return to them. In a truly queueless environment, job flow will be so direct that it will be finished before short-term memory for specifications and production requirements can dim. Increased cost effectiveness and high quality are promoted simultaneously. Job enlargement lends to queueless, flow-straight-through job handling with all of the quality benefits that it can offer.

With increased range of skill application and greater scope of responsibility for work flow, the project shop also offers opportunity for workers to take greater responsibility for all aspects of their jobs. Job enlargement is not just a matter of more and higher skills; it increases the opportunity for choice in prioritizing and sequencing job tasks. The individual worker can easily become the job scheduler and expediter. If shifting from high to low skilled work and back again is a difficult but efficient departure from past practice, joining the management decision-making team is revolutionary. Highest quality project shop work requires full commitment from every participant. Committing to promise dates, original job specs, revision of processes or specifications that are anything but routine, demand the complete involvement commitment of the people doing the work.

BUT PARTICIPATION SHOULD ONLY GO JUST SO FAR

The concept of worker participation in work decisions is mainstream ideology in this age of social change. It is widely proposed and expected that those who do the work will be included in decisions about how and when to do it. Ideology in this case, as in most, goes well beyond practicality and realism. Too many cooks may still spoil the broth. Many decisions require not so much involvement and commitment as timeliness and clarity of communication. The justification of arbitrary management authority lies in those situations in which failure to make any decision is more costly than making a wrong or poor decision. Participation on too broad a scale can slow or stall decisions that merely need decisiveness.

When and whether participation in organizational decision making is or is not appropriate is a well examined and researched question. The works of V. H. Vroom and P. W. Yetton (1973) and V. H. Vroom and A. G. Jago (1988) convincingly settle many of the issues that pertain to worker participation in decision-making processes. The conditions under which involvement is appropriate are fairly clear. When the worker has skill or knowledge that is basic to a good decision and accepts fully the goals of the organization, it is usually desirable to include him or her in the decision-making process. When the worker is capable of obstructing or sabotaging implementation of a decision he or she considers wrong, it is necessary to take any steps required to gain full commitment. When unwillingness to support a decision results from lack of acceptance of organization goals, commitment to the goals is first necessary. Worker unwillingness to share vital information must be first overcome in any way required. Participation in reaching a decision is indispensable when the job can't be successfully done without worker involvement and commitment. Absent these requirements, participation is optional on management's part as a way of teaching or testing decision-making ability.

Obstruction and sabotage are often matters of subtle degree. The worker who is left out of the due date decision makes sure that the due date is missed. Ignoring his or her input to the design problem when special effort or skill is demanded leads to lower effort or failure in application of skill. The project shop offers frequent opportunity for the worker to extend or withhold extra effort to meet due dates, special skill to ensure high quality. Customer service and quality goals may depend on commitment obtained through involvement in the original decision. Quality in its broadest sense requires much higher levels of worker participation and commitment in the project shop than were ever tolerable on the assembly line. The project shop job is a team effort that requires the involvement of everyone concerned.

MANAGEMENT MUST LEAD THE QUALITY PARADE

The dilemma that project shop management must steer around is the natural limitation it faces as to availability of information on which to decide who to include in decision making versus when to make the decision summarily for the sake of efficiency. In the mass output operation, efficiency dominates. If management errs, it errs on the side of making the efficient decision uncomplicated by variations in opinion. In a project shop, efficiency is a low priority. The first priority is to seek involvement and commitment. Management learns from experience when it is a waste of time to ask for input to the decision and next time acts decisively. Considerable experimentation with participative decision making is essential to finding who has critical information, who defeats schedules that are imposed without consultation, who has skills that make a difference in a crisis.

Project shop tasks require flexibility, offer variety and require some degree of real teamwork. To the extent that flexibility requires a range of skill applications, variety means adaptivity and teamwork means cooperation. Worker participation in decision making is indispensable. Clear, shared organizational goals are fundamental to effective participation. Management must know the strengths and weaknesses of its people through probing and testing in depth. These are the exact obverse of the qualities and perspectives required of mass commodity production. Management of a project shop is a major shift in context, theory and practice of management. Only when these new values are appreciated and practiced will high quality begin to emerge in the project shop.

Project shop quality cannot normally be enforced by inspectors the way commodity production quality can. When a one-of-a-kind job is rejected, the cost may double. Quality is as much a result of the way the job is managed and accomplished as it is of quality enforcement and rigorous inspections. The highest quality flows from the project shop where meaningful, appropriate job enlargement is pursued and development of critical skills is pursued. The highest quality arises out of the commitment of every player to meeting the customer's expectations. It is no more effective to exhort quality consciousness in the project shop than it was in the mass output shop. But in the project shop, quality can often exceed or at least become the equivalent in priority to meeting the shipping schedule. There is no longer an inherent contradiction between the exhortation to quality and the imperative of quantity as there is on the moving assembly line. Quality is fully available as long as workers are sufficiently skilled and committed to the success of the job. The job of project shop management is to encourage skill upgrading, validate skill, and elicit real commitment. That is the road to achieving quality in all its forms and dimensions within the project shop.

8

PRINCIPLES OF WORK FLOW

> "Managing work flow requires accurate forecasts—which is why the result is so often erratic!"

Work flow is sometimes confused with scheduling. Scheduling is concerned with the sequencing and completion of individual projects or jobs. The object of scheduling is to complete jobs with a minimum of delay and deliver them on time as promised. Without a time constraint on delivery of a particular job, a schedule serves no purpose. Varying job sequence in a project shop can also serve as a device for reducing, rearranging or opening up slack in task flow to permit better allocation of available labor skills. The work flow of a project shop is constrained by the schedule but serves none of these purposes.

Work flow is a separate set of issues and technologies. The issues that work flow addresses are broader and more strategic on the one hand and more fundamental on the other hand. Work flow takes into account the broader problems of variability in customer demand and inventory levels, along with variation in lead time and work performance.

LEAD TIMES AND OPERATIONS STANDARDS

The moving assembly line was invented to permit exact management of work flow. Scheduling material on the moving assembly line involves establishing lead times for input materials, calculating flow time for subassembly feeders, measuring task time for individual operations and then scheduling backward to coordinate all elements of flow precisely and continuously into the finished product. Each input arrives in time at the point where it is needed on the line. In this respect, the earliest moving assembly

Figure 8–1
The Bell-Shaped, Normal Distribution Curve

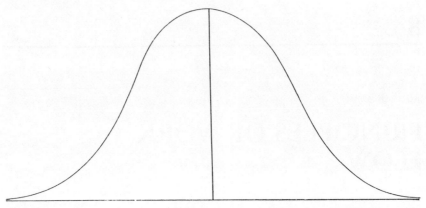

lines were prototypes of a just-in-time production system. The recent re-discovery of JIT by the Japanese suggests that something may have gotten lost in applying the original moving assembly line concept by American industry. What happened in Japan is discussed later in this chapter.

Scheduling labor on the moving assembly line requires that the right number of workers with appropriate skills be in place at line workstations at all times while the line is moving. Assigning workers to repetitive tasks and fixed workstations reduces the skill level required, controls training cost and greatly simplifies scheduling. It is a simplicity that has been bought at the cost of high pay for low skill, chronic absenteeism, lost labor efficiency and marginal quality.

On the moving assembly line, scheduling is subordinated to work flow. In so doing, though, many important operating variables have been over-simplified to fit the rigid mold of continuous flow. Analogous to the fate of victims on Procuste's Bed, that which is too short to fit is stretched, and that which is too long gets chopped. Little tolerance exists for any significant variability in materials, parts or labor skill. The moving assembly line is a strict master. It must be accommodated exactly.

HUMAN PERFORMANCE IS NATURALLY VARIABLE

In nature, variation, not precision, is the norm. The normal distribution curve, illustrated in Figure 8–1, describes in statistical terms the most com-mon pattern of distribution a variable can display. When the variables at play in a situation are numerous, some subtle and intermittent and some more obvious but, overall, complex and most beyond control, a normal distribution around the mean is inevitable. Reduction of variation in ma-terials or parts that go into an end product requires increasingly tighter control of more and more of the underlying variables. Quality control at the level demanded by space flight, for instance, requires an endless attack on quality variation in parts. One by one, variables that remain uncontrolled to create random variation must be discovered and constrained. Extreme high precision in forming or machining may be essential. Even then, close tolerance measures will reveal a normal distribution of deviations around the ideal standard (the mean). Statistical process control as a quality method depends on the pattern of these variations to identify drifts away from the ideal due to tool wear or loss of adjustment. The trick on the moving assembly line is to avoid these variations because their occurrence has the potential to stop the entire line.

Variations are part of the natural order. Avoiding them requires a high degree of discipline in the quality process. The monotony and routine of the assembly line dulls the wit and undermines discipline. If there is a small lapse, everything grinds to a halt. Henry Ford was fabled as a whimsical tyrant. He had to be! It was the surest way to defeat the numbing humdrum of the assembly line. The mass production system requires close, strict supervision to offset the absence of meaningful work, opportunity to grow and healthy variation in work pattern.

Human performance commonly demonstrates normal variation around the mean. A population of humans will vary one from another, distributing normally around the mean of performance. Individual humans will vary in their performance of the *same* task from one time to another. A part of that variation will reflect practice or learning. Part will result from rises and falls in energy, interest or focus from time to time. Daily, weekly or seasonal cycles influence work performance. Assembly line workers, given a modest measure of control of the pace of the line, will often slow it Mondays or mornings and then pick up the pace as the day and week progress, slowing again just before the end of the week. This seems to reflect the typical cycle of performance around the standard workweek. Measures of the natural pace of work sampled randomly during a week would likely distribute normally around a mean.

MASS MOVING WORK FLOW INEVITABLY WASTES HUMAN WORK CAPACITY

The moving assembly line requires that each workstation be engineered to a standard work completion time. Each task assigned must consume the same amount of time as every other task on the line. Otherwise, bottlenecks occur on the line where work either does not get finished or the line must be slowed to accommodate the bottleneck. When a bottleneck occurs, slack (i.e., wasted) time is created ahead of it. Efficiency demands the elimination of waste in the flow. Every workstation must consume as much labor skill/time as every other workstation.

Given the inherent variability of human performance, this is a terribly strict demand on the system. Indeed, one might well argue that it is an excessive and unreasonable demand that can never be met without generating large amounts of waste in labor utilization throughout the system.

That, indeed, is exactly what occurs. A bottleneck must exist in the line wherever a new assignee cannot yet keep up with the work, a skill mismatch prevents standard performance from being attained, an employee is off his or her pace due to illness or distraction or workers refuse to work any faster. Continuous work flow must be paced to fit the lowest common denominator of work performance. There is risk of significant loss of quality if paced faster. One common solution is the 95% rule: the standard at a workstation is set at a level that the typical worker can comfortably attain 95% of the time. The hurdle is set so low that anyone can jump it easily. Once thus set, there is no reason for anyone to work faster. Each individual adjusts his or her pace down to the pace of the moving assembly line. Enormous quantities of labor slack on the moving assembly line are thereby hidden. Workers are barred by the system from exercising initiative or demonstrating superior skill. The requirements of exactly managed work flow ensure that everyone's work is paced in lock step.

Inevitably, work flow proceeds in lock step in mass output operations. Operations management strictly focuses on the mathematics of engineered work flow, ignoring the variable skill and energy of workers. The end result is the full and complete defeat of labor efficiency. Tightly engineered work flow systems are inherently wasteful of human skill. Engineering efficiency has excluded human effectiveness! Indeed, it is not so much efficiency that is achieved by the moving assembly line as it is control. Thus organized, Henry Ford could and did run the whole show with precision that would make a Prussian general envious. By managing work flow he managed everything—or so he fancied.

In paying well for low skilled, tightly controlled work, Ford originally drew easily from the ranks of the unskilled and semiskilled to man his lines with satisfied workers. It was the classic exchange of security for mindless labor. The economic choice then available to the unskilled worker was between low paid, mindless labor and high paid, mindless labor. It was an easy adjustment for most. But there was little room in this work to develop skill or, if developed, to use it. Security was revealed to be a fickle illusion when the market abandoned the utility of a Model T for the comfort of an upscaled modern vehicle.

We can illustrate how to estimate the lost value of human performance input with a simple model of the continuous flow process. Figure 8–2 supplies the outlines of this model. The example is constructed around typical restraints on work standards in a mass commodity flow setting. The direct labor rate, set at $10 per hour, is moderate, neither high nor low. Average worker capacity for output at the rate of one unit per hour sets labor cost

Figure 8–2
Cost of Lost Labor Capacity in a Mass Process Flow System

```
Assumptions:
        Direct labor costs $10.00 per hour
        Direct labor contribution to output
        is 1 hour per unit of output
        Labor content costs $10.00 per unit

The standard deviation of unit labor time is
        6 minutes (65% of laborers produce 1 unit
               within a range of 54 and 66 minutes)

Reference to standard statistical tables shows
        95% of workers can produce one unit in
        69.87 minutes or less

Work Flow Standard is, therefore, set at
        69.87 minutes per unit, even though the
        average worker can produce one unit every
        60 minutes

Work standards are set at an inefficient level
        to assure a steady flow of production

Lost productivity in a 40 hour week for
        10 direct laborers is $658 and for
        100 direct laborers is $6580.

Lost productivity in a 2088 hour work year for
        10 direct laborers is $34,347 and for
        100 direct laborers is $343,476
```

per unit equal to one hour's pay. It is common to find variability in performance even on an unskilled task that is on the order of plus or minus 20.0%. Thus the best worker typically outproduces the poorest by close to 50.0%. When the standard deviation of worker output distribution is set at 0.1 (plus or minus six minutes), 95.5% of all workers are found to perform in the range of 0.8 to 1.2 units per hour of output.

In measuring the work capacity of workers assigned as direct labor to this task, the push flow system must take lesser ability into account by establishing an expected rate that nearly all workers can achieve. Given the mean of 1.0 unit per hour and standard deviation of 0.1, it can be determined from a table of z values that 95% of all workers will meet or exceed a standard that is set exactly 1.67 standard deviations below the mean. The work flow standard, as a result, is set at 0.833 units per hour, which is one unit every 72.02 minutes. The pace of all work moves at that rate. This ensures that work flow can be reliably maintained. Workers will not fall excessively behind necessitating stoppage of the line. Those few (less than 5%) workers who have trouble keeping up can be helped by better workers who are able to keep up easily with time to spare.

The rigidity of a push system of work flow demands just such conservatism in setting standards and the pace of work flow. The result, however, is a significant sacrifice in output from what would be available if the system allowed each worker to work at his or her best pace, allowing the available average level of output to be obtained. At the $10 per hour rate set for this example, this preplanned, closely controlled push flow system wastes $656 in product output value every week for each ten direct laborers. In a year, this represents a loss of $34,243. Extended over one hundred workers, it soars to $342,432, or slightly more than a third of a million dollars.

It must be noted that workers are not withholding this value in labor. The pace of the exactly controlled work flow does not permit any more work to be produced. The only way a worker can produce more is to cover more than his or her own job. It is the carefully engineered, tightly controlled design of preplanned, lock-step work flow that introduces this inefficiency of labor utilization. The materials requirements planning (MRP) system, which sets the exact rate and timing of flow, is a straightjacket that workers cannot break out of even if they want to.

LEAD TIMES VARY NATURALLY TOO

The problem of variability in labor skill/effort under conditions of tightly managed work flow can be generalized as a problem in negotiating and managing lead times. Lead times are a form of performance standard and are typically handled statistically as a problem of averages. The conservative approach to setting a lead time is to establish it as the probable duration of time lapse to delivery that can be expected nineteen times in twenty (95% of the time). Even then, production is delayed one time in twenty by later than expected arrival. The other nineteen occasions, it is on time or early. Because of the one time it is late, slack comes to be built into lead times as insurance against unforeseen events. Everyone in the system negotiates as much safety margin into his or her commitments as possible so that it is possible to meet those commitments comfortably. Pressed to negotiate a very low price to win the work, subcontractors, workers and others who feed the production system may have to increase their performance skill through learning and experience to win the job. But then they will hold to the revised lead time standard long after it has been improved on by experience, using it as a lever on reduced risk or improved cost. The most tightly costed work flow immediately begins to generate slack through learning and methods improvements. The learning curve ensures it. If those improvements are overlooked, the system becomes increasing less efficient with the mere passage of time. Last year's tightly negotiated lead time and work standards are looser this year. Tightening them up may require extensive reengineering of work flow, which is a large cost in its own right.

In traditional industrial engineering terms, this may be resolved down to a problem of optimizing the trade-off. It is a problem similar to determining

Figure 8–3
Cost of Reengineering the System versus Cost of Lost Labor Efficiency

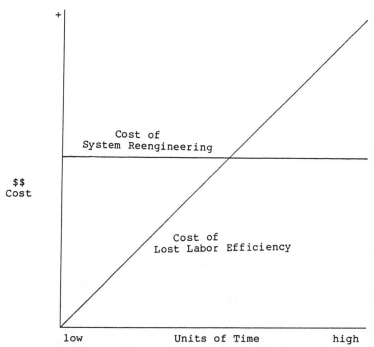

economic order quantity: find the minimum sum of offsetting but unavoidable costs between the cost of labor inefficiencies and the cost of reengineering the process. Figure 8–3 graphically illustrates this trade-off. Costs of reengineering the operation are deferred until the costs of accumulated labor inefficiencies reach or exceed reengineering costs.

The better solution is to find a way to avoid *both* costs. Engineered work flow in the manner of the continuous assembly line cannot avoid them. The value of engineering is in designing better machinery or equipment to do a higher quality job at lower cost. Reengineering any operating process is a maintenance cost of the process, not an investment in improved output. The value of labor is in applying full skill and energy to the task at hand, not in the routine predictability of repetitive performance that wastes labor capacity. Rigidifying the flow of work diminishes or excludes both of these values.

WORK FLOW AND JIT

On a well engineered continuous production line, all work arrives "just-in-time" from the succeeding workstation. When JIT is enforced, every worker is busy and every workstation occupied. Any appearance of idleness is a distress signal. Supervision is acute to idleness. Everyone learns to look busy as long as possible. A poorly engineered line of continuous flow—which could easily just be one not reengineered recently—will have bottlenecks in many places and slack at many others. The WIP inventory, or waiting customers, naturally accumulates at bottlenecks unless earlier workstations either slow work output to match bottleneck capacity, are shut down until the bottleneck catches up or are upgraded in capacity to feed the bottleneck. Tolerating inventory queues is often simpler than solving the problem. The corruptive habit of allowing WIP inventory to accumulate is established. Large amounts of WIP inventory hide both quality and work flow problems. General deterioration of the system sets in. The Japanese discovered the level of deterioration that American managers have permitted to accumulate in auto manufacturing and exploited it.

Discovery of JIT by the Japanese on their continuous flow production lines should be cause for us to pause and reflect. The JIT should be the natural state of continuous flow production. American manufacturers were distracted by the pressure of strong labor unions and grew comfortable on the cushion of high profits. The underlying discipline of tightly engineered continuous flow was forgotten in this country. The Japanese discovered this lapse of discipline and took full advantage of it. Calling it JIT was a brilliant diversion.

To their credit, though, the Japanese did add something to the old formula. Their kanban system loosens the rigidity of exactly preplanned and controlled flow to permit variation in lead time. The flow of the kanban (or reorder) card can be faster or slower than the expected norm depending on demand ahead of workstations. As customer demand increases and finished goods inventory drops, kanban returns earlier than usual to the prior workstation, increasing the work load and signaling the need for increased output. As demand decreases, finished goods inventory accumulates and the kanban lags in recycling to the earlier workstation. Reorders at that station decrease, signaling the need for decreased output. Much the same thing happens when there is a breakdown midsystem. The rhythm of the Japanese factory is set by the flow of kanban cards more than it is by the day of the week or season.

Instead of solving problems by allowing WIP inventory to build up, the Japanese seem more inclined to attack bottlenecks with engineering skill. The bottleneck is recognized as a symptom of work flow malaise and is immediately addressed. Improvements in lead time and work standards are more likely to be the source of the solution. Workers actively participate in the process of work flow problem analysis and system redesign. Quality and flow problems have equal priority. Workers are given the authority to stop the line when either occurs.

PLANNED FLOW DEPENDS ON SOUND FORECASTS

Reviewing this rich history of industrial competition through continuous flow production is useful as a way to identify the critical variables in managing work flow. The planful approach to work flow management has been to forecast customer demand, preplan flow with estimated lead times and work standards and then put every available managerial effort into maintaining the timetable. With this approach, it is essential to control the flow. Excess of output over schedule represents potentially unsaleable inventory. Less than planned output might result in lost sales and even lost market share. If demand seems to change, that change may be accommodated only by going back to the beginning of the flow cycle to change the forecast and then revise everything that follows after it. Materials requirements planning, or manufacturing resources planning, must use a forecast horizon point to target production precisely on that future point. This is illustrated by the caterer who knows that three hundred wedding guests must be served dinner between 7:00 and 9:30 Saturday night. Her standard resources would be woefully inadequate in the absence of exceedingly careful planning for their use. Food must be timed to be hot and fresh. Service must be phased within the capacity of available personnel. The needs and habits of wedding guests must be accommodated. All must be preplanned and managed to control cost and deliver quality. Success of the project is determined by the quality of the preplanning.

By contrast, the responsive approach to work flow management is concerned with meeting demand as closely as possible as it occurs. The normal rate of through-flow is established by history and habit and then is accelerated or decelerated with changes in real customer demand. Lead time between operations expands and contracts to fit demand. An increase in demand tightens lead times throughout the system. The natural variability of human performance becomes the cushion for variation in market demand. This system is illustrated by the fast food restaurant where the cook increases or decreases output as a function of the number of customers in line and the rate at which finished goods inventory is worked off in the different product bins.

"PUSH" AND "PULL" DEVICES FOR MANAGING WORK FLOW

In current popular terms, planning variations are the "push" and the "pull" dimensions of work flow management. These also are the equivalents of forward and backward planning.

The push comes from preplanning and control. Various systems of job flow management, most of an MRP variety, are proposed that push production through the system. The major advantage of the push approach comes from the thorough planning entailed and the predictability of results made possible. Careful estimation of materials requirements and lead times permits the planner to uncover bottlenecks and other problems that might otherwise create major hitches. Jobs that involve complicated, extended bills of materials, multiple feeder flows, numerous sources of materials, long lead times and a penalty for late delivery generally need to be pushed through the system. The existence of any major or critical bottleneck demands a push approach to work flow. When the capacity of the bottleneck must be exactly managed to prevent it from sinking the project, only the right push will do. As with scheduling, flow is planned at the bottleneck first and then adjusted for stations that feed the bottleneck in a pull fashion to fit flow to the requirements of the bottleneck.

The pull comes from careful attention to customer needs. On-line, computerized order entry systems that automatically commit materials, labor and equipment are perhaps the highest technological form of pull. Various forms of automatic reorder point and two-bin storage systems provide a more practical form of pull. These devices work well as long as extraordinary demand can be met through extraordinary reduction in lead time. Extremes of market demand that draw many new competitors into the arena quickly create bottlenecks of materials or labor supply. The most successful competitors typically are those who quickly shift into a push mode with their suppliers and thereby ensure sufficient input of materials to meet production needs when extraordinary increases in demand are encountered.

The economic ideal would be an infinitely flexible set of processes that could supply all the product and services demanded *on* demand. This would be a pure pull system, largely unbuffered by inventory of any kind, responding to the customer's specific need at the time and point of that need. But it does not account for needs the consumer has not yet identified or articulated and for which there is no demand until it is created by existence of a novel product or service. Much of the power of the push approach arises out of the aggressive marketing and sales promotion that accompanies it. The potential for demand is tested in a limited market. If it is a success, that potential is extrapolated, sufficient capacity for production allocated and a fully integrated, preplanned production/marketing effort begun. There is a pull hidden in this formula, though; it is in the market test. The potential pull of market demand is sampled. Planning is based on the result of that sample. Market demand is measured on a limited scale and used as the basis for an extrapolated work flow plan created in a push mode.

The technical side of work flow management is largely the push side. The MRP, materials control, inventory management, production control, all depend on a forecast of output need. Forecasting is an inexact art that, though often clothed in quantitative exactness, nonetheless rests largely on experienced managerial judgment. Judgment must be applied as to what forecast model to apply, what historical data base to use, what near-term economic and political scenarios to bet on as well as to what the upside rewards of the good guess or downside penalties of misjudgment are likely to be. The market share is won and lost on the quality of those judgments. Whether the result is lost sales or excess inventory rides on them.

Still the better method, the economic ideal, would be found in the flexibility to adjust immediately to meet any level of market need. Management of work flow ultimately requires that as much flexibility as possible be built into the operating system, while the most careful planning possible is undertaken to identify snags and bottlenecks that will impair that flexibility. Bottlenecks must be planned and managed exactly while customer need is met with equal exactness. The right blend of push and pull is required to bring this result off.

SOUND PLANNING IS ESSENTIAL BUT DIFFICULT

Management of work flow in the project shop calls for careful examination of the push and pull dimensions of the operation. Low relative equipment capacity utilization reduces, without necessarily eliminating, the occasion of bottlenecks in the flow process. Cross-skill training of workers increases the flexibility with which worker skill can be reallocated to meet changing need. These are operating strategies that increase sensitivity to opportunity from the pull side of the equation. As material suppliers and subcontractors adopt sound project shop management policies, their lead times will shorten. Lead times along the total path of flow shrink requiring smaller and smaller finished goods inventory. Extremely limited inventory and short-term delivery to specification will become the norm. Planning can then focus on any remaining long lead time resources and work flow bottlenecks.

If it were possible to meet all customer demand flexibly in real time, it would no longer be necessary to plan. Much of the planning in a project shop would be eliminated by fast, flexible response to the customer brought about by moderate capacity use of equipment and the presence of multi-skilled labor. An irreducible minimum would still remain. Project shop managers must know how to plan effectively. That is no small task.

Planning is always problematic to the organization. Plans require forecasts of the future. Forecasts are inevitably speculative, sometimes fanciful. A control orientation on the part of management readily translates plans into budgets that become expectations for future performance. The plan easily transmutes into the hard place against which the planner is crushed by the rock of reality. The plan that does not have the commitment of those who must execute it is doomed. The Constitution of the United States guarantees protection from most devices that self-incriminate. The business plan, unfortunately, is not included. Anything you plan can and will be used against you on your annual performance appraisal. One must never lose sight of the fact that *plan* is a four letter word.

It is slightly insane if not wholly irrational to enter into the planning process without some kind of guarantee of immunity. Managers characteristically resist planning and, when forced to it, create the safest, surest plan they can that will impress the boss but will not result in a cut in their budget or status. Planning is clearly hazardous to one's career. If one does it poorly and miscalculates, he or she looks stupid. If the aspiration of the planner is heroic, successful achievement may set expectations for future heroic achievement as a matter of routine. Meeting the plan in the face of changed business circumstance may become ridiculous. There are more good reasons *not* to plan than there are to plan.

Having a plan is not always an advantage. On occasion, it is preferable for everyone to be caught by surprise by the unexpected turn of events. A natural outpouring of commitment and support is likely when everyone is taken unawares. To have planned successfully and anticipated correctly the coming of major crisis might reduce the cohesiveness of response that arises naturally out of the assaults of outrageous fortune. The planner who correctly anticipated might even be suspected of contriving the event, especially where it works in his or her favor by adding influence and power.

These are impelling arguments against planning. They are, though, the arguments of passive victims, not of responsible managers. Facing the future is risky. Every bold call of the shot is an invitation to derision. Planning that merely dresses the window is a waste of time, if not a distraction from the real problems and issues of managing. A good plan is dress rehearsal for the possibilities that may emerge. It catalogues the likely threats and opportunities of the near term in a way that permits allocation or reservation of resources against their eventuality. It need not blind or limit response to actual events.

A good plan searches out and articulates the major possibilities that exist in the business environment. It can never identify all major potential events simply because the range of possibility is so great. Trivial or latent potential can bloom suddenly. In rehearsing what can go right and what can go wrong, a business looks at its resources critically to determine where and how it is likely to be overwhelmed by a high tide of emergent events. It makes little difference whether the assault is from unexpected customer demand or from unpredicted competitive aggression. Good planning uncovers vulnerabilities that must be monitored. Sound planning reveals opportunities that could pass the business by for lack of response capacity. Sound evaluation of planning performance is not whether the plan is fully met. Indeed, any plan that is exactly executed was probably a no-risk dead cinch from the outset. In all probability it had already been achieved before it was committed to paper. Planning is judged not by its successes so much as by its failures. The measure of ineffective planning is the frequency with which significant vulnerabilities are overlooked, ignored or denied. The mark of a poor planner is the emergence of opportunity that cannot be exploited.

MUCH PLANNING IS PATENTLY POLITICAL

Most formal planning is overgrown with the constraints of internal organizational politics. Every government budget (a financial plan) is predicated on the assumption of a healthy, vigorous economy. The slightest economic turbulence brings on fiscal crisis. If it were unlawful for executive and legislative planners to predicate a fiscal plan on anything better than the worst economic conditions of the past ten years, government spending would automatically come under control.

Most corporate budgets reflect the strategic stance of their top executive. Aggressive growth plans produce budgets and commitments that are grandly heroic. A conservative market maintenance strategy expects the average of past results to continue into the future. A retrenchment strategy predicates dire circumstances that call for the greatest of caution. A retrenchment budget reflects the worst that can happen.

Any serious business planning effort that is not fully worked out over all three levels of possibility—best, worst and most likely case scenarios—is a political and public relations document, not a plan. It is impossible for any plan to anticipate all possibilities in the social/political/economic environment. But it is irresponsible not to look at a full range of possibilities in terms of better to worse outcomes.

A GOOD PLAN IDENTIFIES THREATS AND OPPORTUNITIES

Project shop planning must recognize the risks and opportunities that lurk in the business environment. There are enough unmonitored unpredictables to be dealt with anyway. Customer whimsey drives the economy. The project shop has little protection against the winds of sudden change. Failure to look for significant emergent risk or opportunity is also hazardous. Operations in the project shop must focus specifically on capacity restraints—bottlenecks—that can arise out of likely new sources of business. It must identify lead times that could solve or snarl response to those challenges.

In many ways, planning the project shop is simplified by the variety of threat and opportunity that naturally faces the business. The planning process can be formulated as a simulation of various combinations of business opportunity. Planning begins with two simple models: one of the equipment capacity availability and another of labor skills on hand. This need not be a problem in scheduling. It requires only that over some defensible span of

Figure 8–4
Planning the Work Mix in a Clerical Project Shop

```
Forty hour work week is assumed
Heavy week is 240 hour of labor demand
Light week is 120 hours of labor demand
```

Worker		Available Labor Hours	Maximum Station Hours	Heavy Week	Light Week
#1	Type & Proof Max Typing	80	40	60	25
#2	Type & Proof Max Proof	80	40	40	20
	Wkrs 1&2 Max Type & Proof	80			
#3	Graphics & Copy Max graph	40	40	40	25
#4	Fax & Copy, Max Copy	120	40	60	35
#5	Fax & Copy, Max Fax	80	40	40	25

Work Mix;	Heavy Week	Light Week
Term Papers	40 hrs type, 20 hrs proof	10 hrs type, 4 hrs proof
Bus letters	20 hrs type, 10 hrs proof	15 hrs type, 6 hrs proof
Signs, tables & charts	40 hrs graph, 10 hrs proof	25 hrs graph, 10 hrs proof
Straight copy	60 hrs copying	35 hrs copying
Fax; send & receive	40 hrs faxing	15 hrs faxing

```
Bottlenecks Identified in the Heavy Work Week
     Typing station, 60 hours are required vs. 40 available
     Type and Proof, 100 hours required vs. 80 available
     Graphics       40 hours required vs, 40 available

Primary worker skill is indicated by "max" function
```

working time, possible business mixes be applied to available resources to identify the likely bottlenecks in work flow. Figure 8–4 illustrates how variability of work mix might be analyzed for the clerical service shop.

PLANNING TO COVER THE HEAVIEST ANTICIPATED WORK LOAD

In this illustration, the normal maximum and normal minimum from historical data are analyzed for their effect on workstation loading, labor requirements and general work flow. The number of workstations available is assumed to constrain the total number of people who can work in the office. Equipment constraint can easily be suggested to limit the work available on stations like fax, copying, graphics and typing. Space limitations of the office might restrict the number of workers to five total. This does not necessarily put an absolute limit on the number of workers who could be employed, though. A full second shift might be employed, or workers might work staggered schedules, permitting a sixth or seventh worker to be assigned part or full time to cover work in the flow. Saturdays and overtime are possible for regular or supplementary personnel. For this example, it will be assumed that no more than five people can be contained in the office at one time and that five workers in a normal five-day workweek is the simplest available schedule. Working a normal eight-hour day, five workers scheduled five days offer the potential for two hundred available hours of labor.

On a heavy workweek schedule, 240 hours are called for. This is the equivalent of six full time workers on a forty-hour schedule, or five workers on a six-day, forty-eight-hour schedule. Management of work flow, though, must not stop there. It is already apparent that scheduling may exhibit logjams that create unavoidable slack downstream in the schedule. The most likely source of logjams will be bottlenecks. It is essential, therefore, to compare anticipated work in the heavy workweek with available skill and station hours.

In station loading terms, all five stations are loaded to maximum for the week, with two stations, typing and copying, running beyond forty hours in the standard week by twenty hours each. To accomplish work at these two stations it will be necessary to either stagger worker schedules or schedule overtime. Overtime might be scheduled evenings or Saturday. Another alternative could be to use part time workers on a second shift or Saturday basis. The remaining three stations may have spillover in the schedule due to unavoidable slack in the flow and, depending on how bad the spillover is, might be covered in the same manner with overtime, staggered schedules or part-timers. With a little luck, perhaps limited overtime will do the job.

Next, the fit of work demands to available skill hours must be assessed. Eighty hours of typing labor are available to cover sixty hours of need, and eighty hours of proofing labor can be called on to cover forty hours of proofing work required. Since the two workers who are qualified to type are also proofers, though, the real limitation is found in the total of hours available for both typing and proofing, which is eighty. The sum demand of typing and proofing is set at one hundred hours, which exceeds the available total labor hours by twenty hours. A major bottleneck has thus been located in the sum of typing and proofing hours available under assumptions of maximum work loading.

This bottleneck must be managed. Possible solutions might be to schedule both qualified typists/proofers for ten hours of overtime each. But fifty hour weeks are potentially stressful for people in this kind of work. Quality might suffer. It might be preferable to cover excess station hours of typing with an off-shift part time typist. If these off-shift hours could be scheduled to match the twenty excess hours of copying time required, supervision and assistance of the part-timer to maintain quality could be worked out.

Another bottleneck can be identified when labor hours available are examined; forty hours of graphics labor are available to cover forty hours of work. Whereas the graphics worker might otherwise divert to copying between graphics projects, that will be impossible under these restraints. Any slack in the graphics schedule that might be applied to copying would be offset by required overtime to finish the graphics assignments. For practical purposes, the maximum available copying hours should now be reduced to eighty to account for the substantial unavailability of the graphics worker to cover copying work.

In the forty-hour workweek schedule, only eighty hours total of fax and copy labor are available to cover one hundred hours under the heavy workweek scenario. Again, overtime might be scheduled or a part-timer used. Staggered schedules add nothing to the restriction on available labor hours, though they might be used for other purposes.

If two part-timers were employed to cover the excess hours of typing and of fax/copying outside the normal workday schedule, problems of supervision and quality could be encountered. One regular worker on a staggered schedule covering either area of work beyond the normal day schedule could supervise one part-timer. A second part-timer could be scheduled during normal day hours filling the gap left by the staggered schedule.

THE LIGHT SCHEDULE IS EASIER BUT COULD STILL BE TRICKY

Covering the light week work schedule in Figure 8–4, by contrast, creates very little scheduling stress. Hours required are well within the availabilities. The major concern will be to schedule workers fairly to fit earnings and leisure time preferences and still cover all the hours of work available. Altogether, only three full person weeks of labor are required. Total typing and proofing, however, exceeds a forty-hour workweek and must be covered either by splitting work between employees or adding five hours of overtime when one person covers the schedule. Flexibility to cover graphics, fax and copying seems adequate with skill hours available.

Planning in this manner identifies the bottlenecks that can constrain work flow and permits preidentification of possible solutions. The likely shape of the work schedule is made apparent at the outset by the planning process. Options can be reviewed, rehearsed and evaluated before the point-in-time of business need overwhelms the situation. It is precisely this kind of planning that is indispensable to effective management of work flow in the project shop.

PLANNING PROJECT SHOP WORK FLOW

The great challenge and advantage of the project shop is the absence of standard, engineered lead times for the majority of work to be accomplished.

Work flow can be scheduled and planned around estimates of probable task times, but considerable variation can and must be accommodated. Estimates may be tightened or loosened to fit demand. The direction of accommodation, though, is counterintuitive; high demand requires loose estimates. A heavily loaded operation must be estimated loosely to ensure that some limited slack will emerge in the flow process. Thus estimates will reflect the longest times likely for work rather than the shortest. Errors of work flow timing will likely be on the side of shorter than expected flow time. Thereby, anticipated long or overtime hours will shrink more often than expand.

A lightly loaded operation can be estimated tightly to maximize quick delivery and increase available leisure time in the schedule. Any errors of estimate can easily be made up either with extra effort or hours.

The project shop offers opportunity for approximate scheduling based on preplanned estimates of task time with the anticipation that workers can adjust for errors of estimate by observing where other related jobs in the schedule stand. Work flow management in the project shop requires that the current status of work be displayed currently for all to see. A kanban styled system offers a simple means for communicating system status as projects move from station to station. A set of task cards is prepared for each workstation showing estimated completion time of the task and time of arrival at that station. As a new task is begun at that station, the start time for the next task in sequence is reestimated on its card and sent to the station where it is currently being processed. Equipment/station availability estimates are thereby updated and communicated at each step of work flow. Any major delays or unexpected open time in the schedule can be spotted. The schedule can thereupon be revised on the spot to account for changes.

An alternative could be a real time status board showing all current projects with estimated and actual completion times. Task cards would now flow to a central scheduling desk as work steps are completed on equipment or stations. A disadvantage of central display could be that workers can no longer own the option to adjust to the needs of the schedule. This is solvable in locating the board where all can make reference to it. When workers have information about likely delays or early open equipment, they can potentially accommodate changes in the schedule. When the schedule gets seriously out of shape, it must be revised immediately, even while work flow is in progress or if it must temporarily be halted. Management of work flow in the project shop is a real time, dynamic and ongoing process that everyone participates in. Computer simulation or visible flow planners that can easily be updated to support the need to reschedule will be indispensable.

Preestimating and preplanning are indispensable to this kind of scheduling, but revision based on actual work flow is equally inescapable. The push and pull of the project shop are in continual tension with each other.

JIT WORKS IN THE PROJECT SHOP TOO

Just-in-time is another useful tool for managing project shop work flow. As long as equipment is being used at moderately low levels of capacity, work should never queue up in front of a workstation that is on schedule. A waiting line of work *must* mean either that a bottleneck has developed at that station *or* that the schedule has somehow failed. Each worker or station may be assigned a small amount of discretionary fill-in work that requires no schedule. This can be used to fill in small gaps. Small overlaps in arrival of work just before other work is finished on a station may be covered by handling documentation or performing quality checks. But anytime a queue of work builds up where it is not expected, attention must be brought to bear instantly to correct the tieup. The discipline of JIT in this setting comes down to every workstation working on an exact now-or-next status of waiting work. Only designated bottlenecks are permitted to have waiting work. All other workstations must either be empty, working on a current job only, or working on a current job with the next job waiting to start immediately. Any other condition of work flow must result in immediate remedial action on the schedule. Now-or-next JIT is a measure of effectiveness and success in the project shop, just as exact uninterrupted flow and absence of WIP are on the moving assembly line.

The engineered solution to work flow represented by the moving assembly line contributed to efficiency in the use of the production system at the expense of limiting the application and efficiency of human skill. The carefully planned and scheduled project shop cannot be allowed to become another straightjacket on worker capability. The push and the pull of work flow management must operate equally. The push identifies bottlenecks of equipment or labor capacity; the pull corrects planning error and takes advantage of unexpected slack capacity. A blended system that allows both to operate in their best respective ways is the only appropriate solution to project shop work flow. Responsive worker participation in managing the flow of work is inescapable in the project shop. It can also become one of its most formidable strengths.

9

HUMAN SKILL AND ADAPTATION

"Worker skill is a project shop's primary asset."

Human skill is an awesome and elusive quality. In the absence of skill, little of consequence can be accomplished. The progress of humankind is the history of skill development and mastery. Physical, intellectual, technical, social, individual and collective skills in problem solving determine the quality of human achievement. Vast parts of Europe and Southeast Asia were demolished or ravaged by World War II. The skills that created the industries not only survived war but grew and prospered through its challenges. In war, it is the *least* skilled whose lives are put at immediate risk. High skill is preserved and protected to ensure continued success. The victor in battle is as often the army supported by the greater pool of skill as it is the result of superior generalship. In crisis of every kind, skill is central to success.

THE WILL TO SKILL MASTERY

Human skill, however, can easily lie undeveloped or go unapplied. Mastery of skill often demands dogged resolution and unflagging confidence. Persistence in the face of repeated disappointment or failure is needed to master the most basic modern tools. Operation of the ubiquitous automobile is seldom mastered without the cost of an accident, however minor. Driving success under conditions of an unfamiliar road or unusual vehicle handling characteristics is largely a function of past practice in similar circumstances. Fixing the balky car is likely to be a technically demanding exploit. Stubborn persistence combined with the appropriate aptitude is indispensable to success in such endeavors.

Personal computers offer the contemporary test of one's will to competence. If the keyboard is not enough of an obstacle (only a practiced typist will find it natural), the operating conventions and internal logic of the machine or its software will be as strange as a foreign language. The quirks of complex electronic equipment, sensitivity to static electricity, temperature or humidity, for instance, have little parallel in common experience. At times it seems as though the hinderances and frustrations are unending. Mastery of the computer as a personal operating tool requires both opportunity and tenacity.

Driving a car or operating a computer are only two of an extended variety of skill mastery requirements in the present era. Spoken language, sung pitch, manually written communication, require years of dedicated practice concluding in the evolution of finely tuned muscular and even neural capacity for the skill. The seamstress's sewing machine and farmer's harvesting machinery demand special skill and experience in their efficient and successful use. Skill with a tennis racket, baseball bat, golf club, violin or piano, lariat, drilling rig, pneumatic hammer, or microscope must all be practiced and developed with patience. Nothing is an adequate substitute for intimate knowledge of the tools needed for the job at hand. The strengths and limitations, peculiarities and characteristics of the tool must be discovered through training, trial-and-error play, accident and discovery. An extended apprenticeship with the tools of the task will consistently precede full skill mastery. In many cases, the physical body of the tool user is reshaped in the process. Person and tool join in symbiotic intimacy as the skill is mastered.

The will to skill mastery often rests on a desperate certainty that one's goals and needs can be more surely and directly met with mastery of the skill. Those lucky enough to be exposed to the skill in childish play may effortlessly achieve mastery. Most must struggle. Some will fail and fall away from the quest. Some mix of dogged resolution, generous help and fortuitous opportunity are usually requisite to final success.

THE WILL TO WITHHOLD POSSESSED SKILL

The circumstances under which possessed skill may be withheld are equally special. Throughout history exceptional skill or knowledge has enjoyed wide repute. Those commanding the skills of rhetoric, mathematics, technology and medicine typically own wide notoriety for their achievements. Fame and fortune often go with acknowledged exceptional skill or ability. Skill possessed can be the source of its own reward. Renown and riches undoubtedly help drive humans to the achievement of skill at the expense of personal sweat and grief. The mystery, then, lies in why anyone would hide his or her skill once it has been mastered.

There are several factors that make possession of skill perilous or inconvenient. The possessor of skill may find its practice harmful to health or well-being. Physicians are often at risk in their exposure to transmittable disease. Aviators risk crashing. Advertising executives hazard ulcers or alcoholism.

The possessor of skill may find its role requirements or personal demands repugnant. The shy academic cringes at speaking before an audience. The nuclear physicist recoils at the prospect of nuclear war. The marksman is a pacifist. Significant skill may be rendered useless by mismatch to temperament or values. The tragedy of one caught between devotion to principle and loyalty to a profession is common.

Skill may be withheld instrumentally—to make a point or achieve a secondary purpose. Application of one's skill is a gift, a benefit to others. When they fail to appreciate or remunerate skill adequately, withholding its exercise serves as penalty for the abusers. An angry employee allows a problem that he could correct to damage equipment or stall output. The successful salesperson changes careers because her commission rate is cut. The physician refuses to respond to the call of a patient who is suing a colleague for malpractice. The garage mechanic doesn't have time for the customer who chronically objects to his billing. The labor union strikes against management that fails to demonstrate respect for its membership.

Skill and knowledge are typically so precious a possession that it is necessary to account for failure to apply it when opportunity presents itself. When application of one's skill is self-injurious or repugnant, there is little choice but to work around it. In hiring for skill, management can either screen out those who want the reward for possession without the toll of its exercise, or it can recognize the barrier and create an assignment that surmounts it. Role conflict and clash with principles can lead to the work pathologies of alcoholism, ulcers, high blood pressure or worse, along with all of their unfortunate consequences. Mismatch of skill and personal makeup is a potentially serious problem that must be either avoided or managed. Refusing to apply skill for instrumental purposes, though, is entirely another matter.

POSSESSING VERSUS CONTROLLING SKILL

Instrumental withholding of skill—holding skill hostage for ransom—can happen with almost anyone under the right (or wrong) circumstances. Those dependent on the skill of others are constantly in search of ways to ensure its continued application to their need at minimum (or reasonable) cost. Those in possession of skill are constantly in quest of devices to prevent domination by the demands of their clients or patrons without adequate recompense. As there is inescapable conflict between the haves and have-nots of wealth, there is inevitable tension between skillholders and those dependent on their skill. From the point of view of those without skill, it may sometimes appear easier to dominate the skillholder than to master the skill. The next best thing to possessing the skill may be to control the skilled.

Ancient Athenian democracy, that paragon of enlightened government, was founded on military might that imported skilled slaves to serve the city as teachers and artisans. The slave who lacked skill was worth little and subject to abuse. Possession of a skill ensured fair treatment and a modicum of dignity. Possession of slaves ensured access to a basic skill and service for the citizens of Athens.

The course of civilization since has alternated between supremacy of the skilled technocrat and resubjugation of artisans to the will of military or economic controllers. The enslaved artisan meters out skilled performance according to the threat or reward he works under. The potential for power employed by the controllers of society prevents worker trust and commitment. Those in power can betray trust with impunity. Commitment may be exploited to the enslaved artisan's disadvantage. The extent of true skill, as a result, is carefully hidden. Withholding of skill in its application is the ultimate weapon against controllers.

The labor union movement is based upon this set of dynamics. Skilled laborers who could successfully withhold labor in their confrontation with owners of tools and equipment blazed the trail for their less skilled brothers and sisters. The absence of self-respect and free choice in the application of one's skill to economic endeavor automatically limits the level and quality of skill that will be applied. The social dynamics that underlie this limitation are clear and natural. No amount of force will change them. Indeed, demonstration of superior power over the worker/artisan can only decrease self-respect and sense of choice to lower levels. Productivity inevitably decreases in tandem.

The other side of the coin is the arrogantly independent technician who expresses only contempt for the customer. The free artisan who insists on doing the job *his* way must be renowned for quality of skill if he is to survive his customer's countercontempt. The musician who plays only on specified instruments or performs only his or her choice of music may lose the audience. The architect who ignores the client's needs will not have many clients. The large middle cluster of the average skilled will find it necessary to accommodate the customer or go without income.

Economic advantage in a free society tends to flow first one way and then the other. The swing of the economic pendulum keeps controller and artisan both aware of the limits of their respective powers. Skilled worker and customer are the Siamese twins of social and economic progress. Neither may dominate without diminishing the other.

Cultural values or habits can and do influence the confrontation between skill and value. Americans are notoriously independent and sensitive to exercise of power. The major difference in the attitude of workers between Japan and the United States, for instance, is in the greater self-respect and sense of choice Japanese workers seem to enjoy, despite their subjugation to authority. This is in part because power in Japan is veiled. It is typically exercised along strict class and seniority lines. In part also, it arises because Japanese workers accept subjugation to authority more comfortably than do Americans. Acceptance of Japanese styled management by American workers is often positive because Japanese management operates with a few very consistent, strict rules and demonstrates greater sensitivity to the need for self-respect by their employees. The exercise of raw force to achieve a business end is rare among Japanese executives. Workers who are sensitive to the presence of authority have no greater love for Japanese bosses than for American ones. Those who wish only to be treated consistently and sensitively by their boss seldom seem to have any complaints about the Japanese style.

SUBSTITUTING MACHINERY FOR SKILL OR SKILL FOR MACHINERY

In the broader scheme of things, economic progress may go forward through investment in either more powerful machinery that requires minimal skill or increased skill that permits application of simpler, more versatile tools. The age of mass commodity production has been an age of low skilled labor working with expensive plant and machinery. Elemental skill that can be quickly verified or trained is the foundation of mass commodity output. Substituting labor with alternative labor or more advanced machinery is generally made easy by this operating strategy. The worker who withholds that limited level of skill is easily replaced.

Mass commodity production processes increase the power advantage of owners and managers in the skill-dependency power equation. The sole path of progress, however, is toward replacement of labor with increasingly more expensive and specialized machinery. Eventually, mass commodity production comes down to competition for the best engineering design, maintenance efficiency and sourcing of raw materials to produce the lowest cost, highest reliability product or service. Mass output system flexibility of response to market change is low. Vulnerability to innovation or to a massive shift in consumer taste is high. Once the age of mass production fades, the former advantages of continuous process mass output mutate into liabilities. In the coming of the age of the project shop, high skill with flexible tools is the strategy of choice. Skill must become the dominant factor.

THE ECONOMICS OF HIGH SKILL

Aside from loss of power advantage when high skilled labor is employed, the major argument against wholesale development of worker skill is cost— the cost of training and learning and the higher wage cost of more skilled workers. As the pendulum swings away from mass production, the conventional wisdom concerning wage cost shifts toward skilled workers being the better cost value. At a higher wage per hour cost, high skill is more likely to generate more and higher quality output per dollar of cost. Qualified, this can be an important management principle. Workers who have high self-respect and a sense of free choice in applying their labor can, if genuinely superior in skill, produce more of a better product per dollar of cost. It is a matter of management skill in providing the essential standards or setting a competitive wage level. A major shift in management perspective away from mass toward project shop strategy is required as a foundation to success with high skilled labor.

The cost of training is real and substantial. As such, it would appear to be a major barrier to developing worker skill at employer expense. On the contrary, the cost is incurred regardless and is frequently observed to be acceptable. Development of managerial talent, for instance, requires the high expense of a tuition refund for advanced study or travel to costly seminars or the extravagant price of rotational assignment to gain breadth of work exposure. When there is enough at stake, the high cost of learning is not so high after all.

The major cost of not developing worker skill arises out of the absence of self-respect and sense of free choice. The typical present day factory suffers from the hidden cost of scrap and rework, which is largely the result of skill withheld by workers. Estimates of these costs in the range of 25% of total cost reflect the expense of *not* developing worker skill. Training cost that results in genuinely increased worker skill has a large potential for reducing scrap and rework. The popular trend reflected by quality circles combined with assignment to workers of responsibility for quality maintenance reflects awareness of this cost improvement potential. Low skilled, minimally trained workers who approach work with a sense of powerlessness will avoid responsibility for the final product and withhold skill beyond the minimum expected. In a supervisor's parlance, "they don't use their heads." Why should they? They were hired as "hands," easily reprogrammed to simple tasks and readily replaceable if they get out of line. The absence of self-respect and sense of free choice makes wage vassals of them.

The Japanese, by overcoming most of the major psychological barriers that block worker commitment to production goals, have successfully rehabilitated mass commodity production to an earlier level of cost and quality effectiveness. The structural disadvantages of mass output remain, though, even in Japanese production operations. Progress is no less limited to improved machinery. Competition is still on the basis of best engineering design, efficient maintenance and low-cost material sourcing. The advantage shifts from one Third World economy to another with each passing year. The glowing twilight of mass production output systems can be discerned on the international economic horizon. The future is passing into the hands of the project shop.

A RENAISSANCE OF TOOL USAGE SKILLS

A good tool in the hands of a skilled user is a wonder to behold. The Asian merchant keeping accounts with an abacus is as remarkable to watch as an agile acrobat. There is a sense of purposeful flexibility in the whip of beads supplemented by mental shifts in the operator's mental context. A mistake when it occurs is an affront to both skill and esteem. The best blended qualities of human adaptiveness and mechanical exactitude are obtained in the symbiosis.

By contrast, a complex tool in the hands of the inexperienced may do harm. The ineptly read cell count in a powerful microscope, incorrect entry of data into the computer terminal or badly installed robot on the assembly line does more damage than good. The tool and its master must be parts of an integrated whole before their magic can be worked. The tool that is ill designed is destined to abandonment. The worker who is lazy or without purpose will never discover the tool's utility. To the master, a good tool is a valued friend and coworker. In the combination of user and instrument, skill generates synchrony, even harmony.

The secret of high quality (and quantity) of work output lies in the partnership of user and tool. There must be an opportunity for play and exploration in using the tool before mastery can come about. It makes no difference who holds title to the equipment; as often as not it will be the bank. Mastery requires free access and reasonable experimental use. With access there will be an opportunity for a passionate liaison to emerge.

The explosion of personal computer applications in the decade of the 1980s is the direct result of putting computer power into the hands of several thousands of hackers who thereupon created software of unparalleled power and quality. In the two decades preceding, dedicated computer users haunted the computer room in the dead of night to play and experiment without interruption. Wildy fanciful "dungeons and dragons" games reflect the playful exploration of computer firmware that emerges from intimate user/machine symbiosis. Present day computer users (including me) become wholly addicted to the power of the computer for computation and word processing uses. Returning to raw pencil and paper would be the equivalent of crossing the great plains in a covered wagon.

Every generation discovers the tools that enhance life. In earlier centuries it was the implements of seafaring that captured the imagination by conferring freedom and power. Guns are a perennial object of fascination if not the tool of choice for many thousands of people. Endless hours and rounds of ammunition are spent in their mastery. Abraham Lincoln must have spent long hours wielding his favorite ax and reading his favorite books. The locomotive on its tracks and telegraph key have enjoyed their day as power implements. Had Thomas Edison not cut his inventive teeth on them, the age of electricity might have been delayed. The automobile for a typical teenager is second skin and legs. Young mechanics master their trade maintaining an old car and practicing on the vehicles of friends. Becoming a qualified aviator is impossible without hundreds of hours of flying time. The purpose of flying is unimportant; only the time and experience of being at the flight controls count.

Tool mastery is a time consuming and sometimes costly investment. From the perspective of future performance capability, it is one of the best investments that can be made.

Mass commodity production discourages, even prevents, tool mastery. Typically, the production line itself is the tool. Workers are its tenders. They are more likely to learn how to sabotage and defeat the tool than to master it. For production supervisors the line is likely to be no better than a troublesome necessity. They must depend on it but have no time to learn its idiosyncrasies. The maintenance department, which has a minimal stake in production output, keeps it operating—after a fashion. A production engineering department with no accountability for operating goals designed and installed it. If it works right it is because someone, a maintenance engineer, a production supervisor or a manufacturing engineer, has developed a personal interest in the system as an integral tool. As a result, he or she spends countless hours tinkering and playing with it to learn its operating peculiarities. He or she is the *real* owner. As likely as not, ownership of the production system will reside nowhere. The result is that no one takes the trouble to master its use.

The fundamentals of mass output require that the machine structure and pace production activity. It is a policy that defeats tool mastery. It is unlikely that anyone will ever accept ownership of the whole tool and learn how to use it with skill. Truly efficient, effective mass flow production lines have generally been the work of one person or of a highly skilled team of experts. Often, they and they alone understand the tool they have created well enough to make it work right.

An inherent inefficiency of use is designed into the mass production process when this is the case. No one but the designer can understand the system. For the real machine designer, the thrill is in moving on to the next design, not in maintaining the last. Continuity of ownership is thereby discouraged. Perhaps the prospect of an automated factory with no human workers holds out the potential for one person or a small team to take ownership of the factory as an integrated tool. When the entire factory can be turned over to someone (or a team of someones) who has the opportunity to tinker and play with it at leisure, the potential for genuine tool mastery may be restored.

The best analog of team mastery of tools in the current economy resides in the maintenance of commercial aircraft. Teams of specialists train on a particular model of airplane with the assistance of designers and builders of the craft. These specialists, stationed at the airline's system hub, work continuously on the same or similar craft, following them, sometimes individually, over their lifespan. An intimate knowledge of the aircraft type and even of the peculiarities of individual planes is thereby achieved. Pilots supplement mechanics in their mastery of the machine in daily use. The best airlines have the most experienced, stable maintenance teams and flight crews.

The existence of hundreds of comparable, if not identical, airframe configurations combined with the imperative of flight safety creates conditions whereby mastery of this remarkable tool of transport is both necessary and feasible. In the age of the project shop it is an example to be emulated.

SKILL IN MASS PRODUCTION VERSUS PROJECT SHOP SYSTEMS

Mass commodity production systems, unfortunately, are subject to exploitation for near-term profit. Minimum maintenance, the quick fix of poor quality, narrowest specialization of labor to avoid training and strict quantity shipment goals milk the operation for maximum early payoff. If the basic system is soundly engineered, it can be driven at this pace for an extended period before breakdown is imminent. The illusion is thereby produced that training cost can be dispensed with, quality can be tacked on where needed and maintenance trivialized to the handyman level. Operating in this mode is frequently warmly celebrated as good, efficient management. It is no more nor less than milking the business. The concealed expense of diminished production capacity is eventually borne by owners and customers. It is absolutely the wrong model for product shop operations management.

The project shop must provide opportunity for playful exploration of tool capability. It must encourage and invest in skill development. Time and equipment must be allocated to employee growth in skill. Workers must have an opportunity to master as many different tools as they can. In traditional factory terms, this sounds like a grossly inefficient waste of time. But project shop work demands flexibility. Maximizing skill is the lowest cost path to maximizing flexibility. Time invested in tool mastery is never wasted.

The unpredictable work schedule of the project shop offers many opportunities to apply time toward tool experimentation and skill mastery.

Work flow is naturally uneven, irregular, feast or famine. Feast demands the continuous application of possessed skill to meet demand. Famine is an occasion to invest in growth. In the ebb and flow of natural economic demand cycles there is first one opportunity and then another when response is appropriately flexible. In mass commodity production there is work at a consistent, moderate pace or no work at all. Project shop work calls for a pace that matches the level of demand. Fall in demand is an occasion for skill growth and mastery.

A REVOLUTION IN TRAINING IS AT HAND

Programs and incentives for skill training already exist under a variety of state and federal laws. The precedent for government support of skill enhancement is well established. Most apply to training of the wholly unskilled. The era of the project shop only calls for extension and enhancement of these policies to workers at all levels.

Workers who would otherwise be on temporary or short-term layoff and eligible for unemployment compensation, for instance, might better be compensated for acquiring a new skill in their present employment. That would be an improvement over watching TV at home. It would certainly be preferable to working covertly for an unrecorded cash payment at routine or menial tasks. This would require changes in existing unemployment compensation laws that would take emerging project shop work values into realistic account.

Many employees would prefer to apply slack time to learning, even without pay. Wage-hour laws may need to be loosened to permit workers to apply their time voluntarily at their workplace enhancing work skill and mastering tool use when paid work is unavailable. The feast and famine flow of work that requires eighty hours of work one week and ten the next is ill served by the assumption of a standard forty-hour workweek. Specifying overtime for all hours over forty in a workweek is a convenient way to recognize that fringe benefit packages are loaded onto the first forty hours of work in a workweek. Indeed, the principal reason for requiring premium pay for time over forty hours in a workweek is to restore workers' wages to the full measure of value over those hours in which an employer bears no cost of fringe loading on base pay. Ways to accommodate overtime and fringe costs to project shop needs are discussed further in chapter 10.

The philosophical foundations of mass output compensation systems must be understood to appreciate their weaknesses and limitations as far as skill and human adaptivity are concerned. Henry Ford's world famous $5.00 a day wage for assembly line work made news for its time because it represented high pay for limited skill. Ford could not hire or keep his line manned without attractive pay. The mind-boggling sameness and simplicity of an assembly line required a payoff of sorts to offset the absence of interest in the

work. Operation of the line required a grasp of the entire production flow—
a preserve that Ford as chief engineer kept jealously to himself. Everyone else
was either a machine tender or a technical assistant to the chief engineer.
Ford drove the concept of mass commodity output to its logical limits and
established the precedent of paying for the bleak austerity of narrowly specialized jobs. The wage slavery of mechanically paced assembly line work led
inevitably to low self-respect, which was naturally offset by militant labor
union representation. A single powerful labor union that dominated the core of
the auto industry demanded yet higher wages for its wit-dulling, low skilled
work. Third World manufacturers with low skilled laborers eager for upward
economic mobility easily outcompeted Detroit in cost as a result.

The era of mass commodity production introduced undesirable policies
and practices into the way that managers think about worker compensation.
It is widely accepted that money can and should be used as a "motivator"
of high job performance. Unfortunately, it is a motivational theory that
becomes partially and mischievously self-fulfilling when it is applied. When
employees expect to receive extra pay for a better than average work effort,
they often reduce output when they don't see regular pay increments added
to their compensation. Regular, significant pay increases become the requisite of acceptable performance. To the average citizen, "average" does
not signify the midpoint of a normal distribution as it does for a statistician.
Average is a derogatory term. It has come to connote marginal or even poor
performance. In many quarters of industry, an advertised policy of pay-for-
performance has been corrupted into a system of bribery for merely acceptable performance. The project shop holds out the promise for remedy
of this distortion through honest compensation for full skill.

Carrying over the customs and principles of mass production compensation to project shop work would be the worst imaginable operating policy.
The project shop restores worker skill to its preassembly line level of importance. Tool mastery by every worker is central to rapid, flexible adaptation to changing and variable customer need. It is no longer necessary to
pay off workers for the absence of intrinsically interesting work. It is essential
only to pay them their fair market worth for skill applied. For more on that
theme, see chapter 10.

THE AGE OF FRAGMENTED SKILL AND IQ
MEASUREMENT

Compensation for applied skill must be the foundation of the project
shop. But most work is still poorly defined and only dimly recognized. The
elements of skill that make a real difference to a business are seldom known,
much less recognized and promoted. Fundamental work skills go untested,
unidentified and unacknowledged. Two factors in near history contribute
to a lack of attention or definition of skill. The first is the fragmentation

and trivialization of skill by continuous process mass production. The second is the dominance of verbal and intellectual skill in measuring human ability.

Mass commodity production processes bypass skill mastery in favor of simple, highly repetitive actions. Minimum physical strength and coordination are required. When the potential for a difference in strength or coordination exists, individual workers can undertake the job on a trial basis and rotate out or quit when it is difficult or uncomfortable. Trial and error on the work itself sorts out the most successful and unsuccessful skill fits in the mass output operation. Key technical skills like engineering problem solving or administrative control are spread across multiple staff or managerial positions allowing strength in ability to emerge by chance out of the pack. Fragmentation and trivialization of work responsibility in the elaborately organized commodity production operation assumes that every job can be accomplished with a minimum of narrow skill specialization. When the work calls for more than minimum ability, chance is relied on to supply someone from among the large numbers of specialists who will rise to the occasion.

From among a hundred assemblers, twenty supervisors and ten engineers the majority will stick to the narrow province of their assigned specialty. A handful, though, will possess the knowledge, interest and experience to see the source of a production problem and move individually or in ad hoc coalitions to resolve it. The formal organization structure makes no provision for extraordinary effort beyond the assigned job. Indeed, if an attempt to solve the problem fails, those who abandoned their assigned roles to wrestle with it may suffer penalty for their trouble. Success when it occurs may go unrecognized. When an unsolved problem is recognized by others outside the work group, an expert may be imported to solve it. In the formal structure of things, the work group is free to obstruct or cooperate with the expert. There is no guarantee that a problem will be addressed with appropriate skill and judgment. Mass commodity output is a populist phenomenon; everyone, regardless of skill or experience, is assumed to be equally competent to do the work. Experts, at workers' discretion, can be aided or sabotaged. The able compensate for the weak. Planned availability of skill mastery is presumed to be needlessly expensive and even unnecessary.

The ubiquitous IQ test alone stands as the universal arbiter of possessed skill. Differences in ability are more likely to be attributed to "smarts" or "brightness" than to something like skill with logic design or tool mastery. Measurement of human ability is dominated by tests of academic aptitude. Concept definitions and word associations along with basic mathematical functions constitute the core of IQ measurement. Performance tests are sometimes used to estimate IQ but are invariably validated against verbal and quantitative performance tests. In popular terms, *ability* is almost universally defined as a high level of skill in using words and numbers.

INTELLIGENCE TESTING AND SOCIAL STATUS

Challenges to intelligence testing as a measure of work ability were common in the midsixties. The source of these challenges was the efficiency with which such tests define blacks and non-English speaking workers as lacking intelligence and, by implication, work ability. The absence of a defensible connection between IQ and work ability was made embarrassingly clear by these challenges. Indeed, it was apparent in many situations that mere average intelligence was an asset to the typical commodity production worker. Those with severely limited IQ were sometimes more costly to train or lacked the middle-class social values of their coworkers. Those with too high an IQ, though, were often automatic troublemakers and misfits. IQ is perhaps more a measure of social status than it is of work ability.

In the hierarchical structuring of mass commodity production systems, status is useful to the extent that it predisposes those of lower status to accept direction and control from people of higher status. In strict terms of performance ability, nothing is more curious than the relationship between a new West Point second lieutenant and the seasoned twenty-year veteran top sergeant. The second lieutenant is rigorously trained in actions that accord with his status. If his judgment in crisis if faulty, the top sergeant may not overrule it on grounds of skill or experience without risking court martial.

A similar anomaly exists between the recent engineering graduate and the experienced production employee in industry. The young engineer by virtue of educational status may legitimately attempt to impose her solution on the experienced employee. The long service production employee can sometimes afford to object to the idea, or a strong labor union may embolden resistance. But the employee must be careful not to violate the status boundary excessively for fear of retaliation in the form of discipline or harassment. Status outranks skill in the hierarchy of mass commodity output systems. Skill is, by design, fragmented and diffused so that the system will not be overly dependent on it. Skill testing in industry has more to do with social status and social adjustment than with performance capability.

ALTERNATIVE SKILL MEASURES

Although it is indisputable that formal tests of verbal-quantitative fluency dominate testing technology, there are many significant beachheads of success with other kinds of skill testing. Tests of speed and accuracy of hand movement—manual dexterity—are available to help identify those with good finger/hand coordination. Such coordination is often only a matter of practice, though, and may not identify applicants with good potential for the work. Training or practice cost may be cited as sufficient reason for being unwilling to invest in potential, though, and only those already quick of digit may pass the test to become employed.

Keyboard skill, spelling accuracy, knowledge of grammar, and clerical checking speed can be measured with clerks, typists or secretaries. The relative low status of these jobs in comparison to importance of skill raises the importance of skill assessment to unusually high levels here.

To cite several examples, useful measures exist of spatial visualization, logical thinking, coding and visual field independence capabilities. Simulations of social settings can be used to measure social judgment, interpersonal sensitivity and social influence capability. Tests of specific technical knowledge, as for instance in electronics, economics or accounting, are available through which to verify training or experience. See Figures 9–1A, 9–1B and 9–1C for examples of these measurement instruments.

The era of the project shop offers an opportunity to apply skill testing technology in wholly new ways to the measurement of job skill. The easiest approach is simply to sample real job activities and build a test around them. Have the candidate for head chef prepare one or two typical menu items. Ask the applicant for the engineering design job to do a simple design. Require the prospective designer to create the design documentation from rough specifications on a computer aided design (CAD) system.

When experience is available in the labor market, carefully constructed, representative work samples permit direct measurement of skill and knowledge. When it is not, aptitude tests must be sought. Measures of aptitude assume the presence of a fundamental, underlying skill that is a foundation to future performance. Reversion to IQ testing is the major hazard with aptitude. IQ may be relevant when verbal communication skill or basic math are themselves fundamental. If not, it is an assessment dead end that must be avoided in the project shop.

The most critical aptitudes in the project shop will be those that support basic working tools. Work with machine tools generally requires strong spatial visualization—initially in two dimensions, later in three. Several good paper and pencil tests of two dimensional space imagery exist. None is available yet in three. Most product design requires three dimensional aptitude. Measuring it is important but difficult.

Plastics or surfacing of materials requires an understanding of chemistry and physics as basic. It moves up to mastery of materials characteristics. Textiles are nearly as complex in physical quality and may demand an aptitude for understanding material performance under tension or stress. Food preparation of all kinds is based on an aptitude for chemical phenomena.

Job circumstances that require social coordination or influence require listening aptitude, empathic openness and understanding of social structure. Supervisors seldom successfully develop human relations skills if they lack these foundation abilities.

Figure 9-1A
Tests of Nonverbal Intelligence

STORAGE TEST

In this test you will be asked to plan how objects can be stored in a given space. You will be asked to think of as many different ways as possible to arrange the objects in this space.

How many different ways can 4 boxes, like the one on the left below, be stored in the container shown on the right? The numbers on the sides of the figures and the dotted lines are to help you compare sizes.

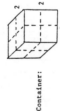

Box:

Container:

The drawings below show three correct solutions to this problem. Note that drawings (1) and (2) use the same rule. The rule is that all of the square ends of the boxes are on the same face of the cube. Drawing (3) uses a different rule.

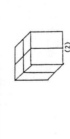

(1)   (2)   (3)

Your score on this test will be:

2 points credit for each drawing which shows a new rule;
1 point credit for each drawing which is not exactly the same as earlier drawings but which uses the same rule.

You will have 3 minutes for each of the two parts of this test. Each part has one page. When you have finished Part 1, STOP. Please do not go on to Part 2 until asked to do so.

DO NOT TURN THIS PAGE UNTIL ASKED TO DO SO.

BUILDING MEMORY

This is a test of your ability to remember the position of things on a street map.

You will be given a map with streets and buildings and other structures to study. After you have had some time to learn the street layout and the different kinds of structures, you will be asked to turn to a test page. On that page you will find the street map and numbered pictures of some of the structures. You will be asked to put an x on the letter that shows where each of the structures was located on the study map.

Now look at this simple and enlarged sample:

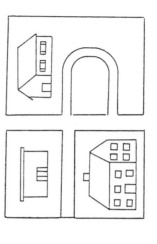

After you have studied the sample above for a minute, turn to the next page.

From Kit of Factor-Referenced Cognitive Tests, Educational Testing Service, Princeton, N.J. Reprinted by permission of Educational Testing Service, the copyright owner.

Figure 9-1B
Tests of Nonverbal Intelligence

PICTURE-NUMBER TEST

This is a test of your ability to learn picture-number combinations. In each part of the test you will study a page of 21 pictures with numbers. After studying the page showing both pictures and numbers, you will turn to a page showing the pictures in a different order. You will be asked to write down the numbers that go with them.

Here are some practice pictures with numbers. Study them until you are told to turn to the next page (1 minute).

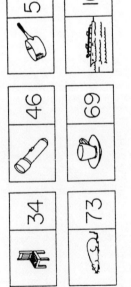

DO NOT TURN THIS PAGE UNTIL ASKED TO DO SO.

HIDDEN FIGURES TEST

This is a test of your ability to tell which one of five simple figures can be found in a more complex pattern. At the top of each page in this test are five simple figures lettered A, B, C, D, and E. Beneath each row of figures is a page of patterns. Each pattern has a row of letters beneath it. Indicate your answer by putting an X through the letter of the figure which you find in the pattern.

NOTE: There is only one of these figures in each pattern, and this figure will always be right side up and exactly the same size as one of the five lettered figures.

Now try these 2 examples.

A   B   C   D   E

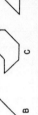 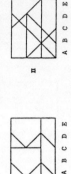

  I   II

A B C D E   A B C D E

The figures below show how the figures are included in the problems. Figure A is in the first problem and figure D in the second.

  I   II

X B C D E   A B C X E

Your score on this test will be the number marked correctly minus a fraction of the number marked incorrectly. Therefore, it will not be to your advantage to guess unless you are able to eliminate one or more of the answer choices as wrong.

You will have 12 minutes for each of the two parts of this test. Each part has 2 pages. When you have finished Part 1, STOP. Please do not go on to Part 2 until you are asked to do so.

DO NOT TURN THIS PAGE UNTIL ASKED TO DO SO.

From Kit of Factor-Referenced Cognitive Tests, Educational Testing Service, Princeton, N.J. Reprinted by permission of Educational Testing Service, the copyright owner.

186

Figure 9–1C
Testing Alternatives to IQ Measures

X. PAPER FORM BOARD

In each problem, think of the figures in the upper section as the pieces of a jigsaw puzzle. They can be slid around, but they *cannot* be turned over. If you slide them around, they will fit together to make one of the four figures, A or B or C or D, below. PRINT the CAPITAL LETTER of that figure in the upper right corner. EXAMPLES (with correct answers):

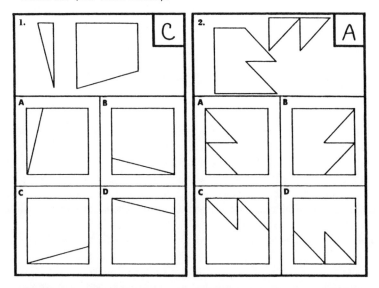

Mark an answer for every problem. If you don't know the answer to a problem, make the best choice you can.

VI. MECHANICAL COMPREHENSION

Each problem consists of a picture with a question under it. PRINT the CAPITAL LETTER of the correct answer in the box at the right of the question. EXAMPLES (with correct answers):

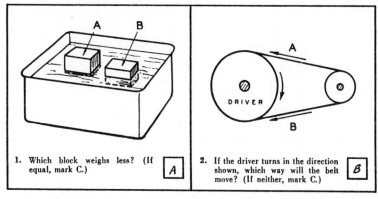

If you don't know the answer to a question, make the best choice you can. Leave it blank only if you have no hunch whatever about any of the answers.

Figure 9–1C (continued)

IX. CHECKING

Each problem consists of a pair of names or a pair of numbers. If they are *exactly* the same, PRINT a CAPITAL S on the line between them. If they are different in any way, PRINT a CAPITAL D on the line between them. EXAMPLES (correctly marked):

1. 80172 __D__ 80192

2. Jones Co. Ltd. __S__ Jones Co. Ltd.

3. 314250 __S__ 314250

4. Paul L. Kelley __D__ Paul L. Kelly

Reproduced by Permission of the Author, Dr. Edward E. Cureton

Technical problem solving in the present age demands an aptitude for computer based problem solving logic (programming languages for instance) and a grasp of the disciplines of experimental science. Many college graduates can give impressive lip service to the values of science without aptitude or appreciation for the disciplines of experimental testing. Even the practice of courtroom law increasingly demands appreciation of the discipline of logical truth testing, which underlies the rules of evidence. Those few tests of logical hypothesis testing applied are rudimentary but fundamental to justice.

Job analysis in commodity production settings has gone only skin deep into the work. Given the shallowness of skill demanded, that was usually appropriate. Job analysis in the project shop can and must go to levels of requisite skill and underlying foundation aptitudes that are considerably more substantial. This requires that the task of job analysis itself take on added dimensions of skill. Knowing how to test and identify underlying work aptitudes will certainly be one of them. Constructing measures of those aptitudes may well be another.

Skill is the foundation of the project shop. Status presently diminishes the importance of skill and will continue to do so until skill is raised in importance and priority. Skill mastery is the surest source of job satisfaction and work involvement. Consistent compensation of skill for its market value is the foundation of equity and fairness. But status must take a back seat to skill before skill compensation can fully occur.

The project shop era promises a revolution in the relationship of worker to work and to the tools of work. It is a revolution that has long been foretold and awaited. For the revolution to effect meaningful change, the old methods and principles of the mass commodity process must be replaced by an opportunity for choice, by learning and skill mastery, by compensation for skill and by realistic assessment of skill capability. Those changes have the potential for massive change in the ways of work life in America.

10

COMPENSATION AND REWARD SYSTEMS FOR THE PROJECT SHOP

"Pay for anything other than skill and risk is a waste."

Opinion pollsters know that when they inquire about sexual practices of the average citizen, they will usually obtain willing and comprehensive answers. Change the subject to job pay and earnings, though, and the door is likely to be shut in their faces. Few issues are as sensitive as that of one's income.

PAY IS A PERSONAL ISSUE

A variety of reasons can be called on to account for the ticklishness of pay as a subject for discussion. Some people who hide their income are fearful that the IRS or creditors will discover their secret. Others pretend to make more than they actually do to obtain increased status or credit. Some do both at the same time with different audiences. Especially as compared to earnings of friends or relatives, wages earned are seen as a measure of one's personal success, even one's value as a human being.

Earnings can be a competitive issue. One who measures his or her skill and ability as equal with another is likely to experience severe upset to discover that the other is paid higher. Openly comparing pay levels can put serious stress on a relationship. Many have learned to avoid the subject just to preserve their own peace of mind.

Talking about one's pay, thus, is not likely to be comfortable, even under favorable circumstances. Work cultures vary in the degree of confidentiality to openness that characterizes information about pay and pay systems. Civil service is notably open on matters of pay bases and practices. Real pay, though, includes significant perqs and overtime that may create huge differences in pay for people at the same level of classification. Middle management pay in private industry is highly secretive. Individuals with exactly the same title or level of responsibility can differ by a factor of two or more in their pay depending on work history and other special factors. Those who know they enjoy an advantage are not likely to talk about it. Those who fear they suffer a disadvantage may prefer not to confront the discrepancy. The suspicion always lingers that anyone who professes to tell all about his or her income is distorting the facts for effect.

BUT DETAILED INFORMATION IS WIDELY AVAILABLE

Management of compensation systems is a fairly systematic art. Compensation data are widely gathered at all levels of business. Top officers of publicly traded corporations must report real income in their Securities Exchange Commission (SEC) filings. This becomes publicly available knowledge to anyone who wishes to search it out. Industry associations and private firms conduct pay or salary surveys on a confidential basis, summarize their findings and either give it back to members or sell it on the open market. University faculty, notorious for their curiosity and unsecretiveness, insist on full disclosure of their colleagues' pay by administrators. Data are accumulated and summarized for all to see in the American Association of University Professors' national publication *Academe*. But medical doctors vigorously fight any attempt at income disclosure. Fee schedules are widely available for specific medical procedures, but disclosure of income by doctors is carefully avoided. Nevertheless, hospitals exchange information extensively about pay for the salaried medical staff.

Anywhere that work is organized, pay information and schedules are published for reference by those who make pay decisions. Equity of pay is a matter of comparison between those with equivalent skill or experience. Individuals compare their pay by asking close friends what they make or by answering want ads and finding out what pay is offered. They look at the standard of living of others with similar work or skill and make inferences about their paychecks. Between organizations, comparison is easy and accurate. General managers, human resource managers, compensation managers, can simply talk with their counterparts at association meetings or on the telephone to compare jobs. Almost every industry has its pay or salary survey data sources. Information on average pay and range of pay for industry or a specific occupation is not hard to get. When positions and working conditions are comparable, pay is likely to be comparable. If pay is low for the position or industry, skill and experience are likely to migrate to centers of higher pay. If it is high, it is likely to create a competitive cost disadvantage reflected in the company's prices.

THE LABOR MARKET DOMINATES PAY RATES

The court of last resort in setting pay is the labor market. Like any market, the labor market is subject to its ups and downs and occasionally even produces weird anomalies in the way of isolated high or low prices. On the average, though, it soundly and reliably establishes the level of pay that must be met to keep good workers without becoming uncompetitive in price. The expectations or negotiating skill of the individual worker may result in small differences in the rate of pay, though rarely more than 20% from comparable jobs. When individual assertiveness translates into higher energy and output on the job, such differences may be entirely defensible. For individuals in the same work with the same skill and experience, it is reasonable to expect individual differences in performance. Individual pay can and should reflect both equity in the worth of skill or experience on the labor market and individual differences in worker energy or ambition. But the balance must be carefully struck.

THE ILLUSION OF MOTIVATION FROM MERIT PAY

The principal hazard in setting pay arises out of straying too far from the market rate for skill and experience. During the past half century a variety of systems have been proposed and tried that purport to motivate higher output through higher pay. Supposedly, pay can be matched directly with output to elicit the best worker effort without incurring a higher cost of production. Merit pay and incentive pay systems have been the most common movement in this direction. In the widespread attempt to implement them, serious weaknesses have been uncovered.

Merit pay is intended to scale up pay in percentage increments to reflect "improved performance" or a "sustained higher than average" work contribution. The heyday of merit pay occurred in the decade of the 1960s, which was simultaneously the high point of wage-price inflation in the United States. Inflation running at a 10% + rate added to skill and productivity improvement averaging 3% to 6% per year resulted in rapidly escalating dollars of pay. Because interest rates were low (limited by law) and home ownership among workers widespread, it was an escalation that produced real gains by permitting old, low interest rate mortgages to be paid off with inflated, cheap dollars. Young workers entering the labor market who did not yet own property barely kept even in their purchasing power in spite of 12% to 15% "merit" increases. Older workers who owned real estate saw dramatic gains in their financial status. At best, merit pay was a blend of illusion and benefit dependent on large annual dollar increases combined with real increases in worker-homeowner wealth produced by the combination of low interest rates and high inflation.

Historically, real interest rates (adjusted for inflation) had run around

4% to 5%. Productivity increases hovered around 3% to 4% per year before midcentury. Return on capital, thus, was close to equivalance with return on investment in skill. The sixties disrupted that balance. In doing so, it created expectations for rapid wage escalation and a real increase in worker wealth. The increase in wealth experienced was the result of a redistribution of wealth brought about by the discrepancy between interest and inflation rates. When it ended, worker expectations were bound to be disappointed.

The only real justification for merit pay increases is in higher work output by workers. This comes down to an attempt to tie pay directly to level of output. When the tie is not made directly to output through an incentive pay system, it can only be successful if substantial pay increments are periodically (annually as a rule) available to give the appearance of a reward. The average worker has minimal sense of any change in income when the increase is less than 10% (the classic threshold of perceptual discrimination). A 3% or 4% increment has little or no effect; it may even be seen as an insult to some workers. Rates in the 6% to 8% range are dependent on a summation of productivity and inflation for economic justification. Variable interest rates have corrected the old discrepancy between inflation and interest rates. Merit pay is now wholly an illusion that would disappear if inflation dropped near zero.

Inherently, there is no economic reason for pay to be linked with level of work output. Worker perception of pay equity is a function of pay comparison. It is an entirely different matter to want more pay than it is to believe one is underpaid for the market worth of his or her work. When there is concern that higher output will result in revision of the incentive rate, workers who are put on an incentive system will set and enforce a maximum level of pay and output that is satisfactory to the majority. On the other hand, normal, virtually inevitable increases in productivity that result from new methods, new machinery, new material and augmented worker skill demand regular adjustments in that incentive rate. If the rate is kept sound, there is no way to avoid regular—often annual—adjustments to redistribute equitably the natural and expected gains of productivity between capital and labor. In the absence of those adjustments, all of the gains go to labor. Incentive pay without regular rate adjustments can raise pay excessively above the going market rate for comparable skill and experience. An overpaid worker has absolutely no reason to want to test the going rate in the market. He or she will simply demand employer adherence to the original bargain of above average pay for above average output. Demonstrating to the worker that incentive pay is out of line with the market may be very difficult.

QUANTITY VERSUS QUALITY

Another equally serious problem is raised with incentive pay. Pay is based fundamentally on a count of output—quantity is crucial. An easy way to increase pay is to slight the quality of work. If quality is not easily maintained, or if poor quality can be hidden or disguised, incentive pay invites the trade-off of reduced quality for increased pay.

Indeed, any quantity oriented production system, which includes just about every commodity mass production system, suffers in quality because of the emphasis on quantity of output. The message of continuous flow production as well as the message of incentive pay is that quantity comes first. Management may exhort and preach as much as it wants. Until there are exact controls on quality that match those on quantity, the system itself undermines quality. When quality is highly visible or otherwise easy to maintain, incentive pay has a place. When it is not, incentive pay will readily turn into an abomination. If incentive pay were universally safe and successful, it would be universally employed. The domination of hourly wage rates throughout industry exists for sound reasons. Too often, incentives don't work. Occasionally, they turn into a nightmare.

DOES PAY REALLY MOTIVATE?

There is no inherent reason for pay to be linked to work output. When the attempt to make the linkage occurs, pay must also be linked precisely and reliably to quality. Once the pay/output linkage is made by management, it will be made by workers. Workers expect, then, to be paid proportionate to their measured output. Perception of low pay will result in a withholding of effort and, often, a real drop in output. If the incentive rate itself is adjusted, output can fall, regardless of the equity of pay compared with the outside labor market. The literal bargain between workers and management is pay for output. Unless it is regularly renegotiated, it can become an excessively favorable bargain for labor over the long run. The economically naive manager who attempts to drive production with the carrot on a stick finds that nothing moves at all when the carrot is taken away.

Most workers work for a fair living wage at the best job they can find. A good job is a function of wages, working conditions, tools, friendships, high self-esteem, challenge and opportunity to enact personal purpose. Jobs that lack any of these qualities in significant degree must often pay more to hold competent workers. Jobs that exhibit them often attract good workers at less pay. Making pay the totality and sum of worker motivation puts more of a load on money as a control and motivator of performance than it can reasonably carry. For the truly ambitious or greedy, money is the central measure of success. Their attempts to motivate others on the same foundation are likely to founder and fail. Using pay alone as the primary driver of performance is a serious mistake based on too limited a personal set of work values.

A subtler use of pay to drive performance arises out of scale gradations of pay rate up the organizational hierarchy. The assembler or technician earns less then his or her manager because the manager feels that anything else would be inequitable. When the job of the manager calls for clearly higher skill or knowledge than the worker has, the difference is justified. When a manager takes greater risks and faces greater insecurity and threat of loss than the worker, the difference is obviously justified.

PAY FOR SKILL VERSUS PAY FOR RISK

One scholar (Jaques, 1961) has proposed that hierarchical levels of pay should be based on a time span of discretion in decision making. This is the equivalent of saying that anyone who is in a position to make more or bigger mistakes must be paid more. The justification for higher pay with a longer time span of decision-making discretion is ambiguous, though. Does the manager who could make more expensive mistakes require more pay to account for greater decision-making skill, or does he or she need higher pay so that fear of loss of employment from a bad decision is heightened, thereby increasing caution? Depending on the industry and business culture, it could work both ways. The former is higher pay for higher skill, the later higher pay for greater risk. The better strategy would certainly appear to be one of ensuring the presence of decision-making skill. The bad decision is a cost not only to the decision maker but to the business and everyone in it.

Management decision-making skill, though, is difficult to teach, hard to verify and tricky to test. Good managers sometimes make bad decisions. Developing (the euphemism for training) managers to be good decision makers sometimes seems to come about faster and more efficiently by letting them make mistakes. The bad decision is seen as an investment in managerial growth. The story is told of the very successful manager who was asked the secret of his success. He replied, "sound decisions." How did he learn to make sound decisions? "Experience," he replied. Whence came the experience? "Bad decisions," he retorted. The story always ends here accompanied by a chorus of appreciative laughter from experienced managers. No one ever goes on to ask how he won the opportunity to make bad decisions without penalty. What would the answer be? "It was my father's business!" Or, "I successfully covered them up." Or, "I was lucky they were never serious and I could learn from them without being fired!" The logical transfer of the humor to flying an aircraft might be, "I became a good pilot by crashing airplanes."

The inevitability of mistakes on the part of the business decision maker has introduced a wholly new dimension to pay; the decision maker is partially insulated by status from blame for his or her mistakes. Those admitted to the councils of business decision making are chosen with the expectation that their appointment is an investment in learning how to make decisions. In attempting to appoint those who will make fewer, less costly mistakes, high starting pay is introduced as a hiring inducement for the more apt. The more apt are assumed to be the most intelligent and best educated. In family businesses they may also be blood relatives. Unfortunately, there is no evidence whatever to demonstrate that IQ, a college degree or genetic relationship improves management decision-making aptitude in the least. Nevertheless, higher pay with the assumption of the right to make some bad decisions creates a status differential in the pay structure that sharply increases pay without improving cost or ensuring better management decision making.

High pay for unskilled decision makers is patently unnecessary. But the opportunity to learn from mistakes is not necessarily and always a mistake. By tradition and largely due to the wisdom of J. C. Penney, entry into retail management training often requires starting at a fixed pay rate below that of regular sales personnel. Lower pay on this special progression path is justified by the expectation of bad decisions on the part of neophyte managers and the requirement that new managers will be chosen competitively and only from among those who learn by following this route. Special status in retail management training does not equate with higher initial pay but does confer an opportunity to learn from mistakes and does mean higher pay later when skill has been demonstrated. Lower entry pay tests the level of motivation for following the management track and learning to make good decisions.

The prevalence of nepotism in family business is unlikely to change. Fathers foolishly think that awarding special status and protection to a son or daughter will improve the quality of the decisions made. Dad wishes someone had been there to shield him when he was starting out and fails to see the value of the agony he endured from learning in its absence. Overprotected offspring in family businesses are seldom prepared to meet a real business crisis. They don't discover the sinking sensation that goes with impending doom until it is upon them.

A century ago, only lawyers, ministers, doctors and the children of the rich went to college. Fraternities and secret societies in college created special relationships that lasted a lifetime. The sons of the wealthy were expected to attend college, to make their lifetime alliances and friendships and to enter the family business in the company of their trusted college cronies. Many of the excesses of business arose out of the special status of business tycoons' sons and their friends. Politics, finance and law were bent to fit the weaknesses of the wealthy and their children. Fortunately for our democratic traditions, entry into military academies largely escaped this nepotistic heritage.

Continuing to choose future managers largely on the basis of status conferred by a college degree is merely a continuation of a long standing aristocratic tradition. It offers no better assurance of superior future management decision making than random selection might. It raises salary cost without increase in skill or exposure to risk. It is a burden on business cost that is unnecessary and indefensible.

There are two very sound reasons for variability of pay: skill and exposure to risk—either personal or business risk. There are two traditional but treacherous grounds on which to base pay: amount of output or "merit" and special status conferred by possession of a college diploma or special relationship that permits entry into a management trainee positions. Nepotism will continue until tighter tax constraints are put on pay in excess of market justification given to blood relatives but will never be fully halted even by that. If more stockholders brought suit against trainee managers who are overpaid and make poor decisions, realism might enter that domain. In the project shop, the focus should, indeed, must come to be exclusively on pay for skill and exposure to risk.

REVOLUTIONIZING PAY SYSTEMS FOR THE PROJECT SHOP

Compensation for skill sounds simple and natural. It would seem that pay for possessed skill ought to be the way it is normally done. In an earlier, simpler age that was true. But the domination of commodity production that requires fragmented, narrow skill at each workstation distorts approaches to pay. Skill is less important than mechanical efficiency. Control of production flow is a higher priority than tool mastery. Pay must support consistent exercise of low or shallow skill when interest in the work itself is minimal. Merit pay, incentive pay, indeed, performance based pay of every kind, have been introduced to *motivate* increased work effort and involvement in mass production systems. A large element of pay has come to represent recompense for the lack of meaning or distastefulness of the work itself. Existing pay rates and systems are heavily laced with motivational factors and purposes. Standard jobs that serve as reference points for setting labor market pay rates are shaped by the needs of mass commodity production work. Pay for skill becomes inextricably mixed with pay to motivate workers and to overcome their distinterest in work.

Pay systems in their most carefully developed form are constructed around so-called compensable factors. Along with factors like skill, education, experience, knowledge and physical strength, these systems look at personal qualities like accuracy, ingenuity, initiative, attention to detail, concentration, conscientiousness of effort and cooperativeness, treating them as of equivalent importance. It would seem that a truly skilled worker would naturally exhibit all of these qualities. The intrinsic power and purpose of a skill that is based on genuine tool mastery should easily encompass such personal, work enhancing values. On the contrary, because mass output jobs lack a real skill component, these factors carry considerable weight in determining the pay worth of a job.

The status element that arises out of the control imperatives of organization hierarchy further dilutes the skill factor. The exact same skill at different levels of organization carries with it an entirely different pay. The skilled typist at entry is paid a fraction of the executive secretary's compensation. The brilliant young programmer/computer hacker may work for entry-level pay while the experienced systems analyst draws ten times that amount. Combinations or sets of skill and experience can partially account for that difference. A proven track record of skill application is worth more than the skill alone. But status nonetheless contributes greatly to the disparity. Motivational and status factors are so thoroughly comingled with skill that it is often impossible to separate them out.

In the project shop, hierarchy and status are largely a function of skill and experience. Compensating both is likely to be redundant and, thus, wasteful. Motivation arises out of skill and tool mastery honestly compensated. Flexibility of skill and experience is fundamental to project shop success. The compensation system must be substantially revised to reflect the primacy of skill and experience in support of project shop requirements.

Isolated islands of work experience stand to support this point. Major corporation R&D operations most commonly illustrate the power of pure, applied skill to bring excitement and purpose to work. Hewlett Packard and Polaroid in the decade of the 1970s exemplified it. Many small, growing high-tech operations, like those in the computer industry, have captured the spirit. These operations further exhibit the ability to hold exceptional talent with average wages. It is not necessary to pay a premium to keep employees from going to the competition. The most ambitious will probably pass up proffered modest increments of added salary from the competition in favor of following an entrepreneurial path anyhow. They are either content to be paid for their skill or ready to accept the added risk that goes with the big payoff.

Compensating project shop skill and experience requires that preexisting notions of proper pay be sharply challenged. Identifiable, measurable, tangible skill and experience that directly contribute to business success must become the standard basis of pay. In the beginning, jobs that include the needed skill and experience will be the reference point for pay. Ultimately, a much revised system of compensation that focuses strictly on skill and experience, singularly and in variable combinations, will be required.

The foundation of skill based pay systems will be the worth of the most valuable skill possessed. The going labor market rate for that skill will set the base. As other, work relevant skills are added and demonstrated in the worker's repertoire a percentage will be added, even when they are lesser valued skills. The value of added skills will necessarily be determined by their relative rarity in the labor market and significance to the business. Even low paid skills that are business relevant will merit added pay. A high paid skill possessed but uncalled for in the business is essentially worthless.

Figure 10–1
Trade-off Calculation of Consulting Fees versus Pay for Skill Availability In-House

```
HOURLY EQUIVALENT COST OF CONSULTANT TIME:

Consulting fee for special skill = $750 per day

     Skill is required 15 days per year
          15 x $750 = $11,250

Average Hours worked per year per employee =
                  1920


     $11,250/1920 = 5.86 per hour


   HOURLY COST OF A 20% PAY INCREMENT

Worth of skill assuming pay is $16.00 per hour
      plus a 40% benefits loading:

 20% increment for skill   $3.20 per hour +
     + 40% benefits load   1.28 benefits

TOTAL COST OF SKILL              4.48 per hour to
                                      maintain
               skill
                                 in house
```

A rare, high-cost skill that is needed by the business might add as much as a third or more in pay to the existing rate. The difference between compensation base (the rate of the most valuable skill) and the per unit time cost of an independent consultant specialist who temporarily supplies the skill can suggest the appropriate added skill differential. When the added skill is put to use at least 10% of the possessor's working time and it costs three times his or her rate to hire a temporary specialist, a 20% skill adder would be economical. Figure 10–1 illustrates this calculation.

When the skill is in abundance, the increment added for a second skill must be in proportion to the value of its presence for purposes of labor time scheduling efficiency. Heavy use by the project shop of a widely possessed skill raises the value of its possession in scheduling flexibility. The shop that must adjust rapidly to change of need for a range of skills can work with a smaller labor base when many employees have multiple transferable skills. Figure 10–2 shows how this might work. Based on a reduction in slack labor in the work schedule, the value of the added skill for any three workers is set at about 5%.

Payment for possession of skill could add from 5% in some cases to 35% in others depending on the economic justification found in skill flexibility.

Figure 10–2
Estimation of Savings in Lost Slack Labor

```
If 3% of slack labor is saved by addition of one key skill
to the skills bank for three workers, and the total payroll
is $100,000 per year, then:


The value of the skill is $1000 per worker

$1000/1920 normal hours per year is $0.52 per hour

At average hourly rate of $10.00, this is a 5.2%
increment in pay
```

Summed pay for the multiskilled project shop worker could conceivably double with the demonstration of multiple supplemental skills.

COMPENSATION FOR RISK

Payment for work risk calls for other new compensation practices. Risk for the wage laborer arises from two sources: the potential for injury or disease inherent in the work or workplace and obsolescence of skill or experience. Wage earners endure little or no risk of nonpayment of wages. Wage-hour laws substantially ensure that back wages will be paid under even the most adverse business circumstances. Workers are almost never cheated out of their earned wage. Some potential still remains for injury or disease stemming from the job, but obsolescence of highly specialized skill occurs with increasing frequency as technology evolves.

Adequate recompense for physically dangerous work is, perhaps, a contradiction in terms. There is no such thing as enough pay for risking one's life. Historically, the poor and unskilled who had nothing else to offer could make a living wage by accepting high risk work. Miners, construction workers, race car drivers, aviators, soldiers, police officers, firefighters, all work and live at high risk in return for a secure living wage. Some of them actively seek out high risk employment by choice. An astonishingly large part of the population today embraces the risk of high speed driving, smoking tobacco or casual use of drugs. Taking risk excites and energizes, especially when one is otherwise secure and bored.

Risk from exposure to nuclear radiation or carcinogenic chemicals, from injury when machinery falls or from freak accidents of any kind is a problem for workers for whom the risk is hidden, unforeseen or imposed without choice. Remedy through civil court action is the simplest solution to these risks when the risk is imposed without choice or knowledge. Otherwise, risk of this kind, which is fully revealed to and accepted by a worker, must be accounted for in the wage rate for the job. The labor market determines what the cost of undertaking a known risk should be. In this enlightened age, the cost of these risks is spread over a large population of risk takers in the form of life and health insurance. A large part of so-called fringe benefit packages was originally instituted as a humane, economically sensible answer to the dealing with the risks and tragedies of dangerous work.

Physical risk on the job can only be recompensed through full disclosure of the actual risk accompanied by pay and benefits that are acceptable to the risk taker. The acceptable range of compensation will vary substantially. Some workers seek out risk for its stimulation. Some types of risk offer compensating rewards; the police officer who carries a gun may feel more secure thus armed than he would in a "safe" job that prohibits possession of a weapon. Indians of the Iroquois and Micmac tribes enter the high rise construction trade to act out a cultural norm of exhibiting exceptional bravery in their work. Race car drivers know and revel in the risk of injury or death in their profession. All earn a good living wage for their exposure to peril; some earn exceptional pay for surviving exceptional exploits. All risk life and limb in their work by choice.

Risk can never be completely ruled out in the workplace. It is only a matter of whether the odds of accident are one in a million, one in a thousand or one in a hundred. Acceptable pay and benefits are established by the interplay of individual temperament and the odds of injury. It is a cultural issue that is worked out in the labor market.

COMPENSATION FOR OBSOLESCENCE POTENTIAL

The greater fear, even among macho risk seekers, is likely to be the obsolescence of their skill and work. The investment required to acquire a skill is lost when demand for its application disappears. One's value as a contributor of economic worth plummets. Loss of career identity diminishes self-worth and self-esteem. The psychological impact of skill obsolescence is, in many ways, more cruel than physical injury.

Large segments of the working population have been rendered without income for their acquired skill by recent changes in technology and the world economy. Most were the possessors of a narrow, specialized skill suited only to a specific industry or type of commodity production process. Steelworkers and auto assembly line employees found their economic worth cut by half or more through the obsolescence of their jobs. In retrospect, the high wages paid to narrowly skilled producers of commodity output were probably merited by the risk of obsolescence of their skill. Had these workers fully appreciated the risk of skill obsolescence, they might well have demanded higher pay than they did. Skill that has little transferability is a near certain dead end for the worker. It must be liberally compensated—often at rates 50% to 200% above market value for unskilled labor—to account for the risk of its obsolescence. The value of such work is determined by the lost opportunity for development of a transferable skill and the probable cost of retraining when the job is terminated. Generally, it must be compensated at a rate equivalent to the rate for skills that could otherwise reasonably have been acquired. If provisions do not exist for retraining, the rate should be 50% to 100% higher yet.

Transferable skill is the stock in trade of the project shop. The compensation system need not be built around the nontransferability of work skill. But the problem of unique skill appears on a different level here. Project shop work requires variety and flexibility of skill, some of which may be in wide demand across the labor market, other of which may be unique to the specific business. Wide demand for skill sets an objectively measurable level of pay that reflects supply and demand. This is the base below which a rational worker will quit for higher pay elsewhere. Acquisition of added skill increases his or her value incrementally to a level where the value of flexible skill application to work at hand makes it economically worthwhile to make finding higher pay elsewhere less likely. The increment should not be great enough to make seeking other employment impossible. That closes off a worker's choice by locking him or her into the job. When the combination of skill is sufficiently broad or unique to have no possible match outside in the open labor market, it must be rewarded appropriately with a bonus supplement to base pay. This worker shares in the fortunes of the business fully and should be recompensed as if he or she were a part owner. The appropriate way to do this is through some form of ownership or other profit sharing device that ties the benefits of a unique skill mix to the business success and long-term earnings.

PAY IN THE JOB SHOP

The base level of pay for possession of a unique set of business-specific skills will largely depend on the market worth for the two or three most valuable and transferable skills possessed. When the employee chooses to develop a new skill, pay will reflect its value in an increment that reflects the skill's added economic value to the business. When the employer underwrites mastery of the skill by paying for time, skill or tools needed to develop it, he may reasonably share in the payoff from its availability by grading pay up to its value over a reasonable span of time. For every skill added, there can be an additional increment, though after a basic set of two or three skills is mastered and verified, further skill acquisition will normally be of limited value. Token pay increments up to a modest maximum of added skill increments can be added. The skills that are paid must be business relevant skills that are regularly used by the business. The best balance of depth of skill in the project shop will be the availability of two or three different skills by virtually every worker. Too many workers limited to a single skill will reduce flexibility sharply. Too many with unique skills can increase labor cost without adding flexibility. Care must be exercised in compensating added skill acquisition to keep the worker base of possession as broad as possible. Unique mixes or combinations of skill that are of substantial value to the business are best rewarded outside of base pay through profit sharing or similar ownership styled bonus offerings.

Major changes will also be required in the shape of the project shop's fringe benefits package. Fringes include various medical, life, and disability insurances, retirement plans, vacations, holidays, employee discounts, and other miscellaneous services. The advantage of fringes arises out of their exemption from income tax. The government is the employer's and worker's partner in provision of fringes. Fringes are normally calculated as a percentage of normal pay.

The variable, customer oriented working schedule of the project shop poses the potential for difficulty in funding fringes, especially if the requirement of premium—overtime—pay for hours over forty in a week is retained in the wage-hour law. The economic function of premium pay for time over forty hours in a week is to make up for the absence of fringe benefit costs that, conventionally, are fully loaded onto straight time pay in the standard forty-hour week. Payment of overtime at straight wages represents a real cut in pay in the absence of a premium. For the average worker, though, premium pay is a bonus for working long or unpopular hours. The expectation of premium pay for nonnormal work hours or schedules is so deeply fixed by custom that it will probably be impractical to change the law to accommodate project shop schedules in this respect.

It is probably not necessary. Table 10–1 illustrates how pay can be kept equitable by accounting for working time, benefits loading and overtime on a quarterly basis. Benefits are loaded onto all hours worked under forty per week. Overtime is paid for all hours worked over forty per week. A quarterly benefits credit is calculated by applying an agreed on percentage to base pay. A package of benefits selected by the employee on a priority basis is then purchased for the following fiscal quarter. Legally mandated benefits like the FICA and unemployment compensation tax are automatically included, and a minimum package of benefits is guaranteed.

THE COSTS OF ABSENTEEISM

Pay for time not worked presents a special problem and opportunity for the project shop manager. The central fact of fringes is that they must be accounted for in costing compensation by loading their cost onto normal, straight hours of pay. The conventional approach to loading is to spread their cost over a forty-hour workweek. Actually, the base of the spread is a year's worth of forty-hour weeks minus vacations, holidays and other time off. Paid time off must be loaded onto the actual straight hours worked. Unpaid time off subtracts from the base of hours over which the cost of fringes can be spread. The worker who is absent twenty unpaid days in a

Table 10–1
Example of Benefits Allocation in a Flexibly Scheduled Project Shop

Assumptions: Benefits are selected by each employee in rank
order of importance to that employee. Benefits vary quarter
by quarter based on straight time hours worked in the
previous quarter. Value of available benefits is determined
by a percent (for instance, 30%) of straight time earnings
for the prior quarter that is set to fit the labor market.
Minimum benefits and minimum quarterly earnings are
guaranteed.

Work Week in quarter	Hours Worked	Straight Time hours worked	Benefit Credits at 30% on $10.00 per hour
1	35	35	$ 105
2	40	40	120
3	70	40	120
4	70	40	120
5	20	20	60
6	30	30	90
7	20	20	60
8	35	35	105
9	70	40	120
10	70	40	120
11	0	0	0
12	0	0	0
13	20	20	60
Total Hours	480	360	
Total Benefits Credited			1080

Total Pay for Quarter = $4,200

year gets the same fringes as one who is on the job every day and, thereby,
draws nearly 5% more pay. Figure 10–3 illustrates how this occurs.

To the extent that time and output are closely correlated, absenteeism
represents an increased cost to the employer. The relationship is probably
close for the frequently absent worker in a mass commodity output operation. The dullness and anomie of mass output work produces high levels

Figure 10–3
Effect of Unpaid Days Off on Benefits Costs

```
Assumption: 10 Paid Vacation Days and 10 Paid Holidays
            Benefits must be reloaded on payroll cost
            241 normal days are worked in a year
            Unpaid days off reduce the denominator
            Benefits are assumed to be 1/3 of base pay


Effect of 20 unpaid days off on benefits costs:
     Benefits must be reloaded onto 221 days of actual work
         241/221 = 1.0905
     Normal 33.3% benefits package is increased by 9.05%
         1.0905 x 33.3 = 36.496% adjusted benefits loading
     Employer's benefits costs increase by 3.17%


With current benefits costing conventions, the employee who is
absent 20 additional days in a working year earns an effective
3.39% additional pay in the value of benefits.
```

of absenteeism and much extra cost. The conscientious worker is the loser in the bargain.

The manner in which fringes are loaded onto straight time (hours actually productively worked) is thus inequitable at the outset under existing commodity output operations practices. It is also rigid. If fewer than nineteen hundred or so hours per year are worked, for any reason, wage costs rise directly as a function, spreading the fringe loading over a shorter span of time. The inequity is further compounded by the wage-hour law requirement that all time in excess of forty hours a week be paid time and a half. With fringes typically in the range of 35% to 50% of base pay, straight time payment for hours worked beyond those over which fringes are loaded is inequitable. Even at 35% to 40% of base pay, tax free fringes are the equivalent of 50% real pay to the worker. Overtime, thus, is not justified alone by the inconvenience of longer work hours—many workers would prefer to work more hours, even at straight hourly wages. Overtime reestablishes equity in the rate of pay for those hours worked in excess of the standard base of hours. Workers who are chronically absent must still be paid overtime for hours in excess of forty per week without any sacrifice in level of benefits.

As Figure 10–4 illustrates, absenteeism, paid or unpaid, is a real and substantial cost to a business. When wages are 35% of the cost of goods sold, and if unpaid, uncontrolled absenteeism runs at 10%, then a 6% increase is incurred in wage costs. This means actual wage costs have been inflated by nearly 2 percentage points. Against a bottom line of 8% earnings, this means that a 10% earnings potential was missed. The hidden costs of absenteeism to mass commodity output are high. Paid time off in the project shop could be a nightmare.

Absenteeism is not the issue so much here, though, as the inequities that

Figure 10–4
Costs of Pay for Time Not Worked (Vacations, Holidays, Sick and Personal
Time)

```
Assumptions:

    Normal work year is 261 scheduled days
        (52.2 weeks x 5 days)

    Calculation of Cost of Paid Time Off:

    10 days of vacation + 10 holidays =
        20/261 = 7.66% paid days off
    10 days of vacation + 10 holidays +
        10 sick and personal days off =
        30/261 = 11.5 % paid days off

    For Federal Civil Service Positions:
        20 days of vacation (with 3 years service) +
        13 holidays + 13 sick and personal days =
        46/261 = 17.6% paid days off


Paid time off must be loaded back onto each hour of time
    worked as a benefit cost!

This reduces the size of the denominator and thereby
    increases the percent loading for paid time off

    20 PAID DAYS OFF REQUIRES A FRINGE LOADING OF  8.3%

    30 PAID DAYS OFF REQUIRES A FRINGE LOADING OF 13.0%

    46 PAID DAYS OFF REQUIRES A FRINGE LOADING OF 21.4%
```

the irresponsibility of chronic absenteeism introduce into the conventional compensation system. Constraints on personal time off from the job introduced by the need for full capacity output and fringe benefit loading are an important part of the dullness and unpleasantness of overspecialized work. Every worker should have the right to take unpaid time off whenever it does not interfere with the needs of the business. Every worker should be committed to work long hours and long weeks of project shop work whenever the needs of the business require it. Existing fringes, laws and systems of compensation do not support these basic principles of industrial freedom and responsibility. The era of the project shop offers an opportunity for major revision in all of these practices.

Further inequity can be introduced by the disparity in wage treatment suffered by part time workers. Workers who labor fewer than thirty-two hours a week are usually categorized as part time and need not be included in fringe benefit programs. Frequently, they are paid less than full timers for the same work, and sometimes they produce more per unit of time than full timers. Sometimes the labor rate makes up for some of the disparity. A wage of $7.50 an hour for unskilled part time work is the close equivalent of $5.00 to $5.50 per hour with full benefits. Many younger workers prefer the higher, fully taxed wage to the lower wage with tax sheltered benefits. Part time work with limited benefits can be suited to the labor market it draws from.

Benefits can also be scaled more equitably to wages and hours, as is suggested in Table 10–1. They could be subject to greater personal choice by workers and loaded more flexibly. The payroll deduction for social security, for instance, does not stop at forty hours in the week; it ceases to be collected only when an annual maximum is reached. The benefit of untaxed insurance cost could as easily be scaled up or down over hours actually worked to fit the worker's need or preference. Some benefits could readily be traded off against others. Workers who prefer more leisure time in the work year could opt for fewer benefits.

A REVOLUTION IN BENEFITS IS COMING TOO

Existing pay and work schedules are overly rigid for application to the project shop era. Major reform is called for. The easiest place to begin reform of benefits in the project shop is with pay for time not worked. Vacations and holidays are little more than a feeble attempt to loosen up the rigid schedule of wage slavery. When time off without pay is responsibly encouraged to fit a worker's and the business's needs, there is no need for paid time off. The fringe cost of paid time off can be transferred to other fringes or converted into direct pay. Figure 10–4 illustrates the high cost of loading paid time off onto regular pay. Eliminating paid time off removes the confusion workers have about what they are paid for; the only basis for a paycheck is work output. Pay for nonwork output sends the wrong message. Most directly, it suggests that the rich, stingy employer holds back from equitable pay so that he can dole out occasional bonus favors and thereby appear magnanimous. In the earliest days of mass output, that was probably the exact motivation for paid holidays and vacations for "loyal" employees. In the current age, it is an ugly anachronism.

The worth of fringes must be made clear (truth in advertising?) to workers so that they can make appropriate comparisons of wages between employers. Overtime payment is inextricably tied to fringe packages. Provision must be made for greater flexibility in the loading of fringes, perhaps even on a quarterly or annual basis, rather than a weekly one, before an equity differential is introduced. The equity could well be pegged to actual fringe costs to account for trade-offs between wages and benefits that are becoming more common. Unemployment compensation, which now pays benefits in a week when no work is done, must be revised to fit more flexible work schedules. Keying unemployment benefits to the number of hours worked in a month or fiscal quarter may be a solution. Even more radically, workers may be permitted to accept a pay bonus in return for waiving the right to unemployment compensation as project shop employees.

Medical, life insurance and retirement benefits are already under serious siege in the workplace. It is common practice to sue anyone who may be culpable when death is premature. Life insurance is already largely replaced by liability coverage covering that litigation. Coverage under a group term life policy provided by the job drops sharply after age sixty-five. Various forms of life insurance are available under social security and workmen's compensation. The maximum level of life insurance available tax free under a benefit plan is limited to $50,000. Life insurance today is almost an incidental benefit. It probably should be optional with the employee.

Medical insurance is largely out of control due to epidemics, requirement for provision of routine medical assistance by a maximum cost doctor, malpractice lawsuits, and widespread ill health due to alcohol, drugs, tobacco, or poor diet. As if that were not enough, a shortage of nurses and other medical technicians adds to the problem. The widespread expectation that medicine and insurance will take care of illness and injury brought on by any degree of individual irresponsibility invites foolish risk taking at all levels of society.

Pressure on medical insurance is intense. Major change is inevitable. Medical insurance will soon be taken over by the government and limited to cover only for treatment of life threatening trauma. Elective treatment will be entirely at the individual's own expense or covered by an elective private medical policy. The costs of health maintenance will be shared equally by insurer and insured. Medical insurance costs will be cut to the bone. The typical hospital will be half emergency treatment and half elective. A benefit cost accounting for the largest part of current fringe costs will disappear or shrink drastically.

Social security is today the foundation of every work retirement plan. Federal legislation to restrict excesses in retirement plan funding (ERISA) is eliminating those very plans because of its strictness. The value of a retirement plan was never very great unless one was a long-term employee. Vesting periods of three to ten years robbed short termers of their utility. Profit sharing based on periodic, usually annual, business results is fast replacing retirement plans. Everyone usually shares; the profit sharing bonus can be invested in an IRA plan or held in secure form such as company stock or government bonds. After a specified holding period, the full amount plus interest can be withdrawn. Income tax on the bonus is determined by the way it is handled.

Retirement has never been an issue of importance for young employees. Most express a strong preference for the added cash over the distant benefits of a retirement payout. Retirement becomes of greater importance with advancing age and income. As one habituates to a comfortable standard of living, it becomes important to ensure its relative continuance into advanced age. Flexible laws that permit IRA investments at a level now permitted by Keough plans are needed. Eligibility for an IRA is presently a function of the level of income (up to a maximum). The maximum should be raised and made a joint function of age.

When reforms such as these are effected, fringe benefits as a percentage of payroll cost will either shrink sharply or be replaced by higher pay or other benefits, the tax exempt worth of which may be limited by law. When benefits are traded off for pay, pay will be adjusted appropriately. Wage surveys in the project shop era must consistently call for specification of the full compensation package value, not just taxable wages. The option to trade off benefits for benefits or benefits for pay will become common.

THE SHAPE OF THE NEW COMPENSATION SYSTEM

In the era of the project shop, the entire compensation package will be reshaped. Pay for skill will be the central policy. Fringe benefits will likely become a much less important element of compensation than they are at present.

Compensation for project shop work must anchor basic pay at the rate for the most valuable skill contributed. The failure to recognize saleable skill fully risks early loss of that skill to alert competitors. Paying at the level of least skill is unfair and asks for minimum contribution. The "conservative" employer thinks that paying for the minimum level of contribution controls costs. An understanding of how workers think reveals that when one is paid less than the worth of the present work, employees find a way to work out the difference. Chiseling begets chiseling. Trust and generosity are returned with trust and generosity. Once an employer has invested in skill development it is foolish to encourage its departure by refusing to recognize it in pay.

New hires must be paid at the rate necessary to bring them willingly to the job. At entry, highest work skill must be recognized. When market demand for the highest value work still is soft, that will be accounted for in the going rate. The market must be met, though.

Thereafter, compensation must reward advances in range and level of skill, step by step, first very generously, later more cautiously. Workers who wish to qualify for a skill advance will apply for increases and undergo a stiff, objective and competitive qualifying examination for that skill before the increase is granted. Passing the qualifying exam brings about the pay increase increment. Appropriate waiting periods from one qualification to the next may be established: six months for the first, nine months for the second, a year between exams and raises thereafter. A minimum of time is often required just for seasoning in of performance. That can be recognized in the compensation system.

Advances in both inflation and productivity can be recognized in the fashion most managers and employees prefer; periodic, usually annual, across the board raise increments for all employees are carefully worked out and implemented. Flexibility in compensation must be retained, though. It must be possible to make changes in pay at any time based on changes in the market value of skill contribution. Annual merit increase systems are popular with managers because they permit needed adjustments in a worker's value to be worked out. In reality, the great preponderance of those adjustments are the equivalent of an across the board general increase that accounts mostly for inflation and cost of living creep. A rare few workers will receive either a large increase to bring pay into equity or no increase at all to encourage them to leave. Tying such special events to broad based payroll adjustments only confuses the compensation picture for workers. General increases should be general increases.

When the judgment of a worker's immediate manager or supervisor is an important element in the calculus of work value, a simple device can be employed; the standard annual increase representing inflation and productivity increases can be calculated. If, for instance, it is pegged at 6%, managers may be instructed to assign increases at their discretion to all subordinates within a range of plus or minus 4% of the standard. Individual increases may vary from 2% to 10%. The manager's own increase will be reduced by whatever percent his average of all increases departs, up or down, from the standard. If he gives all employees the standard percent increase, he gets the standard himself. Otherwise, his increase will be determined by how wisely and courageously the standard is differentially allocated.

This device is simply and powerful. Sometimes it will put more pressure on line supervisors or operating managers than they are capable of handling. When increases must, by policy, average to the standard, most managers will give the exact standard to the middle 80% or 90% and then single out a handful of losers to be excluded in favor of another handful of favorites to be rewarded with the extra. It is a zero sum game. Loyalty is rewarded; independence is punished. The judgement of the worker majority logically is one of discrimination and favoritism. The company suffers.

It takes great courage for a manager placed under constraint in awarding differential increases to exclude the goldbrickers and increase the size of rewards for all of the real performers or to reward the stars by taking away from all who won't measure up to the high standards set by stars. If differential wage increases assigned by managers or supervisors cannot be used to these kinds of purposes, there is no reason to have them at all.

Differences in pay increases based on managerial discretion are inevitably an echo of "motivate with money" theories. However sincerely they are carried out, they are likely to become an arbitrary exercise of managerial power over employees unless and until the differential distribution implemented affects every employee in the group in a way that is clearly understood. Discretionary increases are potentially volatile. They are a great test of managerial judgment if used as such but are dangerous when misused. Poor judgment in awarding increases is, unfortunately, the norm of pay for performance systems. The high frequency with which workers perceive inequity in pay flows directly from them.

Paying for possessed skill is a potentially bold departure from many current compensation systems. Skill must nonetheless become the principal basis of pay. Pay progression outside of periodic pay advances in traditional systems of compensation is metered by steps of grade or level. The worker's grade or level establishes not only the pay range but also determines his or her relative status in the organization hierarchy. Status under former systems of compensation is of at least equal importance to pay, conferring esteem and satisfaction that may be unavailable from the work itself. Pay generally follows status in organization, making status a significant lever to compensation. Progressing from one step to another, thus, is a major event. Elaborate rituals and tests exist to ensure that the unworthy do not get past the gatekeepers of status. Wholly irrelevant social issues enter the compensation calculus when status is raised to so high a level of importance. Education (in the purely formal and academic sense) becomes a dominant requirement for advancement. That which a good liberal education confers is increased skill in writing, speaking and understanding language. Sometimes it is a highly specialized language like economics or calculus. The well educated individual is capable of coordinating her work with that of other similarly educated individuals. In the absence of demonstrated ability to communicate technically with peers in one's field, an education is worthless. Communication skill has its own value. Making the degree into a ticket to high status work obscures the value and importance of that skill.

Status is cheap. When status is more valuable than skill, cost is artificially and inequitably inflated. The extended and often elaborate hierarchical structure of mass commodity output systems lends easily to military styled chains of command. Maintenance of control requires obeisance of subordinates. Preservation and enhancement of status differences contribute to control. Control is costly—more costly, perhaps, than we will ever know.

The project shop based on skill mastery can afford to award status on the basis of level and range of demonstrated skill. Control is self-control. Poor quality, poor commitment, poor output, directly tarnish status. Skill is the anchor point of everything in a project shop.

11

WHERE CAN EFFICIENCY BE FOUND?

"Efficiencies, even when available, aren't always worth it."

Efficiency is an illusion created by specifying the variables that the operations manager wants to try to manage. Efficiency on the moving assembly line is defined as continual movement of materials and parts through a process until they come off the end of the line as a completed product. It is purchased at the price of lost human capacity in the development and application of skill. Low skilled work that offers no opportunity for learning, combined with lock-step work standards that waste available human capability, ignores the potential for obtaining a greatly increased contribution from workers. But the moving assembly line is a machine that can be controlled by its creator. It is predictable in its output. Vast amounts of low-cost commodity output can be wrested from it. Kept constantly in motion, it throws off generous quantities of excess cash for its owner. This does not necessarily mean that it is efficient in every sense of that term.

Efficiency can be sought through tight controls over selection and purchase of materials from suppliers. Every effort can be made to obtain the highest quality at the best price. But unless purchases are made in vast sums, most of the savings will be absorbed in purchasing department salaries and overhead anyway. When an opportunity for real economies of scale in materials acquisition exists, a key executive must be assigned to develop the contact from the start. When large sums are involved, cost control is an issue of operating strategy, not efficiency. Price reductions are more likely to arise out of anticipating the play of economic and market forces. The company that fails to exploit the major cost saving opportunity will soon fall on hard times. Cost containment shows up finally in pricing and profits. Efficiency is the result of a competitive response and sound management in this arena.

EFFICIENCY FROM COST TRADE-OFFS: ECONOMIC ORDER QUANTITY MODEL

Efficiency can be sought in trade-offs between offsetting costs. It is common for operations managers, for instance, to calculate the relative cost of reducing the labor force to save payroll costs in the near term and then to assess the cost of allowing the inventory to build in anticipation of an upturn in business at some later time. If layoff and rehiring are cheaper, the payroll rises and falls with change in demand. If carrying inventory is less expensive, payroll is kept level, and inventory varies with changes in demand.

One of the most elegant models of managerial decision making devised is based on a very rudimentary trade-off: the trade-off between the cost of setup (or acquisition of material) versus the cost of holding inventory. This is the Economic Order Quantity Model created by F. W. Harris in 1914.

The EOQ is a device for determining optimum production of lot quantities. It is built on the assumption that offsetting costs are available in deciding how large a quantity of material or product to buy or make in a single lot. The cost first is the cost of holding the material or product in inventory. The inventory holding cost includes the opportunity cost (interest) on investment in inventory, shrinkage or loss while in storage as well as the cost of warehousing, handling, insurance, and so on, which go along with inventory stock. The larger the standard lot quantity, the greater the inventory and related holding cost. Assuming a steady rate of inventory usage, the average level of inventory on hand is estimated to be half the standard lot quantity plus any reserve stock level required.

The second, counterbalancing cost may be either the cost of preparing to undertake production—the setup cost—or the cost of ordering supplies and materials. Setup cost may require retraining of personnel, readjustment of tools or equipment, rehandling of raw materials and so on. Ordering may entail purchasing department salaries and overhead, investment of time to review catalogs, trips to suppliers, inspection of the purchase order to verify correctness and so forth. The number of setups/reorders per year is a direct function of the total annual usage/production divided by the standard lot size.

The cost of holding one unit of inventory in stock for a year and the cost of a single setup or order must each be estimated as elements of the EOQ calculation. Average inventory level multiplied by unit holding cost is total holding cost. The cost of a setup or of placing one order times the number of changeovers/orders yields total setup/ordering cost. Because the number of changeovers/orders is directly inverse to the amount of inventory held, the optimum (minimum) sum of these two costs occurs when they are equal. The elements of the model, thus, can be written in symbolic notation and solved algebraically for the optimum lot quantity. By ordering at this standard lot level, the summed cost of inventory holding and ordering cost is, in theory at

Figure 11–1
Cost Trade-off between Cost of Input Acquisition and Cost of Holding Inventory

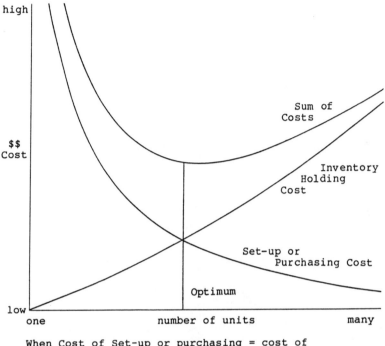

When Cost of Set-up or purchasing = cost of
     holding inventory, then

The sum of costs is equal and minimum

$$\text{Optimum Lot Size}^* = \sqrt{\frac{2 * \text{Annual Usage} * \text{Set-up Cost}}{\text{Per Unit Holding Cost}}}$$

* Algebraically derived from the above model

least, minimized. Figure 11–1 illustrates graphically the trade-off between cost factors and the notational formula for the EOQ model.

The EOQ is an elegant example of logical thought applied to an operating problem. It proceeds from the premise that setup/ordering and inventory holding costs are inevitable. They must be controlled at a minimum level that is determined by the standard production run or purchase lot size. The existence of a mathematical optimum point of summed cost provides an exact and final answer to the operating decision—within the constraints of the assumptions the model is based on.

The EOQ has other lessons for the operating manager who takes time to examine its elements. The EOQ model provides a rare instance of a quantifiable demonstration of an economy of scale. Any annual usage rate can be applied to the EOQ equation to determine the optimum lot quantity. If holding cost and order cost are held constant while annual use is doubled and then doubled again, it is apparent that optimum lot quantity increases at a much slower rate than does usage. The relationship, in fact, is geometric, not linear. Proportionately, a smaller standard lot quantity is required to optimize costs at higher usage rates. Proportionately lower cost is incurred for the sum of setup/ordering and inventory holding cost as well. A large scale operation is feasible at a lower inventory holding and setup/acquisition cost.

Experimenting with the EOQ further reveals that the lowest possible cost is achieved when there is no setup/ordering cost. The inventory holding cost can be eliminated when the setup/ordering cost is slashed to zero. It is thereby made clear that inefficiency of equipment changeover or acquisition cost is the basis of a need for inventory. The most impelling lesson to be taken from the EOQ model, perhaps, is that having to hold any amount of inventory at all signals fundamental inefficiency in adapting the system to changing customer need. The ideal in well-managed work flow is zero lead time. The ideal in lot size is one. These ideals require the minimization or elimination of setup, changeover and ordering costs.

EFFICIENCIES FROM JIT

Just-in-time production flow attempts to achieve these ideals to the largest extent possible. The power of JIT, indeed, resides in its rejection of preexisting policies and systems that depend on inventory at all stages of the operation to keep work flow steady. Some of the devices employed to achieve JIT work flow are, therefore, predictable.

Purchasing to support JIT requires negotiation of a standard price for a blanket order with provision for small drop shipment quantities as needed. A minimum-maximum quantity over a longer span of time is specified. Price variations outside the minimum and maximum may be negotiated. Standard, highly simplified release documentation analogous to kanban is set up in advance to permit routine telephone, fax or computer generated orders that trigger shipments and quantities. In effect, a single order is placed that is then sequenced and sized according to operating needs as they emerge. Materials that arrive in the exact needed amounts at the time of need are automatically inspected and verified at the point of use. Purchasing and ordering are reorganized so that order costs beyond the first order are trivial.

Setup and changeover for JIT are similarly redesigned to permit instantaneous changeover at trivial cost. The Japanese have developed the Single-Minute-Exchange-of-Die for application to heavy manufacturing. This permits the ideal lot size of one to be produced. It is not necessary to produce only one item on a single changeover, but it is possible and cost economic to do so when desirable.

The JIT implies maximum flexibility of response to changing customer need. It is built upon a heavy pull emphasis in work flow. Long production runs and large materials orders no longer imply cost efficiency. The greatest efficiencies are obtained when only that which the customer immediately asks for is produced. There is no need for a large inventory to be held in support of the sale.

CONCERNING THE INEFFICIENCIES OF INVENTORIES

It is potentially much more efficient to eliminate inventory by redesigning work flow than it is to try to optimize the quantity of inventory held. The WIP inventory can hide significant quality and operating problems. Large amounts of unsold, unordered finished goods inventory represent a potential for damage and obsolescence. Inventory can become a major cost of goods sold. Competing on the basis of inventory in stock and producing at maximum efficiency with the expectation of promoting excess inventory through selective price reduction can produce only illusory efficiencies. These are old, bad strategies of operation. In the production of automobiles alone, for instance, excess inventory becomes an immediate drag on value. Discounts and rebates needed to attract buyers more than offset any efficiencies gained from large lot production undertaken to avoid the cost of line changeover. There is no efficiency in the production of goods that must be sold below cost, however economic or efficient the lot size.

EFFICIENCY IS A NEAR-TERM THING

The meaning of efficiency as something skillful, productive and effective has been lost in the language of management. *Efficient* has come to connote near-term low cost. The efficient production operation is run as tightly as possible to generate maximum profit return in the shortest time. Efficiency no longer suggests reinvestment to maintain or improve an operating system. It implies the absolute minimum of training and upkeep required to keep operations going. Efficiency has to do with machines and machinelike systems that are run flat out for a quick buck.

The American financial system reflects these distortions of efficiency in prevailing investment policy. Reinvestment that cuts sharply into earnings is seldom seen as an acceptable alternative business strategy. For those who look only at immediate high return, which has become the standard of the investment community, reinvestment is risky. Efficiency and greed go together in this climate of impatience for greater wealth. An efficient investment program is one that maximizes short-term return. Programmed trading systems look at gains in terms of minutes or hours. Investors have little interest in the long-term stability of a company; if payoff is not certain now, it is assumed to be less certain later. The trading markets of the nation are afflicted with continuous churning that reflects the urgent search for the most efficient return on investment—the quickest, biggest buck now!

This insatiable greed for quick payoff is translated into a strategy of maximum growth by corporate managers. Rapid growth is presumed to rest on a foundation of efficient use of business resources. "Synergy" is the magic word. The search for synergy leads corporations into ever more foolish experiments in expansion or acquisition, most of which are later discovered to have been unwise and unproductive. Growth of existing markets is driven by aggressive sales promotion and advertising. Market saturation is increasingly more common. The saturated market requires faster obsolescence of existing products or services, continual introduction of more advanced technological novelty, sharper differentiation of product offerings and still more promotion to keep the illusion of growth vibrant. Growth is now founded on wasteful excess.

The efficiencies of cost that once arose out of broad standardization of technologies have been lost. The imperative of growth demands that the cost of repair be so great that it is cheaper to discard and replace an item. There are no longer any standard tubes in a television set; every circuit board is unique. The best design uses a variety of specialized components that are difficult or impossible to find in the aftermarket.

Advertising must be efficient. It is not adequate to catalogue the utilities of a product or service in the advertisement; mere information conveyed to the potential consumer does not have sufficiently dramatic effect. The efficient advertisement appeals to status insecurity, romantic fantasy, greed or gluttony. The most stable, profitable industries are those that feed popular addictions like caffeine, alcohol and nicotine. Efficiency resides in the magic of selling the sizzle, not in the creation of real nutritive value in the steak itself.

THE REAL COSTS OF EFFICIENCY

Efficiency has bred an era of waste, litter, pollution, ill health and superficial satisfaction. Efficiency has played its part out on the stage of economic life. It has turned ugly and mean. It is no longer a virtue of business.

Real efficiency never resided in running a machine as fast and as long as it would go. A cheap machine, minimally maintained, producing a popular product or service and run until worn out, can be profitable. It is seldom the foundation of a stable business. Someone, usually the owner or stockholder, gets left holding the bag when this opportunistic, short-term exploitation strategy has run its course.

Competition in commodity production has long since passed the stage of cheap exploitation of near-term profit. Flexible manufacturing requires highly flexible machinery. Machines are subject to wide variability of operating use and conditions. They must adapt or be adapted to change. The best equipment is general purpose equipment. The most efficient equipment is highly specialized equipment. The machine that cannot easily be switched over to alternative use will never deliver genuine efficiency. Henry Ford's Model T was so simply and ruggedly built that a farmer could drive to a remote work site, jack it up, remove a wheel, attach a power belt and operate equipment remotely with the same engine he rode to work in. The current popularity of the ubiquitous pickup truck is based on its working versatility. Lacking a large part of the body weight of a sedan, it is lighter and more fuel efficient. Any handyman can customize the truck bed. The vehicle itself is engineered for pushing and pulling tasks like snow plowing or trailer hauling. The average family sedan, subject to very low capacity utilization at best, is limited to carrying the family and groceries. The typical sports coupe is even more specialized and less versatile. The pickup truck is vastly more practical and versatile.

LEARNING IS INEFFICIENT BUT ADAPTIVE

Human effectiveness depends on adaptability. Using the human body as if it were merely a production machine to be exploited for profit leads to excess wear at points of maximum use just as it must with a production machine. Learning and discovery are the source of quality in human life. Human effectiveness is built on self-development, acquisition of skill, discovery of new ideas. These are inherently inefficient activities.

Learning and discovery are costly, risky activities. Figure 11–2 illustrates the usual shape of the learning cost curve. Initial costs can be exorbitant. Costs fall with task repetition. Mastery of a novel activity, or a significant variation on an existing habit, requires practice. Learning how to play the piano, for instance, begins with plunking out the crudest of one note melodies. Extended practice limbers and strengthens the fingers until more complex multinote patterns become routine. Reading the music is a separate task. Initially, each note is identified and tortuously translated into finger motion. Notes in a chord are first read singly and then later as a unit. If efficiency in making music is your aim, you would do better to purchase a harmonica. Even then you must begin by learning the physical rudiments of breath control. The most broadly useful skill in music is reading the notes. Once that skill is acquired, one can experiment with various instruments to find one that fits existing aptitude. Skills can be specific and general just as there can be specific and general machines.

Some kind of skill will have to be mastered in embarking on new learning or discovery. The best choice is a basic skill that is a foundation for a variety of other skills. Basic, general skill is effective in that it can be carried over to a variety of opportunities and needs. Written and spoken language is an

Figure 11–2
The Experience Curve

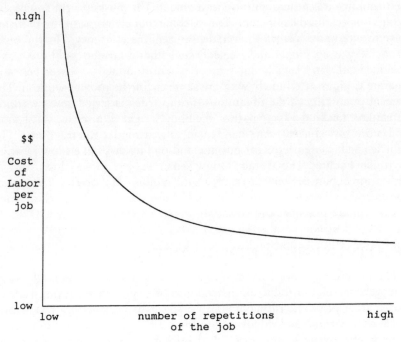

effective base skill that allows many other skills to be added on. In practical affairs, understanding the mechanics of wheels, levers, pulleys, wedges and hydraulics is fundamental to building or repairing machines of every kind. In science, physics supplies the basic principles that other physical science is founded upon. Mathematics is the language of measurement and control. It permits precision in every other basic discipline. When these base skills have been mastered, innumerable other higher level skills can be constructed upon them.

Narrow human skill that requires no mastery in any of these foundation skill areas is more efficiently taught but grossly wasteful of human capacity. One can be an equipment operator without being literate or even mechanically knowledgeable. But when the equipment is obsoleted, the skill and, often, the human being are also obsoleted. Acquisition of the basic skill requires large investment. In current terms, it is inefficient. When measured against the costs of poverty borne by the uneducated, investment in a basic skill is by far the better solution. Possession of general purpose skill increases adaptivity. One may switch from one occupation to another with only minimal changeover cost.

ADAPTIVITY IS A PROJECT SHOP'S GREATEST ASSET

The era of the project shop requires machines and human skill that are general purpose, adaptable, readily transferred to cover changing, emerging customer need. It requires moderate to low utilization of machinery. Human beings demand leisure for recreation and learning to equip themselves for the stresses of adaptation and change. Work schedules must be sufficiently flexible to fit new leisure time expectations. It is all very inefficient, but it is also highly effective in releasing human drive and energy. In the pursuit of effectiveness, efficiency no longer counts.

The classic learning curve (Figure 11–2) points out the great inefficiency of learning in the early stages. Every time a person starts out to learn a new skill, there must be a period of highly inefficient, frustrating, mistake laden practice. Large amounts of time and resources may be demanded to achieve mastery. But every time one starts to learn again, it is easier. Learning to learn is a basic skill in its own right. Finally, learning, adapting, refocusing on new opportunity, can become a high level skill in itself. Setup and changeover are potentially one minute, one step processes when they have become a way of life.

Efficiency in the project shop does not demand the least frequency of setup. It requires investment in practice and improvement of setup procedures. Setup is an integral part of every custom job and a substantial element of any short-run job. Setup, changeover or preparation of any kind is inherent in the job. Setup is no longer a separate part of the job. Skill at minimizing setup or changeover cost is the competitive edge of the project shop. Setup and changeover must be effectively executed, not efficiently avoided. This is a wholly new and different point of view in managing setup and changeover. It introduces entirely new opportunities for managing the multistep setup process in the project shop.

The extent of the change of perspective demanded by the project shop to deal effectively with setup and changeover costs must not be underestimated. Every experienced operations manager has learned the hard way that setup, changeover and materials acquisition are significant sources of cost and must therefore be contained. Setup is the enemy of efficiency. The EOQ model demonstrates that inventory can only be kept minimal when these costs are driven as low as possible. But these are lessons that apply best to long, efficient commodity runs. Product or service that is repetitively produced must pay back the investment in the setup cost required to put the production process in place. Commodities will still be produced in mass flow fashion, which minimizes overall cost by treating setup as an investment that must be recovered over a lengthy term of operation. Automated commodity factories will fill this need. Project shops must take a new and divergent approach.

SETUP BECOMES ANOTHER ELEMENT OF JOB COST

In the project shop, flexible equipment and worker skill are the best sources of cost control with setups of every kind. Setup, changeover and materials ordering are integral aspects of every job. Some small degree of cost amortization may be possible with short project shop runs. That must never be permitted to obscure the fact that setup costs are basically part of the total job quote. Cost competition in the project shop does not, cannot, must not, depend on long production runs to justify setup costs. Cost competitiveness will be based wholly on the flexibility with which setup is effected through existing skill and equipment. The basic investments that permit rapid, accurate setup and materials flow management must be made through improving skill and equipment flexibility at the outset for the project shop to be price competitive.

It is a fool's dream to expect to be able to drive down setup costs in a project shop. The setup cost will increase more often than decrease as an element of project shop costs. With one-of-a-kind products or services, the setup cost must be handled as part of the unit price. Defining, preplanning and training all become integral aspects of the job itself. With one-of-a-kind prototypical jobs, even the likelihood of rework can usefully be calculated into the cost. To the extent that the setup cost is a function of experience with the product, process or operation, a shop may absorb some or all of this as a learning cost required to buy into the market. Mastery of setup flexibility becomes a strategic move. Otherwise, the setup cost is merely added into the base cost. Close attention to setup is necessary to cost control, but driving setup costs down to zero is an unrealistic goal in a project shop.

A critical investment in competitive capability will be rethinking the entire setup process. When tasks require multiple setups or changeovers in sequence, it will no longer be effective to let all jobs flow through the system unscheduled for setup time. Scheduling the setup requirements of work will become as systematic as the MRP scheduling of materials flow now is in mass commodity output.

When there is even just a moderately high potential for rework and resetup at earlier workstations, it can be demonstrated that the cost of resetup will easily offset or exceed any ROI sacrificed to maintain the setup by withholding equipment from production. Under conditions of low equipment capacity utilization, lost machine time is much less a significant management issue. Even so, withholding machine capacity to maintain a series of setups for queueless, uninterrupted flow of a job can be economically preferable to risking resetup by releasing equipment when the job has yet to be completed on subsequent workstations. The cost of resetup alone can justify holding equipment in readiness *in case* the job must be rerun. Setup practices in the project shop offer an opportunity for reform that can reduce cost

Table 11–1
An Example of Collapsed Setup Scheduling

Job Element	Job Station	Set-Up time in hours	Processing Time in hrs	Total Time in hours
1	A	2	2	4
2	B	1	0.5	1.5
3	C	4.5	5	9.5
4	D	2.5	2.5	5
Total Time		10.0	10.0	20.0

and do so within the newly adopted norm of queueless, low capacity, high quality output.

SETUP CAN BE SCHEDULED AS A SPECIAL KIND OF LEAD TIME IN WORK FLOW

The greater change in treatment of setup costs comes with those production runs where setup or changeover is required on multiple, sequential operations or workstations. Long standing habits of maximizing equipment capacity utilization would dictate scheduling setup or changeover immediately in advance of the actual operation followed by teardown immediately after to set up for work waiting in the queue. The effective emergency room physician, however, immediately stages all equipment and personnel necessary to treat the seriously injured accident victim and requires that all be kept in readiness until explicitly released. Queueless, delay-free, maximum quality project shop service will often require that the schedule for setup of operations be sequenced for uninterrupted flow-through and preserved so that all setups are continuously available until the job is fully completed.

Whenever significant potential exists for rework, it may be cost effective to set up workstations at the outset and leave them in place until the entire operation is successfully completed before tearing any down. When long processing time makes this impractical, setups can be scheduled to be finished exactly as work comes off the immediately prior station. Setup lead times are then scheduled as precisely as material lead times now are on a moving assembly line. When there is a question as to the significance of resetup costs, it can be analyzed and calculated as an expected cash value and compared to the ROI lost because machinery is withdrawn from normal service while the entire job is processed.

Table 11–1 presents a four-stage task that is 50% setup and 50% processing time. This is a ratio that is common with many short-run jobs and might easily shift sharply toward dominance of setup costs for many one-of-a-kind jobs. Figure 11–3 illustrates the analysis. It shows continuous sequencing of setup on all four tasks. Collapsing and overlapping setup reduces twenty hours of simple sequence time to twelve. If the product is unacceptable after the final station, rework of the entire job could still be finished in twenty-four hours including resetup of all stations, compared to forty hours with nonoverlapped, simple sequence. In JIT terms, continuously sequenced setup scheduling is a winner at the starting gate.

Note, though, that two hours of resetup delay *and* the cost of all station resetups can be avoided by leaving setups intact and withholding machinery at these stations from other production until the satisfactory conclusion of the job. These savings are gained at the cost of eighteen hours of lost machine availability.

How can it make economic sense to withhold machinery to avoid a resetup cost? We begin by calculating the cost of the extra hours of station commitment required to withdraw all stations from production until the assigned job is complete. Station A is finished at the end of 4.0 hours and must be withheld for 8.0 hours. Station B is finished at 4.5 hours and must be withheld for 7.5 hours. Station C is finished at 9.5 hours and must be withheld 2.5 hours. The hourly ROI required of each station by ROI goals is next calculated. If, for instance, the average station investment cost is $20,000 and the ROI goal is 24%, the ROI margin on each station for a 2,000 hour work year is 0.24 × $20,000/2000, which equals $2.40 per hour. Lost ROI in the example is 18 × $2.40, which equals $43.20.

The expected cost of resetup can now be estimated. With a four-stage job, six possibilities exist for rework requiring resetup; we may return to station A after stations B, C or D, to station B after station C or D, and to station C after station D. Each possibility represents a unique cost. A probability must therefore be assigned to each possibility. Starting with an overall probability of 15% that any of these rework possibilities will occur on a given job, the individual probabilities and costs may be calculated. The sum of the expected costs for all six conditions is the expected cost per job of station resetup.

Table 11–2 shows the result of this costing approach. The hourly cost of setup, estimated at $50, is multiplied by the hours required for each rework condition times the probability of its occurrence of any job. For the summed probabilities of rework, the expected resetup cost calculates to $47.25 versus an average machine withholding cost of $43.20. Substituting continuously sequenced, withheld stations setup for the cost of lost machine capacity utilization represents a slight expected cost advantage in resetup costs saved.

THERE ARE OTHER BENEFITS BEYOND COST SAVINGS

Continuously sequenced setup scheduling alone can greatly reduce delay on every job processed through the system. Savings in resetup costs are over

Figure 11-3
Sequenced Four Station Setup Schedule

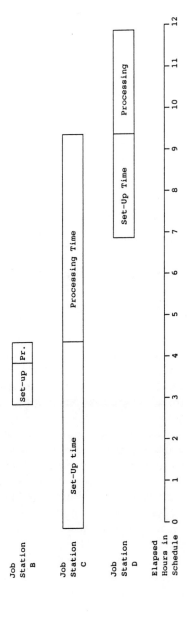

Job
Station
A

| Set-up time | Processing |

Job
Station
B

| Set-up | Pr. |

Job
Station
C

| Set-Up time | Processing Time |

Job
Station
D

| Set-Up Time | Processing |

Elapsed
Hours in
Schedule

0   1   2   3   4   5   6   7   8   9   10   11   12

Table 11–2
Decision Table for Expected Cost of Resetup under Conditions of No Equipment
Withheld

	p =	re-set-up hours	per hr cost	cost	p x cost (ECV)
Restart					
Station A from					
Station B	.02	2.0	$50	$100	$ 2.00
Station C	.02	3.0	50	150	3.00
Station D	.03	7.5	50	375	11.25
Restart					
Station B from					
Station C	.02	1.0	50	50	1.00
Station D	.03	5.5	50	550	16.50
Restart					
Station C from					
Station D	.03	4.5	50	450	13.50
No Restart	.85				
Sum of					
Expected Cost					$47.25

and above the JIT benefits of continuously sequenced setup scheduling. Thus
even where the cost of lost ROI is substantially greater than the expected
cost of resetup, the customer may prefer the cost of lost ROI added to the
price as insurance against delay. The added benefit of sequencing the setup
schedule for continuous flow-through is a zero queue at every station after
the first, creating a condition of near absolute minimum job flow time. This
may have extra value for the customer in its own right. But when the
expected cost of station resetup exceeds lost ROI from withheld equipment,
continuously sequenced setup held until release of the finished product or
service is more cost effective than seeking increased capacity utilization of
equipment through immediate teardown of the setup and can be justified
in its own right.

To implement continuously sequenced setup practices, established materials flow techniques that allow close scheduling of material flow to account for lead time are directly carried over to the scheduling of setup.
When maximum capacity utilization is the goal of management, however,
it would be inconceivable to think of sequencing setups continuously to
implement JIT. Withholding equipment from use for such a purpose would
be unthinkable. Queueless project shop work flow virtually demands attention to this new kind of scheduling opportunity. The limiting variable in
establishing the best possible due date for the job may more realistically be
the longest task setup time in the job sequence. One-of-a-kind jobs are
notorious for miscues and problems. Multiple resetups to complete a job
are entirely probable, even predictable. A policy of sequenced setups released
only after the job itself is released will become a fundamental of many
project shop operations.

In principle, indeed, these rules apply to setup of any production run that is too short to permit optimized allocation of setup costs against inventory holding costs. Cost analysis of the benefits of simultaneous, scheduled setups dedicated to one job is fundamental to the improvement of project shop cost and efficiency. Depending on the patterning of setup times required at successive stations, a substantial reduction in flow time is possible. When rework is required, preserving the sequence of setups contributes to the successful completion of the job and also reduces process time substantially. These are savings in process time and operating costs that result solely from reformed setup practices. They are independent of the additional savings in time or cost achieved from elimination of queues at each of the successive workstations. Finally, the sum of the added savings in time and cost achieved by continuous sequenced setup practices and queuelessness is independent of the increased quality available from the whole of these reformed practices.

Any situation that calls for allocation of equipment, work space or specialized teamwork will benefit from continuous sequence setup planning. Complex prototype construction, publishing, an R&D project, a multistep medical laboratory procedure, scientific research, repair of heavy machinery, road or bridge repair, all have potential for cost savings in strict flow-sequence scheduling of setup. Many such projects are presently managed by setting up all equipment in advance and holding it through to completion because of the excessively high cost of resetup. The potential for still greater cost and time savings by closely scheduling in those jobs is high.

PEOPLE NOW TAKE PRECEDENCE OVER MACHINES

As the age of mass commodity production emphasized efficiency in use of expensive tools and equipment at the expense of human health and growth, so the project shop era must focus on effective use of human resources ahead of machine or equipment efficiency. Ownership of productive tools has, for a century or more, been a sure high payoff investment. A 10% to 50% standard return on investment has been the payoff for wise investment in the tools of production. The pendulum has swung widely away from that position. A hundred years ago, mere ownership of productive equipment conferred vast wealth. Today sharp swings in payoff from application of production tools flow directly from differences in the management skill with which they are applied. A few years hence, tools will be in such abundance that ownership will routinely convey only a modest 2% to 4% ROI. Finding a standard 10% to 50% return on those tools will depend entirely on the level of skill with which they are employed. Human effectiveness is the wave of the future.

Human skill is *not* efficiently employed when it is dedicated to simple repetition. Some joints and muscles are overused to the point of fatigue or damage; others are underused to the extent of severe degeneration. Repetition of any kind requires counterbalancing activity that rests the over-worked but stresses the unused physical capacity. Much the same seems to be true of mental capacity. Too much practice with word use in school neglects broader pattern recognition skills that underlie intuitive power. In the age of mass commodity production, it was efficient to train the young as willing robots of production. The skills of judgment and insight were neglected by public schools. The era of the project shop demands much stronger communication and analytical skill, far less mechanical drilling of spelling, grammar and math. The existing system of public education must undergo major reform to meet this need.

POWER OF CONCENTRATION MUST BE DEVELOPED

A paradox of human effectiveness is that although it is diminished by the wear of excessive repetition, it is greatly increased by the ability to concentrate intensely on a narrow activity for more than a few minutes. Human efficiency suffers from seven and a half hours of repeated routine on the job simply because work becomes a mindless habit while consciousness is disengaged for application to other, more stimulating activities. With training, it is possible to learn the exact, total conscious focus on one's immediate activity for periods of two to three hours at a time. The high skilled individual who puts 100% of his or her attention on the task at hand for three solid hours can produce awesome results. Such spans of intense concentration must be interrupted by counterbalancing activity or diversion before they can recommence. Health enhancing regimens of exercise and eating may be necessary. In the absence of discipline, burnout is very likely. It is instructive, for instance, that the work of a court of law is generally divided into two periods of three hours maximum, morning and afternoon, with a minimum two-hour break in between. Critical, formal consideration of evidence and judgments requires absolute concentration on the process at hand. A more intense schedule would be physically and psychologically distressing to many of the participants. In occupations such as aircraft control, classroom teaching, medicine or law enforcement, burnout is common among those who fail to develop the disciplines of exact concentration counterbalanced by recreational diversion. If the task is excessively stressful, it may be too painful to concentrate on without distraction. Distraction creates the potential for error. Error is an occasion for externally applied discipline. Maximum human inefficiency ensues.

EFFICIENT ACTIVITY IS BALANCED AND VARIED

Human efficiency demands concentrated focus counterbalanced with variety in activity. This generally means two to three hour spans of concentrated effort on one kind of task alternated with similar spans on a physically and mentally different task. Alternating skillfully can permit a lengthy string of four, five, even six, such successive spans of time to be scheduled in a day without noticeable decrement in performance. Successful executives manage their time in exactly this fashion. The sequencing of activity is crucial to staying fresh and alert. Activities are balanced in the schedule to offset one another in source and type of fatigue. Twelve to fifteen hour days on a continuous schedule would be impossible otherwise. The executive offices of a soundly managed corporation, indeed, are largely in a project shop mode. Many important lessons in efficiency can be discovered from observing them.

Real efficiency resides in using human time, energy and skill at their maximum. Too much sleep, too much work of one overly narrow kind, too much idle play, are all inefficient. The variety of activity, like variety in food, must be carefully balanced. Physical, mental, sensory, imaginative activities all need to be brought into play in the course of daily events. Vigorous physical activity must be employed to offset tranquil or sedentary work. The effects of vigorous physical work should not be cancelled out by an alcoholic stupor or with excessive eating, as it often is. Thinking can be combined effectively with physical movement, but when it is the physical activity that is hired and paid, thinking may be only a distraction. Some care and planning need to be put into the balance and construction of the schedule.

Indeed, some of the most significant planning any human being does has to do with his or her schedule of work and personal activities. Two to three hours must be set aside every week to review current activities for balance and contribution to health. Any significant sense of fatigue or depression must be examined for its implications for inbalance in one's weekly pattern of activity. Three to six occasions of vigorous physical activity balanced against another three to six periods of quiet reflection and study each week are fundamental to good health. Work that is sedentary must be offset by breaks or transit time that is active. If one commutes to work seated in an automobile, work should permit active movement and vice versa. Most paid employment demands heavy dependence on sensory input through the eyes and ears. At a minimum, there should be variation in the use of those sources. Eyes should be alternatively used for both near and far vision. If work activity demands sight and hearing, leisure must emphasize touch and smell. Olefactory/tactile stimulation unavailable in many current jobs is too easily supplied through overuse of food or tobacco. Both defeat health and human efficiency. A walk in the park or a period of brisk, sweaty exercise is better by far.

Economic sufficiency no longer requires dawn to dusk work. The project shop era permits planful design of human activity patterns to maximize efficient use of time and energy. Habituated to imposed schedules of time and work, many people will at first find their new options confusing. The project shop will, in some cases, begin to offer a more humane and humanly efficient activity schedule. Two intensive work periods of three hours separated by two hours of counterbalanced activity, either personal or work, would serve as a transition from the current standard eight-hour-plus-lunch workday. Eating need not be a major ritual in such a schedule. Nutritious mealetts served at planned intervals during work would serve to sustain energy without needless commitment of passive time to heavy eating. The poor eating habits of many workers may require planned nutrition on the job in times of heavy customer demand. Long workdays might be scheduled in segments of alternated activity built on a series of five two and a half hour work modules. Efficiency in use of human skill and energy requires radical redesign of work schedules. Designs fitted to the mass commodity production age are inadequate for the emerging project shop. Wholly new approaches are needed.

In planning work schedules that elicit maximum human efficiency, a variety of priorities will compete for satisfaction. Work demands will likely be one of the easier priorities to cover. Ensuring healthy variation in activity or purpose will not always be easy or even possible because of the primacy of work demands. The priorities to be met must be carefully catalogued. Managing them will be the trick. The 80/20 rule, sometimes called the Pareto principle, offers an answer to handling them successfully. Figure 7–2 in Chapter 7 illustrated this phenomenon graphically.

APPLYING THE 80/20 RULE TO ADAPTIVE ACTIVITIES

The 80/20 rule specifies that any set of varied activities or requirements can be divided into the 80% that requires 20% of the time, effort and planning to manage, versus the 20% that demands 80% of management attention. The 80% of an activity schedule can and should be a routine that is dictated by habit or custom. This portion of the schedule is generally carried along by its own momentum. Any effort that goes into directing it will typically involve varying the established routine. The remainder of the schedule requires careful planning and close monitoring to keep it in place.

The 80/20 rule is also a guide to the proportions of human activity that should normally be committed to the familiar routines versus exploratory novelty. In the mass commodity output operation, the proportions are more on the order of 99/1. Almost all energy in managing schedules on the moving assembly line, for instance, must go into changing the routine. Little is left to permit entertainment of variation. The project shop should, perhaps must, set a goal of 20% variety in all work. Individuals who plan their own schedules must set an equivalent goal. Public schools must discover how to set habits of adaptive change in scheduled activity in its students. Efficiency is no longer to be found in robotlike repetition of elemental actions; change and adaptation to escalating variety cannot build or survive on such efficiency. Efficiency in the project shop era will arise out of establishing a foundation of strong skill and habit in those matters that occupy 80% of working time or energy and then planning and managing the inevitable mix of novelty that will occupy the remaining 20% of one's work life. Of the planning energy, 20% will go into adjusting or revising the central skill and habit core, and 80% must be applied to managing novelty and change. Out of this shift in emphasis will arise the opportunity for rescheduling individual life patterns for greater personal satisfaction and health.

Ultimately, an efficiency that is based on machines and tools is one that enslaves human beings to the demands of machines and tools. Human efficiency demands that all of the potential of the unique self be realized. In the project shop human efficiency gets first priority. The human being who is continuously responding to the need for change and adaptation does not need to follow the rut of repetitive labor to achieve efficiency through a balance between setup and inventory. Response to change is routinely efficient. Customer need can always be satisfied in a minimum of time. Inventory will never be greater than that required to satisfy existing orders. The ideal of zero setup/changeover/materials lead time is thereby approximated, and the maximum efficient lot size of one is achieved. This is the best prospect for increased efficiency in the project shop era.

12

CONCLUSION: OPERATIONS POLICY AND PRACTICE IN THE NEW ERA

"There's nothing cosmetic about this package of changes!"

In the two hundred year span of time we call the industrial revolution, the quality of working life has continuously taken a back seat in favor of rapid growth in material wealth. At the outset of this historical detour there was little sense of personal discomfort because there was immediate gain in basic human security. As the journey nears its end, the experience of discomfort and loss brought about by the discipline of narrow specialization and dedication to efficiency in tool use becomes increasingly more painful. The industrial revolution *always* carried within it the seeds of its own demise. Those seeds are now flowering.

Still, formulation of economic policy in the United States at the highest levels turns heavily on concern for plant capacity utilization. The assumption that continued economic growth depends on high utilization of physical and machine capacity is deeply fixed. In reality, the largest proportion of machines and plants sit idle during the majority of any workweek. Age old practices designed to keep labor and machinery steadily applied in outputting goods and services dominate the decisions of business managers. In the United States, the age of the project shop is already at hand. But old, inappropriate methods and policies impede success in bringing that age to a profitable bloom.

Efficient use of capital and capital investment will not buy quality of life. Growth beyond some point becomes grotesque in every sphere. Population expansion probably has some ultimate and absolute limit, but the present risk is more that of poisoning ourselves well before the limit is reached if we continue our undisciplined and headlong rush for material wealth. Mass economy and mass society are, inherently, instruments of inhumanity. In a world of plenty, no one need tolerate them. An industrial revolution is justified through its attainment of freedom from material want and dispelling of human ignorance. The real wealth is found in our expanded base of knowledge about how to manage the material world around us. Once that door is opened wide, no one need remain a slave to the machine any longer.

Well designed, general purpose tools do not demand a short-term payoff. Mastered in use and properly maintained by an owner/user, they may last a lifetime. There is no need to debate the economic utility of the privately owned home purchased with a thirty-year mortgage. Mass rental housing is a social abomination. It is typically worn out in a decade or less while it produces a distortion in human lives and values that is a burden on the whole of society. The privately owned home brings a base of stability and responsibility to its habitants that strengthens the whole of society by preserving and increasing the value of housing as a social resource.

In like fashion, people do not need steady jobs. They need knowledge and ownership of flexible, powerful tools that can be put to productive use. Skills that lead to the mastery of tools and information that lends flexibility to their economic application are the imperatives of the emerging age of the project shop. Government policies are needed that encourage, even subsidize, individual ownership of productive tools. Flexible, automated factories run by a team of owner/operators must become the norm, even in commodity production. Absentee ownership of the tools of production, in corollary fashion, must be severely taxed. Income from absentee ownership of the tools of production should be taxed at a premium rate. Allowable depreciation schedules must be maximal in length. Tax sheltered allowance for depreciation that is not reinvested as maintenance or replacement within a very brief period must be fully recovered. Voluntarily deferring depreciation allowances that will not be reinvested should be encouraged. There should be no attraction in a purely financial short-term payoff from investing in the tools of production.

Public investment must continue to emphasize human skill and knowledge. Even the process of education itself must become project shop oriented. Mass production of educated students worked well one hundred, even fifty, years ago. A public system that attempts to turn out a politically acceptable, homogeneous student is limited to the production of mediocrity, if not less. There is no longer any such thing as the all-American boy or girl. Achieving a consensus as to what is all-American is politically impossible if not ridiculous. A system that permits individual teachers no latitude in meeting the individual needs of students, no opportunity to adapt to local culture, cannot produce excellence in skill or knowledge. Vouchers from the state that permit parents and students to shop for a school or a teacher who is monitored by independent examinations of student achievement, openly published and identified with the school or teacher, are the real future of general education. Tax monies will no longer be allocated for university level studies that "develop the mind," accomplishing little more than preparation of graduates for a life of social and intellectual dilettantism.

Schooling systems at all levels that are modeled on mass production processes from industry will soon become as limited in use as mass production itself. The basics of education may well be taken over by computers and television—fully automated, employing direct human intervention principally to guide the progress of the student qualitatively. Indeed, transformation of public school systems will likely be the signal of full transformation from a mass production to a project shop economy. Public schools are already a political battleground, under siege from taxpayers, students, parents, employers and teacher's unions. A politically bland, centrally controlled monolith, legally mandated to demonstrate equality of treatment, can never deliver value to its customers. It must finally fragment into customer oriented, cost effective project shops.

The traditional system of schooling was organized to achieve fullest possible use of the available classroom space and time. The project shop demands that sufficient capital resources be committed to permit immediate engagement of student interest with learning opportunity. Teaching skill must come to be applied at its highest level of effectiveness. Devices that monitor student progress automatically, permitting daily or even hourly assessment of status, will permit timely intervention of the skilled professional to solve learning problems of every kind. The classroom, the computer and video technology must become the tools that are owned and mastered by the individual teacher in the delivery of education if education is to be made effective again.

Public or, at least, traditional educational systems stand as examples of the opportunities and challenges of the project shop era. Artificial shortages of the tools of production, created by demand for near-term payoff on the capital invested, need not be tolerated. Indeed, public policy and tax subsidy must support a long-term investment climate for such tools. Limited capacity of productive tools in the project shop raises costs by reducing quality and diminishing the level of service. A narrowly defined efficiency that rapes the tools of productivity for maximum near-term payoff to investors is no longer tolerable as private or public policy. Capacity need not be wasted, but the shallow economies obtainable in maximum use of *things* need no longer be a first priority. We have learned how to produce things in commodity quantities efficiently. Material wealth need not be a first or even a high priority of life. Quality of life in the era of the project shop arises out of the skilled use of resources, not out of mere ownership of increased quantities of them.

Effective scheduling and smooth work flow remain important concerns to the project shop manager. When scheduling is, above all, constrained by a shortage of resources, all other values and purposes are reshaped to meet the imperative of using the critical resource. Shortages of material resources need no longer be allowed to distort the quality of life in the ways that mass production systems inherently do. The natural rhythms of life—the seasons and customer demand—serve better to constrain schedules in the project shop. Work teams that produce continuously through the night to meet critical demand—a common occurrence in the crisis of war—will respond to genuine customer need and business opportunity. Work that is abandoned in midcourse merely because the quitting signal has sounded will remain to obstruct tomorrow's flow and may take longer to finish tomorrow when resetup is required or specifications have faded from memory. A major, documented difference between American and Japanese workers is the willingness of the Japanese to continue working to conclusion on any project that is behind schedule when it will save time overall or could impede normal production flow the following day if held over. In a project shop, the habit naturally emerges of never needlessly leaving a project unfinished. One is always prepared to accept leisure in the absence of work or to begin immediately on the next job opportunity when it appears. A lock-step schedule of fixed hours or days is no asset here.

Range and depth of skill are inconsequential in the mass production operation except in a handful of isolated, key positions. By contrast, range and depth of skill are fundamental assets of the project shop. Encouragement of skill development on and off the job, payment for demonstrated possession of relevant skill and special pay increments for infrequently but critically needed skill specialties are essential to the success of the project shop's operations. The work of the project shop is genuinely enriched, up and down the scale of skill levels. The opportunity for variety can be employed to refresh physically and mentally, *on the job*. Leisure is not necessary as a release from the dulling routine of work. It is, rather, an opportunity for growth—an occasion for yet greater variety. Retirement need not beckon as the light at the end of the dreary tunnel of a paid job; retirement is more likely to mean a reduced work schedule that focuses on the application of one's best or most enjoyed skill. Retirement and layoff need not consign narrowly specialized workers to the human scrap bin; in the project shop era they will represent merely a shift in intensity or emphasis of work effort.

Planning in the project shop need not be a public relations process carried out for the benefit of bankers, backers or customers. Project shop planning must honestly face up to the best and worst events that come upon its industry or the economy. The typical project shop will be smaller. It will be more sensitive to the ebbs and flows of economic change. It must respond quicker to emerging opportunity and be prepared better for business adversity. Contingency plans based on the best and worst cases are indispensible. Although hiring cannot be done "in hopes," available skill and labor capacity must still be maintained equal to the big chance. Growth or investment strategies that depend on everything working favorably must be avoided. The best plans serve as preparation for all but the most unlikely circumstances. Good plans need not predict exact outcomes. A business must always set high performance goals that stretch resources enough to truly risk falling short. Plans must never be distorted, though, to fit the utopian assumption that exceptionally difficult business goals will certainly be achieved. Planning allocates resources to fit all business contingencies, including fantastically high achievement. When plans are locked in to the assumption of that achievement alone, they are likely to become an albatross that impedes the best available performance.

What it comes down to is that major changes must occur in the policies that shape the management of operations in a project shop. Cost optimization in the service of near-term profitability is an unacceptable guide to managing the project shop. Instead, policies that result in a rapid, undelayed flow of high quality, customized work must be sought. The operating objective of the project shop might be summed up as the achievement of an essentially queueless work flow that services customers fast with high quality products or services. Work enters and leaves the project shop with absolute minimal delay due to capacity constraints of any kind whatsoever. If work is delayed, it waits at the point of entry, not in the middle of the work flow, because of some lacking critical skill or unavoidable labor constraint.

Fortunately, the fundamental operations tools that assist in managing an effective project shop are very little different from those that have helped solve past generations of mass production operations problems. Only the emphasis has shifted as to which are more or less useful. These tools are part of the training of business graduates from every accredited school of business. The American Assembly of Collegiate Schools of Business, the accrediting institution for business education, requires that they be taught as elements of the common body of knowledge imparted to a fully prepared business graduate. This is a relatively recent emphasis *beyond* the pure mathematics of statistics, probability, linear programming, and related operations research technology that once served a similar purpose for designers of the moving assembly line. Management of project shop operations requires the application of simple but powerful tools, the mathematics for which can usually be handled easily on a personal computer station.

Managing operations in a project shop remains, nonetheless, a technology that requires familiarity and opportunity for mastery in its application. It is a special if not presently an unusual way of looking at work organization and flow. Without a hammer, saw, level, square, tape measure and lever bar, it is very difficult to build a house. Lacking the appropriate tools of operations management, it is very difficult to organize and manage a project shop profitably. The right tools must be mastered and kept at hand.

It has to be apparent by now that capacity issues are central to managing a project shop effectively. Managing bottlenecks is critical to managing work flow overall. Bottlenecks are nothing more than relative points of capacity constraint in the flow. Capacity decisions, directly or indirectly, determine both the level of capital investment required of the business and the level of service available to the project shop customer. Waiting line, or queueing, theory describes the relationship between level of capacity utilization and average delay in serving customer need. Queueing theory is the basic model within which capacity-service trade-off decisions are rationally made. Absent a grasp of waiting line phenomena, the project shop operations director has no tangible foundation for those decisions. He or she can either chase a market share willy-nilly by boldly adding to capacity or squeeze costs by insisting that capacity be used as close to current demand as possible. The strategy followed depends more on personal habit and temperament than on business opportunities and requirements.

Scheduling the project shop permits little dependence on standard, repetitive work routines. At the ultimate, every task is uniquely shaped; it calls on a different range and sequence of project shop resources. Instead of a continuous parade down main street, passing every viewer on the line of march, it is a grand fairground where each visitor chooses his or her own mix of events. The pipeline model used to describe materials flow in MRP type systems no longer fits here (though it may be useful elsewhere). Tasks are now a crazy quilt of variety that needs creative assembly to minimize delivery delay or waste of labor time.

The better operations model against which to evaluate project shop operations is the project PERT, a network plan that details activities and their sequence through the shop. Critical path analysis identifies the bottleneck path through the project. A hybrid model based on PERT that superimposes and accumulates work in-shop is developed and used as a tool for locating potential bottlenecks. A dynamic computer model that models the flow of existing work under differing rules of sequence or varying levels of slack is needed to discover the most effective scheduling sequence. Shortest processing time, formerly assumed to be the universally safe scheduling heuristic for the project shop, must be superceded by comprehensive computer simulations of different flow patterns. Discovery of chronic weak points or gross excesses of capacity requires Monte Carlo simulation on the same kind of dynamic computer model.

The scheduling illustrations offered in this text suggest that small shops may sometimes get by with manual modeling of the work flow in developing schedules. Up to a point, this is probably true. The effective project shop operations director, though, will likely need to be comfortable using or even creating simulators on his or her personal computer. With time, scheduling software for the project shop simulations will be created for PCs. The flow simulator in one form or another will be central to managing project shop operations.

Capacity planning in a project shop will call for another type of simulator—one that illustrates the effects of the best, worst and most likely case business circumstance on available machine and labor resources. Sound capacity planning in this mode will frequently put limits on some kinds of jobs accepted or suggest an opportunity to seek out work that better uses available capacity. Capital investment decisions are likely to require a preliminary set of simulations under variable business mix conditions to estimate their effect on interdependent resources. The potential, even inevitable, complexity of the project shop calls for a much more comprehensive approach to capacity analysis. "What if" simulations based on best and worst case forecasts are a practical way to address this need.

Labor skill is the critical resource of the project shop. The ergonomics of person/machine interface cannot be ignored. Methods whereby new equipment is rated for quality of ergonomic interface by both human factors experts and experienced employees alike will be required. Training and skill verification methods are needed to upgrade worker capability and authenticate acquired capabilities. The project shop operations director must have a working understanding of training methods and psychometric measures. Some form of skills bank or skill inventory will be needed to keep track of available capacity in-shop. The skills bank could readily become an element of an in-house work flow simulator.

Compensation systems for the project shop are integral to supporting the levels of skill required. Approaches that take the base market rate of skill into account but allow incrementally for added, multiple skill acquisition must be a part of the compensation system employed. The compensation system must take into account the special benefits loading needs of a project shop. Paid time off and benefits plan financing will have to be reshaped substantially to fit the needs of the project shop.

Management of quality in a project shop requires less of the traditional quality enforcement tactics and more standard statistical/analytical analysis of processes employed. Quality will be less inspected into the product or service since sources of quality problems will be identified through research. Data on quality problems must be gathered by equipment station, individual worker, type of material, components vendor, engineering designer, customer, day of the week, time of day, previous schedule of machine and worker and anything else that might be relevant. Statistical process control can always be applied to any output that is exactly covered by specifications. When ultimate utility is the measure of quality, only use will yield a valid measure of quality. When the job goes wrong, the source must be discovered. The variety and uniqueness of project shop flow make this difficult.

A comprehensive data base with a full range of potentially useful data, and most certainly one that contains everything that can be routinely measured, must be maintained and cultivated for its information value. Basic statistical methodology in the form of correlational, chi squared or analysis of variance studies will be essential elements of the project shop operations director's tool kit. The same computer that makes accumulation and storage of these masses of data possible also stands ready to apply a variety of statistical tests to the data base. A grasp of the basic experimental method by the project shop operations director and availability of almost any standard statistical analytical package will permit him or her to analyze the quality problems in depth.

Application of the EOQ and 80/20 prioritizing models is necessary to good decision making about operation setups. The most likely application of pipeline styled continuous flow models of operations may eventually be in scheduling setups to achieve queueless work flow of short or one-of-a-kind projects through multiple workstations. Queueless work flow and related JIT practices will revolutionize the control of in-process inventory in ways that substantially refocus EOQ and the Pareto principle applications. They are important tools in the project shop operations director's kit.

The shape of this new role begins to emerge out of this summary of the challenges it must handle. The project shop operations director must have good basic quantitative and analytical skills. Command of the computer as a personal working tool seems indispensible. A knowledge of basic tools and models of operations management is essential. When applied skillfully on the foundation of project shop operations policies sketched out herein, they are the stuff of a potential revolution. Large project shops may employ a team of operations directors and analysts. Small ones may require the general manager, foreman or production scheduler to be their master. If a business is to profit from the emerging era of job shop products and services, it must have someone on hand who is competent in their application. Filling the role effectively is the key.

The emerging project shop will certainly dominate the twenty-first century as the primary form of business organization. The policies and practices that make that kind of operation profitable differ substantively from those that founded the industrial revolution. The effective project shop manager is a new breed of person following a much revised role in managing operations. With a full appreciation of the challenges and opportunities that the new era holds out to him or her, it can be a highly profitable shift of emphasis.

BIBLIOGRAPHY

Ashton, J. E. and Cook, F. S., Jr. March–April 1989. "Time to Reform Job Shop Manufacturing." *Harvard Business Review*, pp. 106–11.

Barnes, R. M. 1968. *Motion and Time Study*. New York: Wiley.

Bassett, G. A. October 1979. "A Study of the Effects of Task Goal and Schedule Choice on Work Performance." *Organizational Behavior and Human Performance* 24, pp. 202–27.

———. 1980. *Part-Time Work in Manufacturing*. Fairfield, Conn.: Consulting Report to General Electric Corporate Employee Relations.

Brown, R. G. 1977. *Materials Management Systems*. New York: Wiley.

Chase, R. B. and Aquilano, N. J. 1989. *Production and Operations Management*. 5th ed. Homewood, Ill.: Irwin.

Conway, R. W., Maxwell, W. L., and Miller, L. W. 1967. *Theory of Scheduling*. Reading, Mass.: Addison Wesley.

Denison, E. F. 1974. *Accounting for United States Economic Growth, 1929–1969*. Washington, D.C.: The Brookings Institution.

Federal Reserve Board of Governors. Bulletin G.3402. "Capacity Utilization in Industrial Production, Mining and Utilities." Washington, D.C.

Fox, Robert E. March–April 1983. "Leapfrogging the Japanese." *Inventories and Production* 3, no. 21.

Gilbreth, F. B. and Gilbreth, L. M. August 1924. "Classifying Elements of Work." *Management and Administration* 8, no. 2, p. 151.

Goldratt, Eliyahu. 1988. "Computerized Shop Floor Scheduling." *International Journal of Production Research* 26, no. 3, pp. 443–455.

Griffin, W. C. 1978. *Queuing: Basic Theory and Application*. Columbus, Ohio: Grid.

Jaques, E. 1961. *Equitable Payment*. New York: Wiley.

Johnson, S. M. 1954. "Optimal Two State and Three State Production Schedules with Setup Times Included." *Naval Logistics Quarterly* 1, no. 1, pp. 61–68.

Karmarkar, U. September–October 1989. "Getting Control of Just in Time." *Harvard Business Review*, pp. 122–31

Kendrick, J. W. 1961. *Productivity Trends in the United States*. Princeton, N.J.: Princeton University Press.

Ohno, T. 1988. *Workplace Management*. Cambridge, Mass.: Productivity Press.

Ross, P. J. 1988. *Taguchi Techniques for Quality Engineering*. New York: McGraw-Hill.

Schonberger, R. J. 1982. *Japanese Manufacturing Techniques*. New York: The Free Press.

Shingo, Shigeo. 1988. "SMED: The Heart of JIT Production." In Y. K. Shetty and V. M. Buehler, eds., *Competing Through Productivity and Quality*. Cambridge, Mass.: Productivity Press, pp. 383–98.

Smith, Adam. 1982. *The Wealth of Nations*. New York: Penguin Books.

Solomon, S. L. 1983. *Simulation of Waiting Lines*. Englewood Cliffs, N.J.: Prentice-Hall.

Taylor, F. W. 1911. *Scientific Management*. New York: Harper and Row.

Vroom, V. H. and Jago, A. G. 1988. *The New Leadership: Managing Participation in Organization*. Englewood Cliffs, N.J.: Prentice-Hall.

Vroom, V. H. and Yetton, P. W. 1973. *Leadership and Decision-Making*. Pittsburgh: University of Pittsburgh Press.

INDEX

Absenteeism, 117, 202–6

Absentee ownership of production resources, 232

Acceptable quality level (AQL), 145

Advertising, 216

Aircraft maintenance, 179

American Assembly of Collegiate Schools of Business (AACSB), business school accreditation, 235

American Civil War, xii

American investment policy, 215

Analysis of variance (ANOVA), 144

Athenian democracy, 179

Automatic reorder point, 162

Avery, Sewell, 55

Backward work flow planning, 161

Balanced work flow, 63

Bassett, G. A., 119, 141

Bell-shaped distribution curve, 154

Bottlenecks, 6, 55–74, 104–11, 115, 165, 167–68

Break-even, 56–57

Buffer inventory, 59

Burnout on job, 226

Business schools, vii

Capacity: adaptive, 2; full, 6–7; output, 1; recovery, 2; structural, 2; systemic, 1; temporal, 1, 3, 5

Capitalism, 46

Carpel tunnel syndrome, 28

Cash flow, 75

Communism, 46, 49

Compensable factors, 196

Compensation and reward systems, 189–210

Compensation for risk, 199–200

Compensation survey, 190

Computer aided design (CAD), 148, 184

Computer technology, 42

Concentration capacity, human, 226

Control of work flow, 156

Control path method (CPM), 60

Conway, R. W., 8, 82, 91

Cost of living creep, 209

Critical path (CP), 115, 131

Critical path analysis, 60

Data bank, skills/experience, 132

Data base management, 237

Decision-making skills, 194

Decision trees, 57

Denison, E. F., 119

Depreciation practices, 58

Design of experiments (DOE), 144

Devil's Advocate, 144

Economic order quantity (EOQ), xv, 212–14, 238

Edison, Thomas, 178
Education, reform of, 226, 232–33
Efficiency, 211–29
Eight-hour, five-day work week, 116–18
Eighty/twenty (80/20) rule, 138, 139, 228, 238
Ergonomic tool design, 27, 30
ERISA, 207
Erlang, E. K., 9
Expected cash value of resetup, 221
Expected value, 57
Experience/learning curve, 217, 219

Fatigue, 71, 225, 227
Federal Reserve Board, 73
First-come, first-served (FCFS), 79, 87–111
Fixed flow sequence, 80
Flex time, 117
Ford, Henry, 39, 155
Forecasting, 161, 163
Forward work flow planning, 161
Fraternities, college, 195
Fringe benefits, 180, 202

Gilbreth, Frank and Lillian Gilbreth, xv, 30
Goldratt, Eliyahu, 115
Gompers, Samuel, 46
Grant, W. T. (department stores), 55

Habit and work routine, 228
Harris, F. W., 212
Hewlett Packard Co., 197
Holiday pay, 122
Human concentration capacity, 226

Incentive pay, 192
Incremental compensation for added skill, 198
Industrial revolution, 45, 231
Inflation and pay increases, 191
Inventory, 153
IQ and social status, 183
IQ test, 182, 184
IRA plan, 207–8
Iroquois Indians, 200

Jago, A. G., 150
Jefferson, Thomas, 45
Job enlargement, 145
Job satisfaction, 119
Johnson, S. M., 66
Johnson's rule, 66, 70, 83–84
Just-in-time (JIT), 6, 141, 142, 154, 160, 170

Kanban, Japanese reorder cards, 160, 169
Keough plan, 208

Labor market, 191, 199
Labor union, 181
Lead time, 153
Learning/experience curve, 158
Lincoln, Abraham, 178
Lincoln Electric Company, 135
Logical hypothesis testing, 188
Luxury and quality, 137

McDonald's restaurants, 135
Machine design, 178
Market saturation, 216
Marx, Karl, 46
Mass commodity output, 5
Materials requirements planning (MRP), 158, 161, 236
Mathematics skills, 218
Matrix organization structure, 132
Maximax decision strategy, 19
Maxwell, W. L., 8, 82, 91
Merit pay, 191, 193
Metabolic cycle, human, 116
Michelangelo, 47
Micmac Indians, 200
Miller, L. W., 8, 82, 91
Monte Carlo modeling, 143
Monte Carlo simulation, 71, 81, 84, 87, 88, 93, 96, 100, 106, 236
Montgomery Ward, 55
More, Thomas, 47
Motivation, 117, 121
Motivation through pay, 196
Multivariate statistical analysis, 144

Narcotic drugs, 48
National Bureau of Economic Research, 119
Net present value, 77
Ninety-five percent (95%) rule, 156
Normal distribution curve, 154

Ohno, Taiichi, 6
Opinion polling, 189
Opportunity cost, 212
Orthogonal arrays, 144
Overtime, 122, 167
Overtime pay, 180
Overtime scheduling, 71

Paid personal time, 122
Pareto principle, 138, 228, 238
Part-time workers, 205
Part-time work schedules, 167
Pay-for-time-not-worked, 122
Pay increases, periodic, 181
Penney, J. C., 195
Performance goals, 235
Personal computer, 236
Philosophical analysis, 51
Physics principles, 218
Planning strategies, 163
Poisson distribution, 82
Polaroid, 197
Postindustrial society, 49
Probabilistic decision making, 57
Productivity, 119
Professional football, 117
Profit sharing, 201, 207
Program evaluation and review technique (PERT), 60, 115, 131, 236
Project shop manager, role of, 238
Prototype, 144
Pull in work flow, 161
Purchasing department, 211
Push in work flow, 161

Quality: and work place, 121; of product or service, 12, 58
Quality performance, 116
Quality programs, 237
Quantity production goals, 140
Queueing analysis, 62

Queueing theory, 9, 67, 236
Queueless work flow, 141

Random sampling, 144
Random sequenced work flow, 71
Reinvestment in plant, 215
Reporting pay, 123
Return on investment (ROI), 17–18, 55, 58, 220

Scheduling rules, 75–111
Scientific management, xiv
Sears Roebuck, 55
Secret societies, college, 195
Securities Exchange Commission (SEC), 190
Setup cost, 75, 219, 220
Setup lead time, 221, 224
Setup scheduling, 70
Shakespeare, William, 47
Shingo, Shigeo, 6, 113
Shortest processing time (SPT), 9, 78, 82–111
Simulated production flow, 60
Simulation, 16; of project shop work flow, 236; static single frame, 87
Single-minute-exchange-of-die (SMED), 214
Skill obsolescence, 200–201
Skills/experience data bank, 132
Slavery, 45
Social status, and IQ, 183
Statistical process control (SPC), 145, 155
Status, and pay, 195–96
Strategy, and efficiency, 216
Stress: from work schedule, 117; job-related, 27
Subcontracting, 71, 73
Suggestion plans, 33
Supply and demand for custom output, 40
Synergy, 216
System slack, 84

Taguchi's methodology, 144
Tardiness, 117
Taylor, F. W., 30, 118

Tools and work, 23–37
Training, government subsidy for, 180
Training cost, 149, 176
Two-bin storage system, 162

Vouchers, educational, 232
Vroom, V. H., 150

Wage-hour law, 202, 204
Wage slavery, 45
Waiting line theory, 9–16, 66, 236
Workaholism, 117

Worker cross-assignment, 110
Worker participation, in decision making, 147, 150
Worker temperament, 122
Work in process (WIP), 214
World War II production, 7, 120
Worst case scenario planning, 57

Yetton, P. W., 150

Zero lead time, 214

About the Author

GLENN BASSETT is Professor of Management at the business school of the University of Bridgeport. Previously he was a member of the General Electric staff doing research in business and industrial relations issues. He is the author of six management books.